THE ENTREPRENEUR'S BUSINESS GUIDE
FROM A STARTUP APPROACH

AUSTIN C. ENEANYA

THE ENTREPRENEUR'S BUSINESS GUIDE (from a Start-up approach)

Copyright © 2019 **Austin C. Eneanya**

All rights reserved. No part of this publication may be reproduced, stored in a retrieval system or transmitted in any form or by any means, electronic, mechanical, recording or otherwise, without the prior permission of the author.

ISBN: 978-1-387-17849-0
EAN: 9781387178490

Printed

By

Lulu Books

For further information or permission
627, Davis Drive, Suite 300, NC 27560 Morrisville,
North – Carolina, United States (U.S.A).

Visit: www.lulu.com

ACKNOWLEDGEMENTS

THE ENTREPRENEUR'S BUSINESS GUIDE (from a Start-up approach)

DEDICATION

This book is dedicated to my immediate younger brother Mr. Victor Eneanya, my father and my friends such as Mike Aham my book cover designer and Seun Noibi who served as a great inspiration for the publication of this book. Who were my greatest source of motivation and inspiration for this book?

ACKNOWLEDGEMENTS

I wish to express my gratitude to Almighty God for the wisdom and inspiration towards the writing of this book. Writing the first edition which was originally titled as **"SECRET BEHIND SUCCESSFUL ENTREPRENUR IN NIGERIA AND IN THE WORLD"** before the tittle was later revised to **"THE ENTREPRENEUR'S BUSINESS GUIDE"** was brought to reality with support from friends, colleagues and especially my family. Special praises to Miss Nonso Akah for her motivational advice to the publication of the book and special thanks to my mom and dad and loved ones who encouraged me all the way with their support and advice.

TABLE OF CONTENT

DEDICATION 3

ACKNOWLEDGEMENTS 4

TABLE OF CONTENT 5

ABOUT THE BOOK 11

CHAPTER 1 12

INTRODUCTION 12

   LESSON 1: WHAT DOES IT TAKE TO START-UP A BUSINESS? 12

   LESSON 2: 12 MOVES SUMMARY STEPS IN STARTING A STARTUP 30

   LESSON 3: ENTREPRENEURSHIP; THE REALITY OF A BUSINESS OWNER 40

CHAPTER 2 43

LESSONS AND FACTORS TO CONSIDER TO AVOID START-UP FAILURE 43

   SESSION 1: STARTING A COMPANY WITH A MISSION AND PURPOSE 44

   LESSON 1: NOTHING IS IMPOSSIBLE IF YOU CAN THINK POSSIBILITY 45

   LESSON 2: UNDERESTIMATING YOUR POTENTIAL (LOW SELF-ESTEEM) 46

      LESSON 3: WORKING WITH THE UNDERSTANDING OF YOUR COMPETITORS 47

   LESSON 4: FIND YOUR NICHE IN THE BUSINESS WORLD AND TAKE IT 48

   LESSON 5: PLAN WHERE YOU CAN, LAUNCH AS SOON AS POSSIBLE, AND MAKE CHANGES AS YOU GO 49

   LESSON 6: FUNDS AND CAPITAL 50

   LESSON 7: NOT HIRING SOON ENOUGH 50

   LESSON 8: FINDING THE RIGHT TEAM 51

   LESSON 9: WATCH YOUR PENNIES, BUT SPEND THE GOOD ONES 52

   SESSION 10: BUSINESS IDEAS OPPORTUNITY THAT CAN MAKE YOU MONEY 52

CHAPTER 3 54

INSIGHTFUL SUCCESS FACTORS NEEDED FOR EXPLOIT IN BUSINESS 54

   SESSION1: CUSTOMERS 54

   3.1.1 LISTENING TO YOUR USERS/CUSTOMERS 54

   3.1.2 CUSTOMER SATISFACTION 54

   SESSION2: LEARNING 55

ACKNOWLEDGEMENTS

3.2 LEARN FROM YOUR MISTAKES 55

3.2.2 NEVER STOP LEARNING 56

3.2.3 COMMIT TO CONTINOUS LEARNING 56

SESSION3: PERSEVERANCE 57

3.3.1 DEDICATION AND GIVING IT YOU'RE ALL 57

3.3.2 EXPECT (AND PREPARE FOR) THE UNEXPECTED 57

3.3.3 TOUGH, BUT REWARDING WORK 58

SESSION4: FOUNDATIONAL INSIGHT QUESTIONS 58

3.4.2 WHAT FUTURE PLANS DO YOU HAVE FOR YOUR BUSINESS? 59

LESSON 1: BRIEF INSIGHT OF GLOBAL BRANDS AND HOW THEY STARTED (E.G COCA-COLA AND GOOGLE) 59

3.4.3: EVALUATING GOALS 63

SESSION5: SUCCESS START-UP FROM SUCCESSFUL C.E. O'S WHO HAD MADE IT FROM SMALL BUSINESS 64

3.5.1. "IDEAS ARE EVERYTHING" - DEREK SIVERS 64

3.5.2. "BUSINESS RISK" - TIM FERRISS 65

3.5.3. "BUSINESS FUNDING" - 37SIGNALS 66

3.5.4. "BUSINESS SYSTEMS" - MICHAEL GERBER 67

3.5.5. "BUSINESS MARKETING" - JOEL SPOLSKY 67

CHAPTER 4 69

PROFITABLE GROWING SMALL BUSINESS OPPORTUNITIES 69

SESSION 1: OTHER BUSINESS IDEAS AND VENTURES YOU CAN START IN NIGERIA 74

WHAT YOU NEED TO KNOW ABOUT STARTING A MANUFACTURING BUSINESS AT HOME .80

SESSION 2: TOP PROFITABLE ONLINE BUSINESS IDEAS IN NIGERIA 82

SESSION 3: GENERAL ONLINE BUSINESS YOU CAN START AT HOME 84

LESSON 2: PROFITABLE WEB-BASED SERVICES BUSINESS IDEAS AND OPPORTUNITIES TO START 87

LESSON 3: MORE INTERNET BASED BUSINESS IDEAS AND OPPORTUNITIES TO START 93

3 STEPS TO REGISTER YOUR BUSINESS IN NIGERIA 94

NIGERIA ONLINE REGISTRATION PROCEDURE FOR REGISTRATION OF COMPANY/BUSINESS NAME/INCORPORATED TRUSTEES ONLINE 96

DARLINTON OMEH PERSPECTIVE ON HOW TO BECOME A SUCCESSFUL ENTERPRENUR (OMEH) 101

CHAPTER 5 104

12 INSIGHTS TO ENTERPRENURIAL START-UP FOR PROSPECTIVE BUSINESS MEN/WOMEN 104

INSIGHT 1. TAKE SKILLS AND INTEREST INVENTORY: 104

SESSION 0.11: DESCRIPTION 107

INSIGHT 3: WHAT YOU NEED TO KNOW BEFORE YOU WRITE YOUR BUSINESS PLAN 109

WRITING YOUR BUSINESS PLAN 112

SESSION1: REFERENCEFORBUSINESS.COM APPROACH TO BUSINESS PLAN WRITING 112

SESSION1.2: CREATING A BUSINESS PLAN FOR A NEW OR EXISTING BUSINESS ACCORDING TO BUSINESSTOWN.COM 121

CHAPTER 6 141

BEYOND THE PLANNING AND WRITE-UP PHASE 141

SESSION 1.1: WHAT ANY ORGANIZATION NEEDS TO SURVIVE AND SUCCEED 141

SESSION 1.2: THE FIVE KEY SUCCESS FACTORS OF BUSINESS 141

SESSION 1.3: ESSENTIAL BUSINESS VITAMINS FOR GROWING BUSINESSES 143

INSIGHT 4: IDENTIFY SOURCES OF START-UP FINANCING 147

INSIGHT 4.0: FINANCE GENERATING APPROACHES FOR SMALL BUSINESSES IN NIGERIA 150

CONTENT PARTNER FOR THE SME TOOLKIT 150

INSIGHT 4.2: OTHER WAYS OF GENERATING CASH: SUCH AS BUSINESS PLAN COMPETITION (AFRICA A. S., 2015) 154

ULTIMATE LIST: *40+ BUSINESS FUNDING OPPORTUNITIES AND AWARDS FOR AFRICAN ENTREPRENEURS* (IKENNA, 2016) 156

SESSION 1: STUDENT ENTREPRENEURSHIP *157*

SESSION 2: ASPIRING AND START-UP ENTREPRENEURS *159*

SESSION 3: BREAKTHROUGH ENTREPRENEURS AND SMALL BUSINESSES *163*

INSIGHT 5: CHOOSE A BUSINESS NAME AND REGISTER IT WITH THE APPROPRIATE AUTHORITIES 169

SESSION 1: INSIGHT INTO NAFDAC REGISTRATION PROCESS FOR PRODUCT BASED BUSINESS 173

SESSION 2: *PRICE- A CASE STUDY OF PRODUCT REGISTRATION WITH NAFDAC NIGERIA (CHIBUZO, 2016)* 177

SESSION 3: IMPORTANT QUESTIONS AND ANSWERS SECTION 181

INSIGHT 6: IMPLEMENTATION OF BUSINESS STRATEGIES IN PROMOTING YOUR BUSINESS 185

    INSIGHT 6.2: PRE-START-UP INSIGHTS TO CONSIDER FOR YOUR BUSINESS 186

    INSIGHT 6.3: WEB SITE BASICS YOU NEED TO KNOW FOR START-UP BUSINESSES 187

    6 BLOGGING TIPS, TECHNIQUES AND STRATEGY 189

    INSIGHT 6.4: BUSINESS LOCATION AND FEASIBILITY CHECK 190

INSIGHT 7: PUBLIC RELATIONS AND TELLING THE WORLD ABOUT YOUR BUSINESS 192

    SESSION1: HOW TO PROMOTE PRODUCTS WITH SOCIAL MEDIA: 4 PRACTICAL EXAMPLES 195

INSIGHT 8: HIRE A SUPPORT TEAM (RECURIT EMPLOYEES) 198

CHAPTER 7 202

BEYOND THE IDEA PHASE 202

    INSIGHT 9: EXECUTE YOUR MARKETING PLANS 202

    INSIGHT 9.1: MARKETING YOUR BUSINESS 204

    INSIGHT 9.2: BUSINESS SALES APPROACHES 205

    INSIGHT 9.3: RE-THINK YOUR SALES METHOD 211

INSIGHT 10: IMPLEMENTATION OF DEVELOPED MARKETING AND CUSTOMER SERVICE PLANS 213

HOW TO START A PRODUCT BASED BUSINESS? 215

    INSIGHT 10.1: WAYS TO APPROACH YOUR BUSINESSES IN SELLING HANDMADE GOODS IN WHOLESALE 215

    INSIGHT 10.2: HOW TO SELL A PRODUCT 219

        SESSION 4: 5 BEST PLACES TO ADVERTISE ONLINE 220

    SESSION5: CONNECTING WITH THE BUYER 221

    SESSION7: IMPROVING SALES 223

    INSIGHT 11.3: CONCLUDING SALES 224

        SESSION 1: (google.com, 7 WAYS TO PROMOTE YOUR BUSINESS ONLINE FOR FREE) 225

SESSION 8: TROUBLESHOOTING POOR SALES 226

INSIGHT 11: PERFORMANCE REVIEW AFTER MEETING YOUR FIRST CUSTOMERS 227

INSIGHT 12: EVALUATE, INNOVATE AND ADD CREATIVITY TO YOUR BUSINESS SYSTEM 228

13 BUSINESS START-UP SURVIVAL RULES EITHER AS AN IDEA OR *228*

INSIGHT 12.1: QUALITY MANAGEMENT SYSTEM 230

SESSION1: TOYOTA COMPANY BUSINESS START-UP STORY 237

FINAL SESSION: NIGERIA TAX, POLICY AND RATES IN NIGERIA 240

FEDERAL INLAND REVENUE SERVICE IN NIGERIA (FIRS)– Information on value added tax (v.a.t) *245*

CONCLUSION OF START-UP INSIGHTS 249

THE NIGERIAN LABOUR LAW 9 TIPS from employers to employees (AS AT 2019) *249*

QUOTES: FOOD FOR THOUGHT 253

CHAPTER 8 254

TIPS ON MANAGING YOUR COMPANY 254

INTRODUCTION: ROLES AND RESPONSIBILITY OF CHIEF EXECUTIVE OFFICER (GOOGLE.COM) 255

SESSION 1: 7 LEADERSHIP PRINCIPLES TO LEARN FROM AN EAGLE 257

SESSION 2: OUTLINE GROWTH STRATEGIES 258

SESSION 3: OUTSOURCING MANUFACTURING FOR PRODUCT BASED BUSINESSES (GOOGLE.COM) 259

SESSION 4: NAFDAC GUIDELINES FOR ESTABLISHMENT OF FOOD MANUFACTURING PLANTS IN NIGERIA 267

SESSION 5: FRANCHISING OR LICENSING FOR AN ALREADY EXISTING BUSINESS (GOOGLE.COM) 277

SESSION 6: CHOOSING THE RIGHT FRANCHISE: TED IWERE TEN KEY FACTORS TO CONSIDER (IWERE) 289

CHAPTER 9 298

WAYS TO GROW A SMALL BUSINESS INTO BIG BUSSINESSS 298

SESSION 1: OVERVIEW (GOOGLE.COM) 298

SESSION2: BUSINESS COST 305

SESSION 2B: DEVELOPMENTAL PHASES OF BUSINESS MANAGEMENT 305

SESSION3: MANAGEMENT SKILLS FOR BUSINESS SUCCESS 311

SESSION 4: (FORBES.COM, 2016) **12 FACTS YOU NEED TO KNOW FROM FORBES' 2016 BILLIONAIRES LIST** 315

    SESSION 6: BIOGRAPHY OF A FEW FAMOUS SUCCESS STORIES OF WEALTHY INDUSTRIALIST IN NIGERIA (WIKIPEDIA.COM, 2016)...317

CHAPTER 10 329

NETWORK MARKETING BUSINESS START-UP 329

    SESSION1: MULTI-LEVEL MARKETING MASTER TIPS (GOOGLE.COM) 330

        SECRET OF THE RICH: *332*

    SESSION2: (CRIBBS, 9 STRATEGIES TO HELP GROW YOUR NETWORK MARKETING BUSINESS) 333

    SESSION 3: INSIGHTS ON FINANCIAL IMPROVEMENT USING MLM (MULTI-LEVEL MARKETING)..338

SESSION 4: LIFE STORY OF KFC FOUNDER 340

    SESSION 5: BILLIONAIRE MINDSET (THE DIFFERENCE FROM OTHERS) 341

CONCLUSION..342

ABOUT THE AUTHOR..345

WORKS CITED..346

ABOUT THE BOOK

The entrepreneur's business guide is a step-by-step start-up business book that addresses business from the start-up phase to ideally the developmental stage. This is a startup business book. This book is a start-up CEO field guide book to scaling up your business, this start-up manual will help you understand what steps to take:

1) Change of mentality between the business world and the employment world conventional way of starting up a business.

2) How to develop a business idea and convert it into a business plan

2) Franchise business model and tips, you need to know before choosing a franchised firm.

3) Outsourcing business model with more than 50 business start-up ideas you can pick from to startup your own business

4) The process and information for NAFDAC registration for product-based business for prospective product startups in Nigeria

5) A Nigerian tax system for Nigeria business owners, a quality management system to service and product-based business.

6) Network marketing approach for start-up building from the ground up

7) This book explains the start-up evolution from idea to profitability using a scalable business approach for start-up founders.

8) Insight about Nigerian Labour and Employment Laws for Business and company setup.

9) Learn how to manage and troubleshoot your business sales as a start-up or as an already growing brand.

10) This is an entrepreneurship book that will guide you on how to develop a business idea and possible funding sources to choose from.

ACKNOWLEDGEMENTS

CHAPTER 1
INTRODUCTION

Starting a business from my experience is not as easy as it sounds others in business makes it look, my first year in business was a ton of struggle until I understand what I was getting wrong when fixed became a walk in the park. Going into business without a clear-cut experience on how best to grow your enterprises, it gradually becomes a full-time job with far lesser pay, then you see yourself living on the business-like parasite feeding on its host. Although Startup business entails understanding with many factors such as: the legal, the financing, the sales and the marketing, intellectual property protection, liability protection, human resources, and many other areas depending on your startup industry. But knowing where to begin and scale is more important, but before I begin, we would first need to understand the mentality and mindset behind running a business before we start talking about other startup factors to consider.

LESSON 1: WHAT DOES IT TAKE TO START-UP A BUSINESS?
In this book, you will find out what it takes, but first from a constructive point of view, I would equate building a successful business to that of erecting a building structure; the only difference is that the business success is not based on the building but on the process, the people and the system. How do I mean exactly? If you want to erect a building, the first thing first in no order is the desire to build; the second is what kind of building are you constructing? Is it a bungalow, a duplex, a triplex, or a castle? Whatever structure you want to build will be highly dependent on three things

a) what is my purpose for building?

b) What Architectural design best fit the purpose to which I am building (Planning)? What is the bill of quantity required to erect such building from foundation to roofing c) The size of your budget? Now linking it; building a successful business can be expressed as the desire for building = Reason for the business, the purpose of building = the objective of the business existence and what type of business, Architectural design of building = business idea and viability, business plan, marketing strategy, and analysis. Bill of quantity for building construction = financial Planning, feasibility studies, budget for cash inflow and expenditure. Size of budget = Amount of maximum time to be imputed, the maximum amount of resources needed, plans and action implementation to maximize the resources. This brings us to other qualities needed to start a business from scratch, qualities such as:

a) Enthusiasm: I call this the fuel of the business, the engine oil of the business that keeps you going despite daring challenges that would make you feel like quitting but as a young entrepreneur filled with passion and energy for your dream little or no technical experience. Then you start feeling it is not necessary to acquire technical knowledge because what drives you instead is the money and prestige you wish to get from the idea/business. Well if that is all that there is, as your reason for wanting to be an entrepreneur/business owner then sorry to disappoint you but you might end up losing both passion, drive and money invested. Instead of making money you would end up losing money rather, be driven not by the money you will make, but the needs your idea will meet and solve? That should be what drives you and grow your passion and not the firm and fortune to be achieved. You need enthusiasm for your business to keep the fire in your heart burning because when the tides are down and the money and firm is not forthcoming from anywhere, enthusiasm will keep you going

b) Taking Risk: Successful entrepreneurs are those that are willing to take the risk for the growth and development of their business, as a small business owner into becoming a big business owner than as an investor. The difference between those that are successful in business from those that are not, is their ability to take what I call calculated risk and not careless risk. You should know that not every risk should be taken; there is some risk that if taken can untimely put you out of business. This kind of risk is what I call careless risk. Meanwhile calculated risk means careful analysis and potent viability of the business risk to be taken and possible consequence of failure and success.

c) Resilient: this means speedy recovery from problems, which can also be the ability to bounce back after facing a setback. If you must be successful in business you must have the ability to preserve through any circumstance you faced with in your business even in the midst of losses, heavy expenditure, rejection, and criticism, how you handle all of this determines how far and how high your business will fly.

d) Energetic: This I define as another driving force that keeps you going, which would have gotten others down, tired, and even depressed but in your case. you are like a tireless worker seeking for excellent results for your business with maximum profit as a reward of working long hours even with the presence of frustrating circumstances and situations.

e) Education: your degree qualification does not necessarily determine how successful you will become in business. which is the more reason why some researchers say entrepreneurs are born and not made while others say entrepreneurs are made not born using formal and informal education but for me, I say out of 3/3 of practical situation of leadership they are (1/3) born and (2/3) made. There are leadership and management theories that back this up such as trait theory and behavioral science but one thing to be noted is that education enhances the way you think, how you approach problems, and how they are solved. Of which a business without training and education as its INSIGHTs is a business scheduled for doom (a ticking time bomb waiting to explode) A few examples are: Charles Dunstone founder of hugely successful car phone warehouse dropped out of school but at least had a considerable level of formal education and high level of personal development. Same applies to bill gate dropping out from Harvard University and many others but one thing you should never forget is that if you want to be an entrepreneur with a difference you should submit yourself to personal development (informal education). Otherwise, you will end up a struggling entrepreneur trying to survive instead of being a prosperous entrepreneur that you were meant to be. The ball is in your court; you are the decider of what your tomorrow holds.

This brings us to type of business based on the duration of input, which is:

37 QUALITIES OF SUCCESSFUL BUSINESS ENTREPRENEURS

1] Commitment, determination, passion, and perseverance

2] Venture into the business you have knowledge about

3] Build your business around your talent

4] Do what you love doing

5] Be totally sold out to their cause to the point of death

6] Willing to pay a price to achieve their goals

7] Determined and unwavering to succeed

8] Persistent, patient and self-discipline.

9] Entrepreneurs have the drive to achieve

10] They are self-starters that are driven by an internal motivation to compete, excel against self-imposed standards, pursue, and attain challenging goals

11] Entrepreneurs are go-getters who do not see impossibility in any situations

12] They are ready to take challenges head on till they experience the set taste of victory

13] They can spot opportunities at every point

14] They examine new opportunities in line with their goals and priorities in trade fairs, exhibition centers, newspapers, and journals, etc.

15] Vision/direction

16] They dream big dreams

17] Have a clear vision and sense of direction

18] Set goals and write them down

19] Translate vision into mission, goals, giving strategic direction

20] Share vision with strategic stakeholders

21] Do one thing at a time

22] Make success out of failures

23] Learn from failures means your business is constantly improving

24] When it comes to developing winning habits, aim at doing everything perfectly every time

25] Believe in yourself (self-confident and values)

26] Be a positive thinker

27] Concentrate on positive activities

28] Act on issues and worry less

29] Accept ups and downs

30] Be a man of integrity with yourself and others

31] Live by principles to withstand storms in business

32] Manage time effectively, avoid time wasters (for examples: visitors and telephone conversations)

33] Develop a reputation for urgency

34] Avoid procrastination

35] Network with others in similar business

36] Tap from the knowledge and experience of those who have excelled in similar areas of business

37] Network with them and relate with them to gain skills in areas of weakness, such as bookkeeping, marketing, and distribution.

UNDERSTAND THE PHASES OF GROWING YOUR BUSINESS

My dad once told me "life is in phases men are in sizes", you must learn to pattern your effort into maximizing each phase you find yourself to make the best of the next phase you enter next. Same applies to business, business is in phases, you must understand the different phases of your business and learn the know-how involved in linking the different phases of your business to one become a success

Phase 1: Start-up Stage - This stage is usually one of the toughest periods, involving capital cost, resources and effort to bring the business into reality, to sustain a business in today's world you must be meeting the need of your target market or better still create a platform that will make your product seems like a need even though it isn't. Another approach is a pleasure; people are moved to buy products that are either pleasurable or very important need. Find your spot in the market that suits your uniqueness and use it to your advantage. As the saying going every system will always have a loophole, find yours and lead your business into being profitable.

Phase 2: Expansion Phase – Now at this stage the business has grown into profitability and here you are thinking of expanding into different locations or a location. The first thing that comes to heart is financial involvement in the establishment of replicating the company standards. At this stage all you need do is make your comprehensive logistics report on the intended branch to be created and ways of execution to reduce error to the barest minimum, of which once established you are good to go.

Phase 3: Consolidation Phase – Business is growing and profit is running in and you wish to settle down and develop the already existing company structures and branches into self-independent and self-sustaining. Even in the midst of crisis, one thing that can affect business of this level is change in technology in such business which would most likely have an effect in the way the company runs her operations which is first felt on the cost of change or transition at the earlier stage, then maintenance and repair become another problem as the company improves in its operations with its newest changes

Phase 4: Reinvented Phase – Here in this phase, research and a development team are created/form to improve the way workers carry out their duties, new blend of products is created, new technology in operations is designed to improve the precision and accuracy of which the products are being created and mass produce, saving money, increasing productivity and maximizing profit all at the same time

SESSION 1: YOUR MENTALITY; THE BEDROCK FOR YOUR BUSINESS SUCCESS

Figure 1: Big Business system

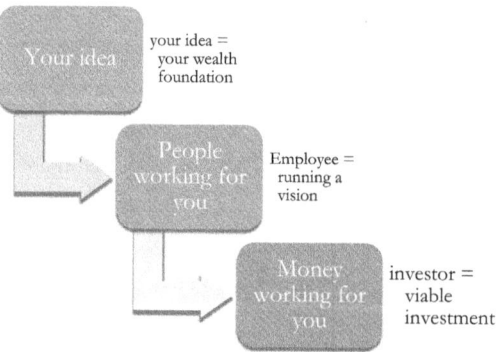

Figure 2: Breakdown of Big business System

To possess a wealth creative kind of mentality, you have to leave your comfort zoon, you need to stretch yourself to think outside the box of your usual mode of thinking? The question I am sure you must have started nurturing is how do I stretch myself to start thinking outside the box? Well, the question is simple, look around you, your environment, and checkbooks authored by men who you seek to be like in the nearest future, consult family and friends on how to generate creative ideas and ways of developing it. More importantly, as a person, you have to THINK, keep changing the style of your thinking by making it richer by attending seminars and workshops from there you would be so surprised how your destiny and mind will pop open into a realm of unlimited ideas. From a well-executed idea using the right approach will take you into the financial freedom that you seek but the first step is to consciously restructure your mind and mentality into ways that generate wealth.

Pattern Your Positive Mentality into generating Cash

> Your mentality= Your Future
>
> Convert your "I CAN'T" to "I CAN" mindset and in return change history positivly

Now that you have restructured your mentality into cash creation the next thing you should be after is how to convert your ideas and newly acquired mentality into wealth unlimited, with the mind of starting your own small and medium scale business. Money is simply a reward you get for meeting a need, it's a reward for solving a problem. Having an entrepreneurial mindset allows you to adapt quickly to changing situations and opportunities around you which when effectively utilized brings cash/profit as a reward. For example, you can't intend to start a restaurant business(food) today and start making thousands of dollars/naira/pound sterling from the first day, you have to be ready to patiently work the growth of that business from earning a few hundred a day to earn a few thousand a month then to a few million a year. Everything about business development is one step after another, it's like climbing a ladder and if all that interests you is in jumping from the base to the top of the ladder, now that, my friend is impossible unless you want to use jet pack to do that and of which you and I know that it's an unnatural and unrealistic thing to do if you consider it. So, you would have to keep climbing the ladder one after another until you get to the peak of that ladder. This is just how it works in the business world never make the mistake of cutting corners and trying to be fraudulent for if you do, your business will never live to see expansion season and development in other words in no time that business will be cut short of continuation and money making which will ultimately lead to the close down of the business. Now in terms of cash generation IDEA = RAW CASH with proper implementation and structured path of actions. *Back to the question how do u convert mentality into cash generation?*

THE CURRENT STATE OF YOUR MIND

70-95% of young graduate hopes to become employees after graduation, being that, right from high school down to having a graduate degree your parents must have been telling you to work hard get good grades, graduate from college, get a good job, and be a responsible person to yourself and to your society. This is the regular mentality our parents unconsciously programmed into our minds; either you go with such mentality or not is completely your choice to make. But don't forget that transcending from being an employee to being self-employed will not be a bed of roses for you so don't expect to start running your business and immediately start making the maximum profit that will yield millions of Naira/dollars without first changing your employee mentality to an entrepreneurial mindset.

JOB = No Employee can be richer than the Organization they work for. It means that if you start-up your business with an employee mindset it's just a matter of time before the business collapses or you close down the business yourself when the bills start coming in. so if you want to get a job make sure to be the best in what you do and how you get things done in the best time possible.

SELF EMPLOYMENT = Self-Employed owned a Start-up Business. If you don't work out a *business plan, strategy and implementation plan* to grow your business into a working business system then be rest assured that the business will die as a start-up, example of self-employed business that stays small as a result of poor mentality and bad planning or no planning at all is kiosk, spare part business, homemade product like liquid soap and so on. Any small business can grow. The growth level is dependent on the approach and mindset of the visionary.

BUSINESS OWNERS = Big Business Owners have a business system, with employees working for them and generating profit. A good **example** of this kind of business is Dettol soap, toothpaste, the alcohol drinks like a star, Guinness, Dansa drink and so on. This kind of business is businesses with well-established business structure and centralized management that grew from small/medium scale business into becoming a big business because of good management, well-planned and organized business environment and most importantly leveraging on the expertise of trained professionals/employees. To grow the company into diversity and variety thereby building a strong brand presence and market share.

INVESTORS = Investors own business systems, their money is working, for them, people, and business are working for them. A good example of such businesses that have grown so much to become working investment is for **Example** Telecom companies in Nigeria, Dangote group of companies, Milo and other network marketing businesses, stock exchange and buying of equity from SME with the prospect of becoming big businesses tomorrow.

From Robert Kiyosaki Quadrant, you can see clearly for yourself that there is a big difference between an employee, an entrepreneur and an investor, when I say there is a big difference I am not referring to the fact that they are in separate quadrant but I'm referring to the educational orientation, mentality, resources, energy, and risk involved in keeping that business running on its feet in each of the cash flow quadrants. For this book, we are mainly concerned with the *second quadrant which is self-employed and possibly grows into being a business owner.*

Background: There is a popular quote that says "you might not be responsible for what happened to you yesterday, but you are completely responsible for what happens to you today. The financial background of your family notwithstanding but you are completely responsible for the financial status of your family for both now and into the future".

Pastor Mensa once said that "if you are not driven by your future then you will surely be controlled by your past"

Your family financial background has nothing to do with your prosperity or your financial prospect (wealth) for the present and future. In today's world, we have heard of men who grew from nothing to becoming world richest men. A typical example is John D Rockefeller who is known as America first billionaire coming from a financial challenge background where to even survive on three square meals was a problem grew into wealth and financial freedom just by choosing not to be an employee, but an employer and grew to become one of the most influential men in his time, Why? Because he made a decision to change the story of his family and generation unborn by taking the first step to go into oil and gas business of which was born out of the need to lightening the rooms of Americans and in no distance, time became so wealthy that his business was the reason for somebody else livelihood. Growing from being a business owner to being a big business owner as seen from Robert Kiyosaki quadrant of cash flow. He was not the only one that grew an empire from nothing to something we have other likes of him such as J.P Morgan the business tycoon, Carnegie the steel man who built a steel plant from nothing into giving him an empire of wealth and affluence. A wise man once said "never let your background put your back on the ground, there are certain things you can't change but there are other things you can certainly change such as your lifestyle and your financial freedom". I would put mine as "you might not have the power to change where you are coming from but you can certainly change where you are going to". I don't know what your dream has always being, either you want to be among the world richest men or to become a big business owner or to be a great investor where money does all the work for you but what I do know is that you can never achieve any of this dream if you keep nurturing an "employee mentality". You can never become a celebrated entrepreneur if you choose to remain in your comfort zoon of collecting a salary for the reason of living comfortably. There are exceptions to this reason, why some people work for others, some do it with the perception of owning their own business after they have acquired expertise and competence while others do it for fear of losing it all or presence of bills at hand to pay while a few others based theirs on lifestyle. But my question is for how long do you intend to keep working for others you have to measure it otherwise you might get carried away with the goodies and comfort that comes with the job to the point that you would forget that you ever had a dream of becoming an entrepreneur and not to talk of becoming a big business owner. If only you understand the business languages well, it would be like taking candy from a child. I would list a couple of noted belief and mentality people keep for never becoming entrepreneurs or chasing their dreams for financial freedom.

a) What of after committing my money to a business and it fails?

b) I have friends and know a couple of family members with relatives that have gone into self-employed businesses and never made it financially

c) I don't have the means and the financial fund to do the business

d) My parents want me to get a job, work for someone and be responsible

e) I have gone into starting my own business in the past but it failed, all the money invested went down the drain

f) I am confused, I have a couple of business I want to do but I don't know which one to do, I want to do all?

g) I am not good enough for business, it's meant for others not me

h) I have a business idea but I am too excited about this idea to the point that I don't know where to start and how to go about?

I) I have started running my own business but I got frustrated because it's not yielding profit so I quit

j) I lose money anytime I start a business but make a lot of money each time I work for others or work as an agent so as for owning my own business I am not interested

k) I want to make quick millions to show off and starting my own business will not give me that opportunity to make the kind of money I want

l) I prefer to make money from scamming others of their money than starting my own business because it's easier and faster, after all, it's a self-employed business

m) I have no clue what I can do or what I want to do, I am waiting for the right moment to get an idea before starting my own business

n) I prefer to own a business started by others than to start my own business from the scratch it's just too much hard work, I would prefer to buy another person failing business but right now I will work for others until I see who is willing to sell one to me even if it's a failing business

Don't let any of the stated excuses be a criterion, all you need is right at your fingertips if only you can see them. If you belong to any of the reason for not starting that business into a change of story into one of the most successful men history will not forget then I suggest you get started. Don't forget that Thomas Edison tried making incandescent light bulb for over 1000times if he stopped along the line he won't be celebrated now and somebody else would have done what he was supposed to have done? Let me ask you if he had given up on himself, would you have any interest in knowing him? Don't forget that there is a quote that says "the fall of a man is not the end of his life", if you fall arise again, check out why you fell and make changes and move on, don't let that fall affect your future for if you don't deal with your past you will pass away with it. So, forge ahead and look forward to having a bright future. Whatever it is you have gone through don't ever forget that somebody has gone through the same thing and even worse and has conquered it and is being celebrated, **what would your story be? How do you want yourself to be remembered? What do you want to be remembered for? Think about it and give yourself an answer** Think about it and start working your way into financial freedom. If you are in doubt go online and find out about people in your situation and you will be so amazed how many people have gone through the same thing and even worse than yours and they conquered. If they did it why can't you do the same?

Structure Your Mentality into Wealth Creation and financial freedom

Wealth Creation; this chart is what differentiates small business owners and investors. This chart is a typical chart of a big investor and a big business owner. The chart that is drawn below is a chart that explains to you that there is nothing extraordinary about big business owners. The only reason why they are richer and far more powerful than you are because they have paid the prize and have all worked on trade secrets that took them to where they are today. In these books you will find out all you need to know just follow every chapter patiently, the hidden things you should know about the wealth creation chart is that there are things you need to do and carry out if you must transcend from having an idea to hiring employees then down to making money that allows you to build people which in-process builds businesses for you.

ROBERT KIYOSAKI MINDSET DIFFERENCES BETWEEN THE RICH AND THE POOR

POOR AND MIDDLE CLASS

1] They want to be rich

2] They believe "Life happens to them" - victimized

3] They play the money game not to lose

4] They think Small, think limitations, wish and hope a lot

5] They focus on obstacles rather than the solution

6] They associate with negative and unsuccessful people

7] They are smaller than their problems

8] They focus on their working income – instant gratification

9] They think they already know it all (Have, Do Be)

10] They choose to get money based on time

FINANCIALLY INDEPENDENT AND RICH

1] They believe "I create my life" - accept full responsibility

2] They play the money game to win

3] They think Big, think Possibilities, dream a lot

4] They focus on opportunities

5] They associate with rich and successful people

6] They are willing to promote themselves and their values

7] They focus on their net worth rather than their profit

8] They manage their money well - buy assets

9] They have their money work hard for them

10] They act despite fear

11] They constantly learn and grow (Be, Do, Have)

12] They choose to get money based on results

To possess a wealth creative kind of mentality, you must leave your comfort zoon, you need to stretch yourself to think outside the box of your usual mode of thinking? The question I am sure you must have started nurturing is how do I stretch myself to start thinking outside the box? Well, the question is simple, look around you, your environment, and checkbooks authored by men who you seek to be like in the nearest future, consult family and friends on how to generate creative ideas and ways of developing it. More importantly, as a person, you must THINK, keep changing the style of your thinking by making it richer by attending seminars and workshops from there you would be so surprised how your destiny and mind will pop open into a realm of unlimited ideas. From a well-executed idea using the right approach will take you into the financial freedom that you seek but the first step is to consciously restructure your mind and mentality into ways that generate wealth.

Pattern Your Positive Mentality into generating Cash

Your mentality = Your Future

How are you able to convert your "I CAN'T" to "I CAN" spirit will depend on your business perception and believes, but if you can change it you are right, if you can't you are equally right. Remember, both lead to different futures (good and bad). Choose wisely.

Now that you have restructured your mentality into cash creation the next thing you should be after is how to convert your ideas and newly acquired mentality into wealth unlimited, with the mind of starting your own small and medium scale business. Money is simply a reward you get for meeting a need, it's a reward for solving a problem. Having an entrepreneurial mindset allows you to adapt quickly to changing situations and opportunities around you which when effectively utilized brings cash/profit as a reward. For example, you can't intend to start a restaurant business(food) today and start making thousands of dollars/naira/pound sterling from the first day, you have to be ready to patiently work the growth of that business from earning a few hundred a day to earn a few thousand a month then to a few million a year. Everything about business development is one step after another, it's like climbing a ladder and if all that interests you is in jumping from the base to the top of the ladder, now that, my friend is impossible unless you want to use jet pack to do that and of which you and I know that it's an unnatural and unrealistic thing to do if you consider it. So, you would have to keep climbing the ladder one after another until you get to the peak of that ladder. This is just how it works in the business world never make the mistake of cutting corners and trying to be fraudulent for if you do, your business will never live to see expansion season and development in other words in no time that business will be cut short of continuation and money making which will ultimately lead to the close down of the business. Now in terms of cash generation IDEA = RAW CASH with proper implementation and structured path of actions. *Back to the question how do u convert mentality into cash generation?*

Enthusiasm about Your Business = Business Strategy = Properly Executed Business Line of Actions = Customer Satisfaction = Money.

Document Important Dates and Action Steps for It Would Become Valuable on the Day of Reward and Celebration

A wise man once said "After every pain of labor is a success", but I believe that "After every well-executed pain of labor on the right path comes to your glorious success". Never forget that an idea is like a virus if passionate about can consume you into actualization even if others don't believe in it, you still do because you only understand its importance and why it needs to be actualized. When that happens rather than dying with the beauty of how sweet the idea is check for its viability, remember that an excellent idea can turn out to produce a rubbish result if it is poorly implemented or executed and an insanely stupid idea can fetch your millions of dollars/naira if adequately executed. Now after putting all of these to actions, you need to consciously document all transaction, dates, where it was done, when you got your idea and so on. Reason being that on the day of celebration where people would call you on radio shows and newsroom to talk, giving them precise information on dates and timing sells these ideas to your listeners that you are a man of details. You keep track of what you do which helps you measure how far you are going either on the right path or actions just implanted wrongly.

Your Financial Growth and Status

For successful businesspeople see opportunities with the eyes of their mind, while non-successful or small business owners see risk and impossibility instead. Making the difference clear between individual business owners. Remember there are just four ways in which you can generate income as an individual of which all the cash generation approaches and cash flow starts from the mind.

I) **Make money as an employee or an employer:** this deals with working for others to build their dreams. **Demerit:** you are liable to be sacked, retrenched, or be retired

ii) **Make money as an Entrepreneur:** Here you are the president, accountant, and the manager, at this point the business is still trying to gain its feet as financially independent and stable. Therefore, the money you make from here goes straight back into the business.

iii) **Make money as a big business owner:** At this point this business can work and generate money with or without the presence of the business owner, meaning that though the business owner would be around for about 65% of the time even for that 35% time of absence the company is still making money.

iv) **Make money as a business system owner (investor):** Here the business has grown to the point where your presence is required as low as 35% to 10% of the time meaning that the rest of the other time remaining these business system owners run other business alongside and equally building investment in many other companies and business.

All of what you have just read above would be made much more achievable and realistic when you P.U.S.H yourself to the point of building your business into millions yielding and later into an empire. I define P.U.S.H as

P - Persist

U - Until

S - Something

H - Happens.

Meaning hardship and challenges will come but what will make all the difference is how you have been able to push yourself to success through persistence and a never quitting spirit to never give up and keep fighting even when it seems like there is no reason to continue as achievement is becoming very blur and unachievable. But I want you to know this the only impossibility that exists are the limitations you set for yourself. The word IMPOSSIBLE just simply means I'm possible. Which means anything is possible if you believe it.

APPROACHES TO EARNING FINANCIAL FREEDOM

1) Start your business yourself.

1B) Do all the business key Positions yourself and create your own business system.

1C) Have most or almost all the knowledge your business needs by yourself.

2) Start it yourself initially but add partners along the way

2B) Know and perfect the business system and get people to do it for you

2C) Take the opportunity to recruit people either on contract bases or full-time employment that your business needs for growth

3) Start the business with others/partners from scratch, but be the founder/highest company stock

3B) Use an already made known business system that works, renovate/refine, and use it to make your business grow(franchise)

3C) Grow the business up to a time frame which must be based on contract and agreement to establish your own unique product different from your franchise product or services

3D) build people to run the business and the people will build the business.

HOW TO SURVIVE IN THE BUSINESS WORLD

1) Create parameters that will allow you recognize opportunities and capitalize on them by creating a need to be seen by those with the opportunity or holding the opportunity that doesn't even know it, or best done by negotiating to strike a win-win situation

2) Start small but make your competitors believe you are not the enemy most especially when they know you until you are fully ready to compete and beat them out of the market but in most times create your own space in the already saturated market

ADDAGE: *A cub that dares challenge a buffalo to a fight will get itself beaten even before the battle begins rather the cub that chooses to win must first grow up and be strong enough to win the battle over the bull if fought.*

3) Create a need with your business and people will need you, meet their need and they will demand you like a man in need of oxygen to breathe.

4) You survive not because you are in the business but because you make people need you because of what you have and also create relevance and need of your product, when that happens they have nowhere else to go except to come to you but if it's a no then you are as good as broke, poor and frustrated making you a complete nobody.

LESSON 2: 12 MOVES SUMMARY STEPS IN STARTING A STARTUP
This varies depending on the country you are currently residing in or doing business in. Every country has their business laws, procedures, and approaches

in starting a startup. It is your duty to discover what those steps are and start following it.

1) First Move to Starting A Business: Come Up with a Great Name for Your Business. Selecting the right name for your startup can have a significant impact on your business success. The wrong name could result in insurmountable legal and business hurdles. Here are some basic tips on how to name your startup:

a) Avoid hard-to-spell names or names that are too long to pronounce all at once.

b) Don't pick a name that can limit your business growth or business expansion.

c) Conduct a thorough google search on your proposed name to check if it already exists online.

d) Get a ".com", ".org" domain name or other domain that is associated with your country.

e) Conduct a thorough trademark search, a good place to start is google search to see what is available and what is already taken, it will shock you to know that the name you are thinking may already have been registered by someone else. Don't assume that the name is available, take the pain to check, just check.

f) Ask yourself if you were an employee would you like to associate with the name, can you confidently talk about your name and be sure that its memorable and not hard to pronounce or remember, if it is revise it or change it.

g) Come up with five names you like and test market the name with prospective friends, partners, investors, or potential customers. All you must do is just ask; you will be so surprised the response you get.

2) Your Second Move will be: Your Vision, Mission Statement and Business Registration (Chapter 2 and 3 talks about this). Determine what services you will offer and what product will you be selling and how is it different from the competition. Once all of this is finished you move to what business model are you adopting in terms of operations, management and picking team players to join your course.

3) Third move will be: Build a Good Website for Your Company

You should devote time and effort to building a good website for your business. Prospective investors, customers, and partners are going to check out your site, and you want to impress them with a professional product. You can check Chapter 5 for more details. Below are a few tips for building a good company website:

a) Check competitor websites and see what they are offering.

b) Draft out how you will stand out with them on a customer competition battle in terms of branding and skill set network.

c) draft five or six websites you can share with your web site developer and express how you want yours to be like in relations to theirs.

d) Be sure your website is search engine optimized (and thus more likely to show up on Google search results). If you don't know how, hire an SEO Specialist to create one for you.

e) Produce high-quality content in form of blogs to drive traffic to your website, if you are too busy pay content writers to write for you.

f) Make sure your content is optimized for spelling errors.

g) Make sure the website does not take forever to load.

h) Keep it clean and simple.

i) Make sure you have a Terms of Use Agreement and Privacy Policy (and comply with the European GDPR rules). If you don't know to create one contact an expert to help you create one.

j) Make the navigation bars on the website prominent and clickable.

k) Obtain and use a memorable ".com" domain name or whatever domain name that is available for your chosen brand name.

L) Make sure it's easy for site visitors to contact you or buy your product.

4) Fourth Move is: Make it Clear with Co-Founders from the beginning on what everyone is getting from the business

If you start your company with co-founders, you should agree early on about the details of your business relationship. Not doing so can potentially cause significant legal problems down the road when the going gets good and money starts coming in (a good example of this is the infamous Zuckerberg/Winklevoss Facebook litigation). In a way, think of the founder agreement as a form of "bond." Below are a few tips your written founder agreement needs to address according to Fotolia.Com:

a) How is the equity split among the founders?

b) Is the percentage of ownership subject to vesting based on continued participation in the business?

c) What are the roles and responsibilities of the founders?

d) If one founder leaves, does the company or the other founder have the right to buy back that founder's shares? At what price?

e) How much time commitment to the business is expected of each founder?

f) What salaries (if any) are the founders entitled to? How can that be changed?

g) How are key decisions and day-to-day decisions of the business to be made? (by majority vote, unanimous vote, or are certain decisions solely in the hands of the CEO?)

h) Under what circumstances can a founder be removed as an employee of the business? (usually, this would be a Board decision)

i) What assets or cash does each founder contribute or invest into the business?

j) How will a sale of the business be decided?

k) What happens if one founder isn't living up to expectations under the founder agreement? How will it be resolved?

l) What is the overall goal and vision for the business?

5) Next move: you must become a Strong Salesperson, if you are not then getting a co-founder or a management team member that has your weakness as his strength. Chapter 7 explains this in details, you can view this for more information on this subject.

If the business is to become successful, you must become a great salesperson. You are going to have to learn how to "sell" your business—not only to customers but also to prospective investors and even to potential employees. If you don't know how to market what you do via word of mouth, if you the shy type, and you don't like talking about your business. Then a strongly recommend you go and get a job and leave entrepreneurship alone for now then later after you have overcome such weaknesses you can pick up from where you left off. Otherwise stay in your full-time job.

It's important to be positive, trustworthy, and to learn how to listen. You must practice your sales pitch, get feedback from a variety of people, and then refine your pitch. Even if you are not naturally an extrovert, you need to show confidence, follow up, and ask for the sale.

6) Next move in your Startup Adventure: Understand Financial Statements and Budgets at least the Basics of financial statement, it will come in very handy when pitching to investors or prospective donors to your brand including family and friends

It's important to keep on top of your expenses and learn how to thoroughly understand financial statements and budgeting. Many startups fail because the entrepreneur can't adjust their spending to avoid running out of cash. Establishing a detailed, month-by-month budget is crucial, and this budget must be reviewed regularly to avoid making unrealistic budgets.

Understanding your financial statements will also help you answer questions from prospective investors. According to Richard Harroch he offered some financial question tips statement you should expect to get from investors:

a) What are the company's three-year projections?

b) What are the key assumptions underlying your projections?

c) How much equity and debt has the company raised, and what is the capitalization structure?

d) What future equity or debt financing will be necessary?

e) How much of a stock option pool is being set aside for employees?

f) When will the company get to profitability?

g) How much "burn" (losses) will occur until the company gets to profitability?

h) What are your unit economics?

i) What are the factors that limit faster growth?

j) What are the key metrics that the management team focuses on?

6b) Determine Which Permits, Licenses, or Registrations You Will Need for Your Business

Depending on the nature of the business, you may need the following permits, licenses, or regulations:

a) Permits need for regulated businesses (aviation, agriculture, alcohol, etc.)

b) Sales tax license or permit

c) Home-based business permits

d) City and county business permits or licenses

e) Zoning permit

f) Seller's permit

g) Health department permits (such as for a restaurant)

h) Federal and state tax/employer IDs

7) Next Move: Market Your Business Like Crazy

To succeed in business, you need to continually be attracting, building, and even educating your target market. Make sure your marketing strategy includes the following:

a) Learn the fundamentals of SEO (search engine optimization) so that people searching for your products and services online might find you near the top of search results.

b) Use social media to promote your business (LinkedIn, Facebook, Twitter, Pinterest, etc.).

c) Engage in content marketing by writing guest articles for relevant websites.

d) Issue press releases for any significant events relating to your business.

e) Network continually by attending events that allows you meet other employers of labour, CEO and entrepreneurs.

8) Next Move: Drive Traffic to Your Website using Digital media platforms

While entire books have been written on this topic, the key ways to drive traffic to your website are as follows:

a) Pay Google, Bing, Yahoo, or other search engines to send you traffic (such as through the Google AdWords program).

b) Build a good website with lots of high-quality, original content that is search engine optimized.

c) Have a smart social media plan to drive traffic from Facebook, Twitter, LinkedIn, and other free social media sites.

d) Get links to your site from high-quality sites.

9) Next Move afterwards: Use Consultants and Freelancers to Supplement Your Team

At the early stages of your startup, you will likely want to have a small employee team to minimize expenses. A good way to fill in for specialized expertise is to use freelancers or consultants. That way, you avoid taking on employee costs and benefits payments. Though you need to know that freelancers will not be loyal to your course or what you are building, it's all about the money for them compare to employees you hire. And there are a variety of sites that can help you access freelancers, such as freelancer.com, Guru.com and upwork.com.

10) A very important move: Secure Capital to Finance Your Business

Here is a summary of the most effective sources of business capital that is available for you as a business:

a) Personal funds

b) Credit cards

c) Friends and family

d) Angel investors

e) Crowdsourcing sites such as Indiegogo.com and Kickstarter.com

f) Bank loans/SBA financings/online lenders

g) Venture capitalists

h) Equipment loan financing

One of the biggest mistakes made by startups is not raising enough capital. You can find more information on this in Chapter 6 of this book

10b) Next move after last step: Seeking Angel Investing Financing, keep these Important Points in mind

In reviewing a prospective investment, angel investors especially care about:

a) The quality, passion, commitment, and experience of the founders

b) The market opportunity being addressed and the potential for the company to grow to become very big

c) A clearly thought out business plan and early evidence of early business traction

d) Interesting intellectual property or technology

e) A reasonable valuation for the company

f) The likelihood of the company being able to raise additional financing in the future if progress is made

Angel investors will want to initially see the following from a startup:

a) A clearly articulated elevator pitch for the business

b) An executive summary or investor pitch deck

c) A prototype or working model of the company's product or service

d) Early adopters, customers, or partners

11) Run the last move and this move simultaneously, Next Move: Understand These Key Points About Seeking Venture Capital Financing

Startups seeking financing often turn to venture capital (VC) firms, which can provide capital; strategic assistance; introductions to potential customers, partners, and employees; and much more.

Venture capital financings are not easy to obtain or close. Entrepreneurs will be better prepared to obtain VC financing if they understand the process, the anticipated deal terms, and the potential issues that will arise.

To understand the process of obtaining VC financing, it is important to know that venture capitalists typically focus their investment efforts using one or more of the following criteria according to Fotolia.Com:

a) Specific industry sectors (software, digital media, semiconductor, mobile, SaaS, biotech, mobile devices, etc.)

b) Stage of company (early-stage seed or Series A rounds, or later-stage rounds with companies that have achieved meaningful revenues and traction)

c) Company location (e.g., San Francisco/Silicon Valley, New York, etc.)

Before approaching a venture capitalist, try to learn whether his or her focus aligns with your company and its stage of development.

The second key point to understand is that VCs get inundated with investment opportunities, many through unsolicited emails—almost all those unsolicited emails are ignored. The best way to get the attention of a VC is to have a warm introduction through a trusted colleague, entrepreneur, or lawyer friendly to the VC.

A startup must have a good "elevator pitch" (as discussed in point #6) and a strong investor pitch deck (as discussed in point #18) to attract the interest of a VC.

Startups should also understand that the venture process can be very time consuming—just getting a meeting with a principal of a VC firm can take weeks; followed up with more meetings and conversations; followed by a presentation to all of the partners of the venture capital fund; followed by the issuance and negotiation of a term sheet, with continued due diligence; and finally the drafting and negotiation by lawyers on both sides of numerous legal documents to evidence the investment.

VCs usually want to see that your business has made some progress and gotten some traction in the market; they will typically not fund a very early stage company or just an idea. For that, you are better off seeking angel investors.

Most venture capitalists won't agree to sign an NDA, so don't bother asking.

For a comprehensive article on the venture capital financing process,

12. Next Move: Pay Attention to Your Business Contracts After getting the Deal if you are been given but if you are the one giving, get an expert to help you craft one, and "avoid shooting yourself on the foot" with terms and conditions that later turns you into a slave in your own establishment.

Business contracts are legally binding written agreements between two or more parties. They are an important part of business and such agreements need to be created and/or negotiated carefully. While smaller businesses will often conduct business based on informal handshake agreements or unspoken understandings, the more that is at stake, the more essential it is to have a signed contract. A contract serves as the rules that must be followed by both parties. It presents each party with the opportunity to:

a) Describe all obligations they are expected to fulfill.

b) Describe all obligations they expect the other party (or parties) to fulfill.

Limit any liabilities.

c) Set parameters, such as a time frame, in which the terms of the contract will be met.

d) Set terms of a sale, lease, or rental.

e) Establish payment terms.

f) Clearly establish all the risks and responsibilities of the parties.

A contract is a written meeting of the minds. While it is typically drawn up by one party and favors the needs and requirements of that party, protecting them from most (if not all) liabilities, it should initially be thought of as a work in progress that changes and grows as each party contributes prior to signing, after which it becomes an official document. "Consideration," whether it is monetary or a promise to do work or provide a service by a specified date, is at the root of a contract.

The term "standard contract" is more myth than reality, and too often people simply sign on the dotted line without reading or negotiating the terms of a contract. A startup must make sure it is comfortable with all the terms of the contract, and depending on the deal dynamics, almost any term is negotiable.

Consideration, compensation, ownership rights, liability, and risk are all areas that need to be worded carefully. You should seek out help from a qualified attorney who is experienced in contracts to make sure you have covered each of these areas in a clear manner.

The contract itself should stipulate how it shall be enforced and what actions can be taken if one party fails to meet their obligations. It is often to the benefit of smaller businesses to have a confidential binding arbitration clause to resolve any disputes.

According to Richard Harroch, The key contracts that a startup should have as its own form of "standard contract" (drafted in the startup's favour) including :

a) Sales or service agreement

b) License agreement

c) Offer letter to employees

d) Consulting agreement with any independent contractors (you want to make sure that you will own the intellectual property rights for anything they develop for your business)

e) Confidentiality and Invention Assignment Agreement for employees and independent contractors

f) Non-disclosure agreement

LESSON 3: ENTREPRENEURSHIP; THE REALITY OF A BUSINESS OWNER

Don't Spend too much time on the planning phase if you do, or you are currently doing that, there will always be a reason to delay your launch until you eventually lose the passion. Develop the product into an MVP (minimum viable product) which means developing a product with only the key features and introducing the others later as you progress.

Consider the Steps needed to Protect Your Intellectual Property

It is important to protect your company's intellectual property (IP). Ever wary of minimizing burn rate, startups may be tempted to defer investment in intellectual property protection. To those who have not tried to protect intellectual property, it feels complex and expensive. Too often, startups end up forfeiting intellectual property rights by neglecting to protect their ideas and inventions.

Some simple and cost-effective techniques can minimize the anxiety, yet help protect core assets. Companies sometimes think that patent protection is the only way to protect themselves. Technology startups frequently ignore the value of non-patent intellectual property. While patents can be incredibly valuable, it does not necessarily ensure that a company's product is a good product or that it will sell well. Trade secrets, cybersecurity policies, trademarks, and copyrights can all be forms of IP that can be protected.

According to Richard Harroch summary involving types of intellectual property protections that is available to an entrepreneur:

a) Patents. Patents are the best protection you can get for a new product. A patent gives its inventor the right to prevent others from making, using, or selling the patented subject matter described in the patent's claims. The key issues in determining whether you can get a patent are:

(1) Only the concrete embodiment of an idea, formula, or product is patentable;

(2) the invention must be new or novel;

(3) the invention must not have been patented or described in a printed publication previously; and

(4) the invention must have some useful purpose. In the United States you obtain a patent from the U.S. Patent and Trademark Office, but this process can take several years and be complicated. You typically need a patent lawyer to draw up the patent application for you. The downside of patents is that they can be expensive to obtain and take several years,

b) Copyrights. Copyrights cover original works of authorship, such as art, advertising copy, books, articles, music, movies, software, etc. A copyright gives the owner the exclusive right to make copies of the work and to prepare derivative works (such as sequels or revisions) based on the work.

c) Trademarks. A trademark right protects the symbolic value of a word, name, symbol, or device that the trademark owner uses to identify or distinguish its goods from those of others. Some well-known trademarks include the Coca-Cola trademark, American Express trademark, and IBM trademark. You obtain rights to a trademark by using the mark in commerce. You don't need to register the mark to get rights to it, but federal registration does offer some advantages. You register a mark with the U.S. Patent and Trademark Office.

d) Service Marks. Service marks resemble trademarks and are used to identify services.

e) Trade Secrets. Trade secrets can be a great asset for startups. They are cost effective and last for as long as the trade secret maintains its confidential status and derives value through its secrecy. A trade secret right allows the owner of the right to act against anyone who breaches an agreement or confidential relationship, or who steals or uses other improper means to obtain secret information. Trade secrets can range from computer programs to customer lists to the formula for Coca-Cola.

f) Confidentiality Agreements. These are also referred to as Non-Disclosure Agreements or NDAs. The purpose of the agreement is to allow the holder of confidential information (such as a product or business idea) to share it with a third party. But then the third party is obligated to keep the information confidential and not use it whatsoever, unless allowed by the owner of the information. There are usually standard exceptions to the confidentiality obligations (such as if the information is already in the public domain).

g) Confidentiality Agreement for Employees and Consultants. Every employee and consultant should be required to sign such an agreement, as discussed above.

h) Terms of Service and Privacy Policy. If you are a company that conducts its business on the internet, it is important to have a terms of service agreement that limits what users can or cannot do on your website and with the information on your site. Closely related is your Privacy Policy, which sets forth what privacy protections are available to your users. The new European GDPR rules may also need to be addressed.

This chapter summarizes the general knowledge of starting up a business from scratch the next coming chapter will explain in details how startup ideas can be generated, developed, and managed which will involve using Nigeria as case study

CHAPTER 2
LESSONS AND FACTORS TO CONSIDER TO AVOID START-UP FAILURE

If you are bothered with the idea of starting a company, worried about things that may go wrong or making the wrong decisions, are you just starting a company but are concerned about how you are doing things? You are not alone, and you are definitely not in unchartered waters.

While you are working on your business plan, how you would establish your business and also looking for ways to raise capital, finding the right people to hire or work with you, etc., part of the process involves asking others for their help and advice and doing lots of research to make sure you are on the right path. But have you ever had the opportunity to pick the brains of founders who created amazingly successful start-ups and companies like Envato, Backblaze, Simple, or Treehouse?

From my findings of founders from the nine well-known and/or growing start-ups based on a one-on-one interview – most of which you'll have heard of – you may even use their services – to ask them about one of the toughest areas of starting your own company' what mistakes did they make and how did they overcome them?

Few people like talking about their mistakes, but thankfully nine founders took some time though but some of them shared their experience on business start-up. So based on the interview conducted some of the most common mistakes and how to avoid them, using the words from the founders themselves from Envato, Dribbble, Freshbooks, 6Wunderkinder, Treehouse, Backblaze, Simple, Shapeways, and Statamic would be explained in the next few lessons in this chapter.

SESSION 1: STARTING A COMPANY WITH A MISSION AND PURPOSE

A company without a purpose is like ship sailing the high seas without having any particular destination. For any company of today's 21st century world must survive, then the need for a mission and purpose would come handle. The next question would be **what is Purpose?**

PURPOSE based on **Microsoft® Encarta® 2009** definition, defined purpose as

reason for existence: the reason for which something exists or for which it has being done or made

a) the *purpose of life*

desired effect: the goal or intended outcome of something

a) The *purpose of the law is to control pollution.*

determination: the desire or the resolve necessary to accomplish a goal

a) You *need to act with purpose.*

Purpose can also be translated based on context usage as ☐ intention, intent (formal), aim, object, objective, and goal. So, with all of these definitions you would see that a business without an objective or an intention or a drive, that simply came into existence would suffer three kind of fate 1) business expansion will be limited 2) business might never survive a 5years existence of growth 3) the business can transform into a pipe, money draining business **(making losses)** instead of making profit and maximum gain.

What does mission mean? Based on **Microsoft® Encarta® 2009** definition

1. **assigned task:** a special task given to a person or group to carry out

2. **calling:** an objective or task that somebody believes it is his or her duty to carry out or to which he or she attaches special importance and devotes special care

3. **space vehicle's trip:** a single flight or voyage of a military aircraft or a spacecraft

4. **group of representatives:** a group of people sent to a country to represent their government, a business, or other organization

5. **Diplomatic representation abroad:** a permanent diplomatic delegation in another.

Now I am sure by now you have started asking what then the difference between purpose and mission is. In a concise **definition purpose** is the picture of the future concerning your vision. It is just the reason for existence, that is to say every business established is done on the platform of a need to establish a solution to a problem. For a business that is not built on this plat form will welder away with time, like it never existed. While **Mission** is the now task/duty you create for yourself that would help you achieve vision which would actually lead to achievement of purpose. Through the use of short-term goals to make it a reality. **From the words of co-founder of Treehouse**

"[…] the biggest advice you can ever get is, the one of starting a company that's on a mission, not just a company that's building a nifty product. *"At Tree house, we're trying to make technology education affordable and accessible to everyone on Earth, and doing that means that we'll be working for a really long time and will likely always have more to do". - Alan Johnson, Co-founder of Treehouse*

From the words of co-founders of Dribble *"Solve a real problem that creates real value in the world. Focus on the problem => and try to make a pass through this sequence sooner than later. Also, be strategic. Find a competitive advantage. At Dribble, we stumbled into ours – we were just building a side project, but it was a site for designers, and Dan is a designer with lots of recognition and credibility. As a result, we attracted a great set of initial users who posted incredible work. Things snowballed from there."-by Rich Thornett and Dan Cederholm, Co-founders of Dribble*

LESSON 1: NOTHING IS IMPOSSIBLE IF YOU CAN THINK POSSIBILITY

If you can dream it, you can achieve it. If you can see it then it's not too far for you to get. The only impossibility that exists is the one you create for yourself. You are who you are. You my friend, is completely responsible for the outcome of your life whether you fail or you succeed is completely dependent on you. So, to achieve the unachievable you have to start thinking the unthinkable, the clear-cut difference between well paid workers sitting in the office and under paid workers working from morning to night is the ability of highly paid workers to think and bring money into the organization/company and as for the under paid workers they are seen as routine workers. Workers doing d same thing over and over again which works best for maintenance of the facility/company but will never make, not even 2% of the money the thinkers bring into the organization on daily bases.

From the words of CEO of Shapeways "Never take no for an answer. Starting a start-up isn't easy and there will always be people who tell you that it is impossible. Don't listen. When I started Shapeways, complex software needed to be built and when I first reached out to developers, a lot of them laughed and told me it was impossible. I never took no for an answer and eventually found a great team that helped me build what Shapeways is today. Always push for yes! "-*by Pete Weijmarshausen, CEO of Shapeways*

From co-founder and VP of operations of Freshbooks *"On a macro level, one of the most daunting challenges was the prospect of entering a market with a fairly large entrenched player. Our strategy was to not even attempt to take them on head-to-head by trying to offer everything they did, instead, we sliced off a piece of the solution that we believed we could do better and that addressed a critical pain point for small businesses – invoicing."-by Levi Cooperman, Co-founder and VP of Operations of Freshbooks.*

LESSON 2: *UNDERESTIMATING YOUR POTENTIAL (LOW SELF-ESTEEM)*
One of the silent killers of potentials and talent is seeing yourself that you are not good enough, that no matter what you do would keep failing. Then you start telling yourself about people that have failed and never made it in business or otherwise. Letting your self be brought down by what others say or think about you. Do you want to know the truth my friend, the past is gone, the present is now, the future is tomorrow, if your past was a "complete disaster" as you may see it what about your future, what becomes of that? The beauty of your future is tied on what you do today. If you want to have a great future then start working, start taking steps towards making life better and beautiful for the generation yet unborn. For the path way to success and financial freedom was never said to be rosy or a bed of extreme comfort. If you have tried everything and you keep failing, then it means there is something you are doing wrong. Albert Einstein *(one of the greatest minds to ever lived)* once said that **"it is pure insanity to keep doing the same thing over and over again and expecting a different result".** If you want to become a success in business then you must change your style, approach and increase your knowledge more on what you are doing or what you want to go into.

In the words of founders of Envato *"Probably the biggest mistake we made earlier was not believing the business was going to be a big success. So we did next to no planning ahead, instead just making decisions as they were convenient."- By Collis and Cyan Ta'eed, Founders of Envato*

Prosperity has no respect for fasting and prayers if you don't pay the price of what it takes to achieve success in business it will never get to you, if you want to walk with the rich then you must start thinking like the rich, start building plans into wealth with careful planning and analysis on how you would achieve it then start talking like a rich/successful person. Stop looking down on your potentials start nurturing "YES I CAN" spirit. If bill gate can do it then why not me, if Larry page and Sergey brin (founders of Google) can do it then I can equally do the same. Remember there is no mountain too high for you to climb or a building too expensive that you cannot buy or build yourself. What you need is to change your mentality about yourself, create a new mentality for yourself, start making adequate research and plans, then start taking steps by surrounding yourself with mentors, business teams and in no time your story will change completely.

LESSON 3: WORKING WITH THE UNDERSTANDING OF YOUR COMPETITORS

Another way of avoiding failure in business is by working with the understanding of your major and minor competitors excelling in the line of business you want to go into, which simply means making a comprehensive research about your predecessors, their success stories, what they did to become who they are and where they are and how they got there? Their failures and the mistakes they made and how they corrected it. A wise man once said that "THE SUCCESS OF A MAN IS IN THEIR STORIES", *Isaac newton* once said that **"I See ahead of me because I stand on the shoulders of them that have gone before me"**. One of the ways to get success information is through biography of men and women that have made impact in the area of business you are aspiring to enter. Another way is through inquiry from books and through the internet to keep update with their activities and growth.

In the words of CEO of Backblaze "*People often say having a co-founder is like getting married. What they don't say is few people know-how to date well. The five of us that started Backblaze had worked together for over a decade. Even so, we realized we weren't clear about each person's goals. Talk to each other about your expectations about work hours, funding or not, exit or not, decision making,* **etc.**"*-by* Gleb Budman, *CEO of* Backblaze.

In the words of founders of Envato **"If you have co-founders, make sure you document who owns what, how you're going to pay yourselves, and who makes what decisions. Personally I believe in having a clear majority holder to make decisions easier (this may just be because I'm a bit bossy!)."**-*by Collis and Cyan Ta'eed, Founders of Envato.*

LESSON 4: *FIND YOUR NICHE IN THE BUSINESS WORLD AND TAKE IT*
My dad once told me that any business you can't cut a niche and be successful in it can't transform your life 360 degrees by making you a monopoly and

giving you advantage to strive favourably in the Nigeria market of today and any other economy you find yourself. As long as the niche you are cutting out for yourself is a need and a necessity to those that need it you will definitely make it in that business with the right team of expertise that's another secret of big business owner. Now some of you would start asking the question what does niche mean, well I will tell you. Microsoft® Encarta® defined Niche as:

1. **suitable place for somebody:** a position or activity that particularly suits somebody's talents and personality or that somebody can make his or her own She *carved out her own niche in the industry.*

2. COMMERCE **specialized market:** an area of the market specializing in one type of product or service designed *to undercut the competition in the same niche*
"*Thanks to the Internet, small niche companies can reach mass markets in a heartbeat.*" (*Forbes Global Business and Finance* November 1998)

So, what that means is if you want to find a niche for yourself you have to check what are your strength and weakness are, what are you good in? What kind of skills or knowledge do you know or have that can give you this niche that you seek? The skills/knowledge you have; will it help you develop this niche? is if applicable to your economy/country you are living in? All of these questions have to be asked by you and answered before you start taking steps on what you want to do.

In the words of CEO of 6Wunderkinder "*I'd say the best advice would be just to get started and once you find something, focus and execute. Don't try to be everything to everyone right away. If you pick one vertical and do it well, other folks will find you. From a narrow niche of IT professionals who were our early target market, we now have a wide variety of customers.*"*- By* Christian Reber, *Founder and CEO of* 6Wunderkinder

In the words of CEO of Backblaze "*Find your niche(s). Early on we believed that because online backup is something everyone needs and we provide the service in eleven languages to anyone in the world, that everyone should use it. While that would be great, especially in the early days you need smaller groups of people where you can get critical mass.*"*-by* Gleb Budman, *CEO of* Backblaze.

LESSON 5: PLAN WHERE YOU CAN, LAUNCH AS SOON AS POSSIBLE, AND MAKE CHANGES AS YOU GO

Planning is very important for any business that wants to see the future and stand the test of time for generations to come. This is what makes the difference between successful business and the failed ones. In later chapter we would talk more on business plans, but for now what you should know that there are many potential big business owners that never saw the light of day because the potential entrepreneurs spend too much time thinking about how imperfect plan they have about their business and when they finally get it, they keep giving themselves excuses and reasons why they are not ready to go into business. my father once said that **"A farmer that keeps looking at the weather and keep saying the sun is too hot, the weather is too cold or its rainy and never sows seed during planting season will die of hunger on the day of harvest"** meaning there will never be a convenient time to go into ANY business, as long as you have made the necessary research, plans and Process of execution then you are ready to start going about your business and while working if you notice that things are quite more expensive than you plan then start by adjusting your financial plans and how to generate financing to meet your current reality.

In the words of Co-founder and VP of Operations of Freshbooks "*And, just do it! Planning and modelling out your business are always a good idea, but don't get stuck planning too long, build something and push it out to your users as fast as you possibly can. If your product is getting good reviews and people are willing to pay for it, you've got something."-by* Levi Cooperman, *Co-founder and VP of Operations of* Freshbooks.

"Bootstrapping can be fun, you get to iterate quickly, turn on dimes, and invent new features on the fly. We should have slowed down just a tad to plan a few steps further out when naming things. Variables, methods, folder organization... all of these areas came out of the gate with a few inconsistencies we've had to work at tightening up. Some things will just need to stay until 2.0 when we have an opportunity to break backwards compatibility a little bit."

LESSON 6: FUNDS AND CAPITAL

Searching for investor to fund your business is good most especially if the business you want to go into is capital intensive, but one thing you should know is that no big time investor/organization will invest in your business without first reviewing your well-designed and structured realistic business plan and also what competency/leadership skill you have acquired to run the business you seek, which means you need a prototype of your master piece and what you intend to achieve with it before you can be taken seriously. That is just one way you can raise capital. Get a business plan and use it as a fund-raising tool, another way of raising capital is through friends and family members and relatives

In the words of co-founder of Dribble "Dribble is what I like to call a "boot up," or "organic start-up" – a company that lives and breathes on revenue. [...] For us, getting cash flowing in sooner than later was critical to give us resources to respond to the site's rapid growth. I think we erred in letting our traffic and operational concerns outstrip our business model, where simply maintaining what we had was preventing us from advancing our product."- by Rich Thornett and Dan Cederholm, Co-founders of Dribble

In the words of co-founder of Simple "We had angel funding lined up before we quit our jobs and started working on Simple full time, but we always knew it was going to take a relatively large amount of capital to build and launch a viable banking product. It took us 10 months and conversations with 70+ VC firms to raise our Series a round. Again, a lot of it came down to persistence, sticking to what we believed in, and being creative about how we created buzz and demonstrated traction."- by Shamir Karkal, CFO and Co-founder of Simple

LESSON 7: NOT HIRING SOON ENOUGH
It is not advisable to start hiring employees in a business that has barely gained its footing simply because a starting business does not have the financial power to pay staff at the early stage of inception most *(especially for services based business with exception to production factory start-up)* simply because the money at hand is the capital that will keep the business on its feet, then after the business has become financially stable to pay workers before the owner can start employing staff one after another until there is an entire sets of staff employed paid from the company account without the fear of bankruptcy. This state of hiring should at least be within the range of 6months to 2years depending on the kind of business you are running.

In the words of co-founder of Dribble "If you like having control over your work and being involved in all aspects of a product operation, running your own business can be a beautiful thing. The flip side is that the work can quickly pile up and overwhelm you if things take off. I had the bad tendency to try to do too much myself, when often stepping back and figuring out how to outsource some of the effort is the best move."-by Rich Thornett and Dan Cederholm, Co-founders of Dribble

LESSON 8: FINDING THE RIGHT TEAM
Every business has some unique features that makes them different from others for example a person selling provision might not need any team to maximize profit while someone else that is running a distribution system of goods or products would need team members to work with, to boost productivity, speed, efficiency and save time in terms of labour. Now this category of persons is who I am referring to. It's a potential Team leader, you have to carefully choose the team mate you want to work with. But in the context of military that are majorly sent to war ground in teams and group, its different based on the grounds that the soldiers care less about what a product sales person would care about because their major objective in this case the objective is to accomplish missions that they are for, to accomplish. What are the reasons for choosing the right team? 1) To get task accomplished on time 2) they are not held back by challenges they encounter on their way 3) they strive to achieve maximum result and minimize their losses 4) failure is not an Option 5) they seek to finish the task delegated to them with speed and accuracy.

"Finding, motivating, and retaining good people has always being a challenge. I think we've done a good job at this and it shines through in Simples product and customer experience. I don't have much wisdom to share beyond acknowledging that it's difficult. One tip I can offer is to be incredibly passionate. Hopefully your passion will inspire other like-minded people who are smarter than you to jump on board.

In the words of co-founder of Simple *"Hire great people… then get out of their way. You should strive to hire people who are smarter than you and, if you succeed, they will get irritated when you get in their way. Delegate and keep your eye on the important stuff."-by* <u>*Shamir Karkal*</u>*, CFO and Co-founder of* <u>*Simple*</u>

In the words of CEO of 6Wunderkinder *"Securing funding and finding the right team was our toughest challenge. Building a product like Wunderlist requires a large upfront investment into technology. What's more it also required a large team of smart engineers that had experience in programming cross-platform software. It was less a challenge to find candidates, it was harder to identify the great ones, the ones who are loyal and really want to build a product like Wunderlist. "-by* <u>*Christian Reber*</u>*, Founder and CEO of* <u>*6Wunderkinder.*</u>

LESSON 9: WATCH YOUR PENNIES, BUT SPEND THE GOOD ONES
For me I have come to realize your personal business require you to spend more money than you would have saved when you make a comparison with employee status. In the employee status risk is not involved but being at the mercy of your boss is what differentiate an employee job from a business owner. How do I mean? As a young business man that I am there is a saying my mom usually tell me **"cut your coat according to your cloth"**, that simply means do not allow yourself to be carried with the idea of buying everything your business needs all at once with limited resources rather consider the capital that is needed to take your business over the start-up phase. How much disposable income do you have left after engaging in the very necessary expenses? Prioritizing the need and importance of what you spend your profit and income for. Never try to live a fake life of being very rich when you know that your business is still struggling to stand on its feet among other competitors. The beginning of the bankruptcy is spending money without first conducting a need assessment survey. If you must spend at all it must be relevant expenditure that will help your business grow in either quality services or profit maximization or brand awareness and building a positive public image that will grow your business.

In the words of founders of Envato *"On a more philosophical note: Sweat the pennies when it comes to expenses, but at the same time don't be afraid to back yourself and invest when you think it's important. If you're bootstrapping, or don't think you'll be able to raise a lot of funds, you're probably better off starting a business which can feasibly make actual revenue early on – i.e. don't go for a consumer-oriented home run business like Facebook!"*
by Collis *and* Cyan Ta'eed*, Founders of* Envato

In the words of co-founder of simple *"Stay lean for as long as possible. Figure out what your milestones are – customers, page views, revenue, etc. – and work towards hitting them as soon as possible. Be creative, and stay lean. Spending a ton of money early on can be a liability down the road. Scale rapidly. This is the flip side of the above advice, but when you start seeing your metrics turn positive, be prepared to invest and grow rapidly. Success can creep up on you, and you need to be prepared when it hits. Staying lean early on will help you when you need to scale.* "By Shamir Karkal*, CEO and Co-founder of* Simple.

SESSION 10: BUSINESS IDEAS OPPORTUNITY THAT CAN MAKE YOU MONEY
Through Network Marketing: here you recruit other salespeople and then receive bonuses based on the performance of his or her recruits. This is also known as MMM which means multi-level marketing see *chapter 10* for more information

Turning an interest or hobby into a business by converting to satisfying human needs

If you can discover a business sector where monopoly exist and is meeting human needs not protected by law, then you have a business opportunity and can establish a competitive product or services.

Setting up a business that fixes or render solutions to failed business/services or product and create ways for such business to locate you and you render solution to them at a price.

Joining a Franchise business or starting up one, information is explained at a later section of this book chapter 8

Buying over an Existing Business either a retail shop or a firm, that are either failing or has failed and there exist a market for that particular business and a need you can pick it up. Make changes and bounce the business back to life.

By starting up in Direct Selling: Opportunity for direct selling exists where a manufacturer misses out the retailer by selling directly to the consumer. These sales are usually worked part-time. The manufacturers give their sales people various titles such "independent" sales rep. being involved with direct selling company has many advantages over setting up a business of your own. The Market research, developing and testing new products, planning, pricing, and working out sales techniques are all done by the same company. All you need to do absorb their sales training and sometimes purchase a starter pack of goods to sell. The sales procedure has been written by experts, so if you follow the training you should, in theory, be able to make sales.

CHAPTER 3
INSIGHTFUL SUCCESS FACTORS NEEDED FOR EXPLOIT IN BUSINESS

SESSION1: CUSTOMERS

3.1.1 LISTENING TO YOUR USERS/CUSTOMERS
A friend used to say *"no matter what it is, you have to say, it still does not change the fact that costumers are always right"*, which automatically counters whatever excuse you want to say concerning your business rather than give excuses provide solution to those excuses. What that means is once your customers' loose interest, trust or credibility in your work or product (your business starts to fall). That automatically means losing them to your competitors which leads to losing money too at the same time. By all standard that is bad for business. For the back bone of any business is your customers for once they leave you, that could lead to the "sudden death" of that business (which could lead to the end of the business).

In the words of co-founder and VP of operations of Freshbooks *"Customer feedback has been critical to our success from the beginning. We occasionally would push out features that were a bad user experience and made our service worse not better and our users told us right away that something was wrong. In fact, our first version included a feedback form upon logout and that along with phone calls gave us plenty of information to learn from. The key in those early days (and even now) was to be nimble and open to feedback."-by* <u>Levi Cooperman</u>*, Co-founder and VP of Operations of* <u>Freshbooks</u>

In the words of CEO of Backblaze *"When Backblaze launched and customers started showing, we thought "Yay!" What we should have done is realization that some of those earliest customers are also thought leaders and fans, and focused on engaging with them. While we focused on providing a good experience with the service and being open to feedback, we did not work to engage, nurture, and build those early fans into advocates."- By* <u>Gleb Budman</u>*, CEO of* <u>Backblaze</u>*.*

3.1.2 CUSTOMER SATISFACTION
Here is the question that you need to ask and answer, every single day: "What can I do to increase the value of my service to my customers today?" Look for ways to add value to what you do and to the people who depend on you every single day. One small improvement in the way you serve your customers can be a major reason for your financial success. Never stop looking for those little ways to serve your customers better. ***"Our success in life largely depends upon***

our understanding of our customers-whether they are families or business partners – and being able to deliver on their expectations" by bob Barnes.

SESSION2: LEARNING
3.2 LEARN FROM YOUR MISTAKES

In business, mistakes are inevitable so instead of getting scared of making one, create checklist mechanism that will help you prevent the mistake in the first place but if it happens not the less learn from it and move forward. For a mistake you don't learn from will keep coming back to haunt you and you will find out later that you are repeating the same mistake over and over again without knowing. And in business you can't afford to keep making mistakes over and over again for every expensive mistake comes at a price or at a cost. A wise man once said *"What you don't want, you don't watch. What you don't want to happen to you, then don't sit down and let it happen"*, meaning if you don't want to continue losing money then stop pointing accusing fingers to people and start implementing solutions. A good example was a mistake Toyota made sometime in 2010-2011 when they made a mistake on one of their models, to correct that mistake they had to recall every single defective model ever sold around the world and even paid their customers for such error but the good thing is that they learnt from their mistake and even right now Toyota is still one of the most popularly driven cars, sold and driven on Nigerian road.

The co-founders of Envato with his statement that: *"Early on we made lots of mistakes. I think that's pretty normal, because we were total business newbies! You make mistakes, and you learn from them. You just have to make sure you're not making the **same** mistake over and over!"-by* Collis *and* Cyan Ta'eed*, Founders of* Envato

"I would doubt that there is any founder who doesn't make mistakes when he or she is starting out ;). Of course, I made thousands of mistakes. But that's part of the process. I strongly believe, as soon as you think you 'know everything,' and learnt enough to create repetitive success, you will immediately fail. Building a company is so complex, it never will be the same. Especially in technology the markets are moving so fast, key learning's from one company are often worthless in the next."-by Christian Reber*, Founder and CEO of* 6Wunderkinder

3.2.2 NEVER STOP LEARNING

In the words of CEO of 6Wunderkinder *"Just keep learning, and you will be successful. Seriously, I have met many people who have told me 'This won't work, I know this, and I've being doing this for 10+ years.' It's wrong. Experience is great and critical for the long-term success of any business, but it can't beat a hungry and fast-learning founder who is willing to do things anyway, no matter what someone tells them."*-by Christian Reber, Founder and CEO of 6Wunderkinder

In the words of Founders of Envato *"And finally, read online! Starting your own business is deciding you want to start back at zero in a new endeavour. You have to be ready to learn everything you can. There are some amazing sources of knowledge for the newbie entrepreneur. I love these sites: Hacker News for start-up/entrepreneurial advice, TechCrunch and The Next Web for keeping up with trends, [and] Inbound.org for SEO/marketing."*-by Collis and Cyan Ta'eed, Founders of Envato.

3.2.3 COMMIT TO CONTINOUS LEARNING

> KEEP LEARNING NEW INFORMATION ABOUT YOUR BUSINESS, AND THEN START APPLYING THEM TOWARDS YOUR BUSINESS. NEVER ALLOW FAILURE AS AN OPTION BY KEEPING THE RIGHT PEOPLE AROUND YOU.

Dedicate yourself to lifelong learning. The fact is that you have more brains, ability and intelligence than you could ever use if you were to work on developing yourself for the rest of your life. You are smarter than you can imagine. There is no obstacle that you cannot overcome, no problem you cannot solve and no goal you cannot achieve by applying your mind to your situation.

There are several keys to lifelong learning. **One of the keys** is that you get up and read in your field for 30 to 60 minutes each day. Reading is to the mind as exercise is to the body. When you read for an hour each day, this will translate into about one book per week. One book per week will translate into 50 books per year. 50 books per year will translate into 500 books over the next 10 years. Since the average adult reads less than one book per year, when you begin reading one hour per day it will give you an incredible edge in your field. You will become one of the smartest, most competent and highest paid people in your profession by simply reading one hour each day.

Another key to lifelong learning is for you to listen to audio programs, especially in your car as you drive from place to place. The average person sits in his car 500 to 1000 hours per year. This is the equivalent as much as three to six months of working time that you spend in your car. This is the equivalent of one to two full time semesters at the university. Set a goal for yourself to become the very best in your business or profession. One small detail, insight or idea can be the turning point in your career. Never stop looking for it. Keep asking yourself these questions,

"What do my customers really want? What do my customers really need? What do my customers consider value? What is it that I can give my customers better than anyone else? What is it that my customers are buying from others today and what would I have to offer them to get them to buy from me?"

Your success in life will be in direct proportion to what you do after you do what you are expected to do. Always look for opportunities to do more than you are paid for. Always go the extra mile for your customers. Remember, there are never any traffic jams on the extra Mile.

SESSION3: PERSEVERANCE
3.3.1 DEDICATION AND GIVING IT YOU'RE ALL

Your [code/product/service] is one of the smallest parts of a successful start-up/app/company/whatever it is you're doing. To be successful you need to give it 110% above and beyond the product you're building. Invest in your customers.

In the words of founder of Statamic *"Give the best support you possibly can. Care too much. I believe it shows, and in a world where dozens of apps shut down every day, it pays to show people you mean business and you're not just slinging spaghetti at the wall, hoping it sticks, and moving on to the next idea. To quote Ron Swanson: 'Don't half-ass two things. Whole-ass one thing.'"- by Jack McDade, Founder of Statamic*

"Sometimes I think I should write a book about all the ups and downs we've had. I know they aren't over yet, but I am sure any start-up veteran has similar stories. Tenacity is the key to success. Keep plugging away, and good things will happen."-*by Shamir Karkal, CFO and Co-founder of Simple.*

3.3.2 EXPECT (AND PREPARE FOR) THE UNEXPECTED

In the words of co-founder of Freshbooks *"[...] there were some crazy stuff that happened: [the] financial meltdown [where] we actually had to cut back on spending and stop hiring as a direct result of the financial crisis at the end of 2009 – it was a challenging time, but we came out the other side a stronger organization. [Then] a truck running into our datacentre [knocked us] out for almost an entire day, but were able to recover and our customers were surprisingly understanding, needless to say we learnt a lot about our IT infrastructure to ensure that never happened to us again."-by Levi Cooperman, Co-founder and VP of Operations of Freshbooks*

ACKNOWLEDGEMENTS

In the words of co-founder of Simple *"One of our biggest lessons learnt is that in start-ups, everything takes much longer than you think it will. We originally planned to launch a beta and start acquiring customers in 9 months. It took us more than eighteen and even longer to refine that beta and get regulatory approvals to do a full launch. This is endemic to regulated industries. Plan your runway adequately."*-by <u>Shamir Karkal</u>, CFO and Co-founder of <u>Simple</u>

3.3.3 TOUGH, BUT REWARDING WORK

"There are so many parts to the overall picture beyond just the app you're building. Building a store to sell and track licenses, setting up a support system, marketing, social media, writing documentation... All of these, honestly, take more time than building your app. It was a big challenge getting coverage on all these areas while bootstrapping the company on the side of your "day job." But we made it work, and we're still here, and cruising ahead!"-by <u>Jack McDade</u>, Founder of <u>Statamic</u>

"The start-up life will be hard on [friends and family]. Insulate them from the ups and downs as well as you can, but you will need to lean on them for support to get through the hard times."-by <u>Shamir Karkal</u>, CEO and Co-founder of <u>Simple.</u>

SESSION4: FOUNDATIONAL INSIGHT QUESTIONS
3.4 Fundamentals Questions for Practical Pre-business start-up
Before plunging into business, you must first note and ask yourself the following questions

1) What kind of business do I want to do?
2) What kind of business interest me that even with little or no profit I would keep striving to make it big time in this business?
3) How much do I need to start-up this business?
4) How much money will this business fetch me within a space of 6months?
5) Where is my market place?
6) Who am I selling to?
7) Where can sell my business?
8) What class of people am I selling my business to?
9) Am I selling to the rich or the poor?
10) How can I sell what I am selling to who will buy it?
11) Where can I get the best people to help me sell my business and at what cost?
12) In business, you are either selling a product or services, how will it be managed?
13) Ask yourself what kind of business will it become in the future?

14) If it's a product business how will I manage my inventory into becoming an asset so as it doesn't become a liability?
   a) What category of distributors do I need to contact?
   b) How do you enhance product development for short-term and long-term?
   c) After you have established, how do I manage my customers?
   d) Then what future plans are you making for your prospective business?
15) Or is it a services kind of business if yes, then what kind of services are you offering or hoping to offer?
   a) What makes yours different or special from others?
   b) How much of the services you offer do you know?
   c) What kind of people/workers are you targeting to render services too?
   d) How much price tag are you willing to place on your services?
   e) How much knowledge, expertise and competence have you acquired over time for the services you intend to offer?

16) How much findings do you have concerning those that are already doing the business you want to do?

17) What strategy are you taking to do the same business better than the way they are doing the same thing you are hoping to do?

3.4.2 WHAT FUTURE PLANS DO YOU HAVE FOR YOUR BUSINESS?

Yogi Berra said *"If you don't know where you're going, you'll probably end up someplace else,"* Set goals helps you to keep track so that you don't wind up someplace other than where you want to be. At its simplest, a goal is just something you aim for. But goals are powerful contributors to successful business growth in several ways. To begin with, the process of setting goals forces you to think through what you want from your business and how growth may—or may not—provide that. This process helps suggest directions for pursuing that growth, which can greatly improve your chances of achieving your goals in the first place. Goals also give you a framework within which to work. This tends to focus your efforts by helping you rule out actions that won't contribute to achieving the goals you've set. A very important part of that framework is a timetable. Any good goal has a timetable, and that timetable will influence your actions profoundly. For instance, if your goal is to retire by age 50, you'll know that any growth plan with a payoff that won't occur by your 51st birthday is not one you should consider, no matter how attractive it might otherwise seem.

LESSON 1: BRIEF INSIGHT OF GLOBAL BRANDS AND HOW THEY STARTED (E.G COCA-COLA AND GOOGLE)

| NAME OF BRAND | TYPE OF BUSINESS | COUNTRY OF |

ACKNOWLEDGEMENTS

		ORIGIN
ADIDAS (Sporting Success) *Name of Founder:* Adolf (Adi) Dassler *Age of Founder at Start:* 20years *Background of Founder:* Trained as a Baker *Countries trading in:* over 170 *Sales and Net Profit:* €10.3Bn and €551million	CLOTHING AND CONSUMER BRAND	GERMANY
BILLABONG (Fashioning the next Wave) *Name of Founder:* Gordon Merchant *Age of founder at Start:* 28 years *Background:* Avid Surf Fan and worked surf board shaper *Year of Foundation:* 1977 *Countries trading in:* 100 *Turnover*: £609million ($1Bn)	CLOTHING AND CONSUMER BRAND	AUSTRALIA
THE COCA-COLA COMPANY *(The Coke Side of Business)* *Name of Founders:* John Pemberton (Creator) and Asa Griggs Candler (Business Founder) *Age of Founders at Start:* 55 and 35 years *Background of Founders:* Pharmaceuticals and	FOOD AND DRINKS	USA

THE ENTREPRENEUR'S BUSINESS GUIDE (FROM A START-UP APPROACH) | **STARTUP BOOK**

Sales *Year of Foundation:* 1886 *Countries currently trading in:* over 200 *Net Income:* £600million ($1.2Bn) and £4Bn ($7.3Bn)		
KFC (The Recipe for Success) *Name of Founder:* Harland Sanders *Age of Founder at Start:* 56 *Background of founders:* Farm hand, railroad operator, justice of peace, insurance salesman *Year of foundation:* 1902 *Countries now trading in:* more than 100 *Turnover:* $520.3million (£260million) (2007)	FOOD AND DRINKS	USA
APPLE (An Apple a Day) *Names of Founders:* Steve Jobs and Steve Wozniak *Age of Founders:* 21 and 26 Background of Founders: Both Computer Technicians Year of Foundation: 1976 *Countries now trading in*: Worldwide Turnover: $7.51bn (£4bn)	TECHNOLOGY	USA

ACKNOWLEDGEMENTS

BLACKBERRY (Research in Motion) *Names of Founders:* Mike Lazaridis and Doug Fregin *Background of Founders:* Both Engineering Students *Year of Foundation:* 1984 *Countries trading in:* 140 *Profit:* £3bn ($6bn) (2007)	TECHNOLOGY	CANADA
SONY (An Electrifying Brand) *Names of Founders:* Masaru Ibuka and Akio Morita Age of founders at start: 38 and 25 *Background:* Engineering and Brewing sake *Countries trading in:* more than 150 *Turnover:* £47bn ($88bn)	TECHNOLOGY	JAPAN
GOOGLE (Searching for Success) *Names of Founders:* Sergery Brin and Larry Page *Age of Founders at Start:* 24 and 25 *Background:* Stanford PhD computer Science students *Year of Foundation:* 1998 *Countries now trading in:* Worldwide	WEBSITES	USA

Income: $4.2bn (£2.1bn) (2007)

In these sections you would observe that some of the global brands of today started with founders who had no formal training to the business they started yet grew the business to the point of global presence and dominance and it had nothing to do with their age. Some of these global brands started up as partnership business and today is a global brand business, how did they do it, they leveraged on expertise of employee and brought in strong brand managers to keep the company going as the company grew even thou most of the founders were either later acquired or merged with another company along the line but the idea is don't let your background put your back on the ground, if you can conceive it in your heart you can achieve it if you can think it and plan it enough to bring it to reality with well laid out corresponding set of actions then it is already achieved even if you are not an expertise in that line of business. All you need do is surround yourself with a team of expert for what you want to do and manage them well. In no time you would be swimming in wealth and success even though it will take time. It will surely come.

3.4.3: EVALUATING GOALS

But it's not enough just to have goals. They need to be the *right* goals and ones that are appropriate to your ambitions and abilities. When entrepreneurs talk about their goals, wheth*er they're for the past year—or* for a lifetime—the most frequent issue is whether those goals were the best ones to have. If your goals appear to be holding you back or directing your efforts into unproductive areas, then there's definitely something you can do about it. In fact, setting new goals for yourself and your business is both easy and essential if you're going to grow. When looking at new goals, make sure they have the following qualities:

Specificity: You stand a better chance of achieving a goal if it's specific. "Raising capital" i*sn't a specific goal;* "raising N10, 000 by July 1" is.

OPTIMISM: Goals should be positive and uplifting. "Being able to pay the bills" is not exactly an inspirational goal. "Achieving financial security" phrases your goal in a more positi*ve manner, thus firing up your* energy to attain it.

REALISM: If you set a goal to earn *N100, 000 per month when you've* never earned that much in a year, that goal is unrealistic. Begin with small steps, such as increasing your monthly income by 25 percent. Once your first goal is met, you can reach for larger ones more easily.

THINKING SHORT- AND LONG-TERM: Short-term goals are attainable *in* a period of weeks to a year. Long-term goals can be achieved 5, 10 or even 20 years from now; they should be substantially greater than short-term goals but should still be realistic.

INCOME: Many entrepreneurs want growth to provide financial security. Consider how much money you want to make each year when planning your growth.

LIFESTYLE: This includes areas such as travel, hours of work, investment of personal assets and geographic location. Are you willing to travel extensively or move if that's what it takes? How many hours are you willing to work? Which assets are you willing to risk?

SESSION5: SUCCESS START-UP FROM SUCCESSFUL C.E. O'S WHO HAD MADE IT FROM SMALL BUSINESS

A time-tested way to learn how to do almost anything is simple: find out the recommended PATH of action from someone who has already done whatever it is that you want to do and then do it!

Learning how to become a successful entrepreneur is often a journey and not a destination, who wouldn't want to shortcut some of the headaches and hassle and jump straight to the making maximum profit with money and success to show for, but the consequence of shortcut is more disastrous than whatever reason it is you think you will achieve for following it.

Let's see if we can cut down on some of the pain and get right to the gain by looking at some of the top tips for start-up's that a "being there, done that" already successful entrepreneurs have doled out as advice.

Here are five tips arranged in the natural chronological order of a typical new business life cycle: "Ideas" to "Risk" to "Funding" to "Systems" to "Marketing":

3.5.1. "IDEAS ARE EVERYTHING" - DEREK SIVERS

Idea is the INSIGHT, foundation and brick holding any business together in one piece, now what that means is once you're your idea execution is faulty and the business just collapses like a damaged bridge. It just folds up along with your resources and investment as time unfolds. Meaning that it is professionally wise to test for the viability, feasibility of the idea and the future profit-loss analysis before you go straight ahead in executing that wonderful idea in your head.

However, actually taking action concerning that idea means that it's time for the proverbial rubber to meet the road and with it the potential for that idea to both succeed and to fail.

Four-time successful entrepreneur <u>Derek Sivers</u> gives his assessment of the value of ideas: *"It's so funny when I hear people being so protective of ideas.*

(People who want me to sign an NDA to tell me the simplest idea.) To me, ideas are worth nothing unless executed. They are just a multiplier. Execution is worth millions. Explanation: AWFUL IDEA = -1 WEAK IDEA = 1 SO-SO IDEA = 5 GOOD IDEA = 10 GREAT IDEA = 15 BRILLIANT IDEA = 20 NO EXECUTION = $1 WEAK EXECUTION = $1000 SO-SO EXECUTION = $10,000 GOOD EXECUTION = $100,000 GREAT EXECUTION = $1,000,000 BRILLIANT EXECUTION = $10,000,000 To make a business, you need to multiply the two. The most brilliant idea, with no execution, is worth $20. The most brilliant idea takes great execution to be worth $20,000,000. That's why I don't want to hear people's ideas. I'm not interested until I see their execution".

3.5.2. "BUSINESS RISK" - TIM FERRISS

Successful entrepreneurs are often stereotyped as having an almost unhealthy appetite for risk. This may be true in some cases, and in fact could very well be true of many successful entrepreneurs, but a risk loving personality is certainly NOT a prerequisite for becoming a successful entrepreneur. Entrepreneurship is less risky than being an employee if undertaken with the right approach and knowledge but if not it would turn out to be like a man who just packed all his money together and set the whole thing on fire and start crying afterwards that's what happens when there is little no planning involved, in order to become a successful entrepreneur there is no need to force yourself to jump headfirst into risky situations because "that is what entrepreneurs do". But you should understand and calculate every move before you make them, *because every entrepreneurial decision to be made comes with a prize to be earned and a price to be paid.* How you go about is entirely up to you.

Serial entrepreneur and best-selling author Tim Ferris gives his opinion of the idea that all entrepreneurs are risk takers: *"One of the most frustrating types of resistance I encounter when talking about lifestyle design or entrepreneurship is a general response along the lines of: "That's great for you, but I have kids and a mortgage. I'm not a risk taker." The fact of the matter is, most of the uber-successful entrepreneurs I know hedge their bets and place small bets while keeping one foot on secure ground.*

This often includes testing the waters while employed full time, as Rick himself did before creating World 50 from nothing. Most of them never gamble in real-life, and a decent percentage don't invest in the public market (like me) because of the lack of control. Are there mavericks who lay it all on the table for the big win or cataclysmic loss? Sure. But don't believe, just because the media likes to highlight such daredevils, that they are the majority of kick-a** founders".

3.5.3. "BUSINESS FUNDING" - 37SIGNALS

"If I could only find a deep pocketed investor then I know that my business would be a success?" Really? Is there any possibility that you would retain full control, after you have got the money because when an investor gives you such amount of money, he automatically becomes a part owner of your business especially when it is given on an equity basis? The only exception to this is if you are given in a form of a grant or a loan? But you can start by growing a little first if you don't want that, you can generate funds for yourself instead of looking for outside funding but if you can generate funds from other means then go ahead, if not then I suggest you try investor instead be careful in your pursuit for this? Maybe a few friends and family members can assist but you need to know that a company with warehouses and machinery is quite different from a company that develops software never compare your business to some company that is not in the same industry with you if you wish to enjoy entrepreneurial success.

The ultra-successful entrepreneurs over at 37Signals have this to say about looking for outside money vs funding yourself: *"Outside money is plan B The first priority of many start-ups' is acquiring funding from investors. But remember, if you turn to outsiders for funding, you'll have to answer to them too. Expectations are raised. Investors want their money back — and quickly. The sad fact is cashing in often begins to trump building a quality product. These days it doesn't take much to get rolling. Hardware is cheap and plenty of great infrastructure software is open source and free. And passion doesn't come with a price tag. So, do what you can with the cash on hand. Think hard and determine what's really essential and what you can do without. What can you do with three people instead of ten?*

What can you do with $20k instead of $100k? What can you do in three months instead of six? What can you do if you keep your day job and build your app on the side? Constraints force creativity Run on limited resources and you'll be forced to reckon with constraints earlier and more intensely. And that's a good thing. Constraints drive innovation. Constraints also force you to get your idea out in the wild sooner rather than later — another good thing. A month or two out of the gates you should have a pretty good idea of whether you're onto something or not.

If you are, you'll be self-sustainable shortly and won't need external cash. If your idea's a lemon, it's time to go back to the drawing board. At least you know now as opposed to months (or years) down the road. And at least you can back out easily. Exit plans get a lot trickier once investors are involved. If you're creating software just to make a quick buck, it will show. Truth is a quick pay-out is pretty unlikely. So, focus on building a quality tool that you and your customers can live with for a long time.

3.5.4. "BUSINESS SYSTEMS" - MICHAEL GERBER

The vast majority of small businesses are owned by landscapers that landscape, mortgage brokers who broker mortgages, plumbers who... plumb, well you get the idea. A truly successful business is one that is successful with or without the presence and involvement of the entrepreneur.

if there isn't a system in place so that there is money being generated with or without me then I haven't really built that great business (I've really just created my own tailor-made job) Sure, when first starting out it's almost required as the entrepreneur's rite of passage that you spend some long hard hours doing anything and everything to get your new business off the ground.

That being said, if that still describes you 10 years later then you probably don't have that great business set up, you just have a way to trade your time for money. Successful entrepreneur and best-selling author Michael Gerber have this to say about the importance of systems: *"The entrepreneur is not really interested in doing the work; he is interested in creating the way the company operates. In that regard, the entrepreneur is an inventor. He loves to invent, but does not love to manufacture or sell or distribute what he invents...*

The entrepreneur builds an enterprise; the technician builds a job... If they don't fail outright, most businesses fail to fully achieve their potential. That's because the person who owns the business doesn't truly know how to build a company that works without him or her... Which is the key element to the business.

3.5.5. "BUSINESS MARKETING" - JOEL SPOLSKY

Marketing is the stronghold of every business. Why did I say that? Because a business without a well qualitative awareness is as good as what is invisible to the consumers meaning that no marketing, no profit, no sales. What's the point selling a product if nobody knows about the existence of such product? what that means is that if you want to get the recognition you deserve, go out and talk to people about it either known or unknown people. As long as your business is concerned everybody is your potential customer including your family.

Different marketing strategies are appropriate for different kinds of businesses, but one thing holds constant: keeping the focus on where the customer is and what the customer wants. Nowhere does abuse of this principle happen more frequently than online. How many Facebook "Like" requests or self-promotional tweets have you got from friends who are starting their own business and want to do "Social Media Marketing" by spamming-excuse me, marketing to their friends and contacts in roughshod blitzkrieg fashion?

Successful entrepreneur Joel Spolsky offers this marketing wisdom in reference to marketing online with a blog and finding customers the right way: "These days, it seems like just about every start-up founder has a blog, and 99 percent of these bloggers are doing it wrong. The problem? They make the blog about themselves, filling it with posts announcing new hires, touting new products, and sharing pictures from the company picnic. That's lovely -- I'm sure your mom cares. Too bad nobody else does. Most company blogs have almost no prospective investors, no traffic, and no impact on sales... So, what's the formula for a blog that actually generates leads, sales, and business success? To really work, [game developer and author Kathy] Sierra observed, an entrepreneur's blog has to be about something *bigger* than his company and his product.

This sounds simple, but it isn't. It takes real discipline to not talk about yourself and your company. Blogging as a medium seems so personal, and often it is. But when you're using a blog to promote a business, that blog can't be about *your*, Sierra said. It has to be about your prospective investors, who will, it's hoped, become your customers. It has to be about making *them* feel good and smiling. So, for example, if you're selling a clever attachment to a camera that diffuses harsh flash light, don't talk about the technical features or about your holiday sale (10 percent off!).

Make a list of ten tips for being a better photographer. If you're opening a restaurant, don't blog about your menu. Blog about great food. You'll attract foodies who don't care about your restaurant yet. If you make superior, single-source chocolate, don't write about that great trip you took to the Dominican Republic to source cocoa beans. That's all about you. Instead, write the definitive article about making chocolate-covered strawberries. For the next 10 years, whenever a gourmand or a baker searches Google for a recipe on how to make chocolate-covered strawberries, he will find your post. Helping your users make awesome chocolate-based confections is likely to attract prospective investors who might buy fancy chocolate, and that's the point of a successful blog.

CHAPTER 4
PROFITABLE GROWING SMALL BUSINESS OPPORTUNITIES

Note: All underlined words in this chapter are reference web links you can follow by clicking on, to follow on to the website for more details.

Agricultural Sector

4.1.1. Catfish and Poultry Farming

The first of the fastest growing business opportunities in Nigeria is catfish farming. The primary reason I listed catfish farming as one of the fastest business opportunities in Nigeria is because it's an emerging industry that hasn't reached its peak or full potential. The major players in this business are usually regional players. What this means in essence is that each major player in the catfish farming industry is focused only on a particular business terrain within the geographical location of the farm.

So, all you need to do is look for a region with a growing demand that haven't being covered by a major player and situate your business there. As for poultry farming, the ban imposed by the federal government of Nigeria as at 2015 with respect to the importation of live or frozen poultry birds has only helped explode the demand. Snail farming is also another under-exploited money maker.

When accessing any of these business opportunities listed above, you must note three important facts. One, food is one of the basic necessities of man, thus making catfish, snail and poultry farming a huge potential. Two is that the population in Nigeria is estimated to be over 150 million and growing so that entails a growing demand for food. Three is that even if the local market with 150 million Nigerians gets saturated (which I strongly doubt as this niche is still in its adolescent phase), there's still a growing demand for catfish all over the world. So, do your own in-depth analysis and put your money to work.

1. Livestock Farming

You can even start this business from your backyard. With 150+million mouths to feed daily, there will always be demand for livestock products. However, lack of technical know-how and the use of crude equipment are the major factors hampering the growth of this industry.

If you can come in with adequate knowledge and the patience to nurture this business, you will reap immensely. Now you can choose to either venture into livestock breeding or better still, you can stick to livestock feed production or equipment retailing.

a) Poultry farming – Egg production, meat production, hatchery or day-old-chicks production, etc.
b) Cattle Farming – Dairy (*milk*) production, beef, etc.
c) Rabbit Farming
d) Goat Farming
e) Sheep
f) Tilapia Fish Farming
g) Piggery
h) Grass cutter Farming
i) Snail Farming
j) Quail Farming

2. Agro-products exportation

Nigeria is blessed with a lot of food and natural resources; and most of these natural resources are raw materials needed for the production of some finished products. Every day, tons of raw materials and food products leave the shores of Nigeria to countries such as India, Vietnam, China, USA, UK, Brazil, etc.; yet, the demand is never met.

You can become an exporter by simply registering with the Nigerian Export Promotion Council and decide on the specific product you wish to export. Examples of products highly in demand both within and outside Nigeria are *Chili pepper, Mango, Kolanuts, Bitter Kola, Cassava flakes (Garri), Cocoa, Groundnut, Yam flour, Cashew nuts*, etc.

However, if you think you don't have the capital or time to engage in agro-products exportation, then you can stay local by buying and selling them within the country. A good example of a product you can buy and sell for huge profits is Palm Oil.

Cassava Production - People are beginning to turn their attention to this aspect of farming in Nigeria that have being neglected for years. Cassava derived foods are some of the most consumed in Nigeria. If you can invest in cultivating 50 - 100 Acre in a fertile area like Ondo State, your harvest will be great.

Textiles Sector

4.1.2. Importation of wears

Importation of clothes (designer wears) into Nigeria is another fast-growing business opportunity you can tap into but I must warn you; you will be breaking the law if you engage in this business because there's a ban by the federal government on the importation of wears. I listed this business opportunity for those who have the entrepreneurial guts to take calculated risk.

Another reason I listed the importation of wears as one of the fastest growing business opportunities in Nigeria is because the ban cut short its supply thereby leaving a gap of demand that can only be filled by brave entrepreneurs.

4.1.3. Sewing of specialized uniforms

If you don't have the entrepreneurial guts to go into the importation of wears; then you can set up a small-scale textile firm that will specialize in sewing uniforms. The demand for uniforms is on the increase in Nigeria; from the crèche to the labour market, uniforms are highly in demand but it's advisable you do your own detailed research before venturing into the business.

Transportation Sector

4.1.4. Outsourced bus service

This is similar to haulage and logistics but the cargo in this case is humans. I am not talking about the regular road transport bus service; in fact, I don't think I have seen the idea for this business being utilized by anyone.

Now in this case, you are providing transportation services to firms and corporate entities. Some corporate organizations can't afford an in-house transport system for its executives and staff, so this is where you come in. You provide the cars or buses; provide the drivers and you are paid on a monthly bases or contract bases for the use of your transport services.

Another area of target is schools. Most schools would like to provide transport facilities for their students but they can't afford it and this is where you come in. You provide a bus service system and send out a proposal to schools to use your bus services. Just imagine twenty or more young schools jointly using your student bus service system and you will catch the vision of this idea.

4.1.5. E-Services

Just as the world is going e-crazy; so also, is Nigeria catching up with the trend? **E-services provision is still a virgin business opportunity that hasn't fully being tapped.** Under the umbrella of providing e-services; you can find the following fast growing business opportunities: E-payment, bulk SMS services, web-design and hosting, database management services, e-portal management, Example of such e-services include *Web designing and development, Web hosting, App development, Digital marketing services, Search Engine Optimization services, Banner design services, Bulk SMS services, Online registration of exams such as JAMB, WAEC, professional courses,* etc.

Educational Sector

The need for education is on the increase and the burden to provide quality education is getting heavier for the government to bear thereby, leaving room for private and institutional investors. The following are ways you can tap into the potential opportunity.

4.1.6. Schools

A lot of institutional and private investors have gone into building quality schools and providing quality education but the potential has not been reached. With a population of over 170 million Nigerians, where 65% are below 40yrs; there's still untapped potential in this niche.

You can access this business opportunity from different entry levels. You can tap into this niche by providing either crèche, primary, secondary or tertiary education but all entry levels holds strong potential. Please carry out your own analysis before investing in any level of this business opportunities.

4.1.7. Seminars

Not everyone loves being educated within the four walls of school. Some prefer street smart education or high-speed learning and that's where you come in. You can set up a seminar company that organizes coaching services according to the current needs and trends of the society.

4.1.8. Training centres

Specialized training or educational centres is another fast-growing untapped business opportunity in Nigeria though they have a few Nigerians in this sector but it is far from being saturated. Examples of specialized learning centres are Leadership training schools, entrepreneurial centres, training centre for the gifted and physically challenged, training centre for hobbies and crafts, etc.

5.1.9. Tutorial centres

With the proliferation of academic and professional exams, **tutorial centres have joined the list of fastest growing business opportunities in Nigeria**. You can access this business opportunity by choosing or specializing on a training need. You can focus your proposed tutorial centre on any of the following: ICAN, GMAT, WAEC, JAMB, GSCE, CIS, job interview training, etc. Every year, millions of people sit for examinations and tests in Nigeria and most of these people usually need some kind of trainings or tutorials. You can position yourself as a provider of such training and make money off this niche. Examples of trainings you can offer include skill vocational acquisition training, corporate management skill training, etc.

Green Energy and Technology

With a global increase in the awareness of environmental degradation and its hazard, the world has resorted to finding an alternative "green energy." Nigeria is not left out in this global awareness that has created massive opportunities for smart entrepreneurs and investors. If you feel green is the next business trend on board, then below are **the fastest growing business opportunities in the green energy and technology sectors in Nigeria.**

4.1.10. Waste management

Waste management is another business with a future potential because Nigerians are yet to imbibe the habit of proper waste disposal. However, states like Lagos have being doing a lot to encourage proper waste disposal and management. Now there are several businesses you can start within the waste management niche and these include waste recycling, waste disposal, junk hauling, organic fertilizer production, etc. which works best when working with the government. With an increased awareness in the need for environmental conservation; opportunity has popped up in Nigeria in the area of waste management. When analysing the waste management business opportunity, I observed that two factors are responsible for the potential in the business and you must make sure these two factors are in place before deciding on an area of service.

One is a bursting population and the second is a strong environmental policy and its enforcement. So far, two states in Nigeria that have taken the lead with respect to these two factors. These states are Lagos and Imo state. But I believe great potential still lie in other states of Nigeria. Do your own personal research before venturing into this industry.

4.1.11. Alternative power

The last but not the least of **the fastest growing business opportunities in Nigeria is alternative power supply**. In recent times; Nigeria has seen an explosive increase in the demand of power supply thus creating an avenue for smart entrepreneurs to capitalize on **solar energy, wind energy and bio energy are some of the alternative power supply systems** that are currently making waves in other countries but the present alternative power supply service providers cannot meet up the demand thereby leaving room for other creative investors. With a good plan, adequate capital and a strong business team; you can break into this niche.

Alternative Power Installation

As the world goes green, and Nigeria battles her power supply challenges; there is an already established opening in Nigeria's power sector. Even though the government has taken steps to deregulate the power sector by granting licenses for Independent Power Plants, granting a free import duty for the importation of power generation equipment and commissioning several power projects, this will never hamper the growing demand for alternative power generators such as solar energy, wind mills, inverters, etc. You can either make money by importing and retailing these materials or you can choose to focus on installations.

SESSION 1: OTHER BUSINESS IDEAS AND VENTURES YOU CAN START IN NIGERIA

1. Sale of Furniture - Buying and selling of locally made furniture is a goldmine. You don't need to be a carpenter to do this, just arrange for regular supply from reliable Carpenters while you display and sell in your showroom. It is a very big business in Nigeria as only few can afford the imported designers.

2. Snail Rearing - Snail farming is one of the choice animal farming for many reasons. It is a low capital investment with high yield and the market is big. There are not too many people currently doing this - and most of them are doing it in a very low scale. If someone invests heavily in Snail farming, he is sure to make good money in Millions within a year.

3. Rice Farming - Rice remains the most consumed food staple in Nigeria and Billions of dollars goes into importation of this product yearly from China and Thailand because the local farmer is unable to meet up the demand due to poor funding and limited knowledge. Though the federal government is organising means in which young Nigerians can tap into the full potential of this sector through loans, grant and skill acquisition to learn the trade of rice farming.

4. Making of Fruit Juice - Nigerians drink fruit juice more than any other people. That's why companies like **Dansa** and **Chivita** who came into the country as nobody are today making billions of naira annually. This business in capital intensive but if you can afford it, it's well worth it.

5. Food processing

Another profitable industry to consider is the food processing industry. The concept of this industry is simply to take raw food materials and turn them into finished products. In fact, there are a lot of businesses you can do in this niche and examples of such businesses include *Tomato puree production, Frozen food production, yogurt production, Vegetable oil production, Garri Processing, oil palm processing, groundnut processing, Fruit juice production, Rice milling,* etc.

6. Oil and Gas Business - We are blessed and cursed with huge deposit of oil in our land which presents some of the finest business opportunity for Nigerians and Foreigners over the years. Owning a Petrol Filling Station, Supplying of Diesel, and Distribution of Kerosene are some the areas you can invest easily and make good money for yourself. However, the filling station business is capital intensive

7. Haulage and logistics

Haulage and logistics are another booming business in Nigeria because regardless of the weather, people must haul their goods from one location to another. In fact, haulage; though it is management intensive. However, you can start with just a truck and see how it goes. The cost of taking a truck from one place to the other in Nigeria is between N20, 000 to N200, 000 per trip. Due to poor rail transport system, most of the Nigerian goods are transported through the road, making haulage business in Nigeria a viable one.

You can choose to focus on hauling containers for clients from the seaports to their various destinations or better still, you can choose to haul products of specific companies such as breweries, production companies, etc. You can also haul perishable goods from farms and villages to the marketplace or you can haul specialty products such as frozen foods, petroleum products, gas, etc.

Now there is also an opportunity for those who want to venture into haulage business but do not want to be bugged down by management requirements. All you need to do is to buy a truck and contract it to a Haulage and logistics company; which will in turn pay you a specified amount weekly or monthly based on agreement.

8. Hotel Business -This is probably the coolest money making opportunity in Nigeria. Invest in small-scale hotel of just ten suites and watch as the money flows in in a central location with well-polished environment. This has nothing to do with tourism boom of any kind; there is just something in Nigerian system that makes this business very lucrative – Most especially when the hotel is centrally located or has an accessible location. Though this is a highly capital-intensive business but if you have the money to do this why not, after all, great hotels of today started in their small way.

9. Fast Food Eatery - Eatery business is another goldmine though poor management can kill it and send the business to its early death stage (total collapse of the business)! If you wish to go into this business, be sure to get everything right and don't forget it's a bit capital intensive and requires good management skills. But if you get everything right, free money is yours. You can make as much as N10, 000 to N100, 0000 a day depending on the size of your customer base

10. Importation of second hand Spare Parts - If you are in USA, this business is good for you. Don't just keep importing exotic cars, gather fairly used spare parts in containers and ship down here. There is a huge market for it in Nigeria. It would surprise you to know that most car owners prefer second hand parts to brand new spare parts at an affordable price though there are some that prefer brand new parts but that is just the way things are currently.

11. Dry Cleaning - Professional dry cleaners at affordable prices is not so scarce to find in Nigeria especially for the urban cities but the reverse is the case for rural areas. It's all dependent on the location you intend setting up your dry-cleaning business. Though some professional Dry Cleaners whose service fees are extremely high or mediocre dry cleaners don't keep to delivery time. Some are given cloths today and you come back for it and meet it unwashed after one week. This business is a money maker if you balance it up.

12. Sales of Building Materials - The rate at which new houses are springing up in Nigeria, you get to wonder why many people still complain of housing problem. Investing in building material is a good business and I can count some guys who are making millions almost daily in this business.

13. Transport Business - What we have in this sector are transport companies that are badly managed by local chiefs and touts. Invest in this business with good management and you will be wondering what hits you with bags of money.

14. Investing in Internet Companies - This is a new crop of powerful investment opportunity that is creating Billionaires around the world including Nigeria. It's simple! You don't have to be a Tech person, all you need is to look for a creative online tech start-up with good ideas and invest into. Within 1 to 2 years you will be counting your profits in millions.

15. Mining

Nigeria is blessed with a lot of mineral resources like Limestone, Coal, Iron ore, Bitumen, etc. Aside this, the mining industry in Nigeria is set to take off because the federal government in June 2013 implemented a policy to drive forward the mining industry by declaring the importation of mining equipment duty free. The government is also going after many dormant investors who were granted mining licenses but are not utilizing it. This act I believe, will spur the growth in the mining sector. If you have the financial capacity and a team, you can position yourself in this sector.

16. Setting up A Private Mini Refinery

There are lots of business opportunities in the oil and gas sector. Building a private refinery and refining crude oil is another business you should look into because there is a lot of potential in it. In January 2012, the federal government announced the partial removal of subsidy and with a long-term plan to totally remove fuel subsidy which they later implemented. What this means in essence is that petroleum product importers will now sell as they buy; thus, bringing in competition and it is a known fact that 80% of petroleum products consumed in Nigeria are imported.

Now with the total removal of fuel subsidy, investors will now have the opportunity to set up their own refinery and produce fuel. Are you among those that think the total fuel subsidy removal is a pipe dream? Then think again because in May 2013, Aliko Dangote raised $9billion for the setting up of a refinery; which will be sited in Ondo state.

Honestly, I understand that not everyone has the financial capacity and technical know-how to invest in a private refinery. Well, you can still tap into the oil and gas sector by setting up a filling station, starting a mini kerosene retailing depot or establishing a cooking gas retailing outlet. Whichever one you choose; you will surely make money.

17. Inland waterway Transport

There are lots of opportunities in the transport industry and inland waterway is one of them. Nigeria has a broad network of inland waterways comprising rivers, creeks, lakes and seas; yet, transportation still remains a challenge because investors are yet to tap into water transportation.

A lot of countries such as Italy, Thailand, etc. have effectively being utilizing their waterways as a means of transport; thus, reducing the traffic congestion on the road. All you need to do is to incorporate a company, obtain license from the state and federal government, import or purchase some locally fabricated boats; and you are in business.

18. Establishing a Television and Radio Station

Now it is a known fact that the mass media industry is saturated in Nigeria. However, this is only true for some cities in Nigeria such as Lagos and Abuja. Traveling through several parts of the countries, it is discovered that most states have no private TV station, and only rely on the government owned TV stations; which are uncreative, unreliable and lacking behind in terms of broadcast coverage. I see an opportunity for entrepreneurs and investors with interest and competence in broadcasting or mass media. You can either choose to setup a radio station or TV Station.

19. Setting up a Security Company

There is a huge demand for excellent security services in Nigeria though there are a few corporate security firms that supplies organizations security personnel. As the government battle to improve the security situation in the country, individuals and corporate entities are now becoming aware of the fact that security is not the responsibility of the government alone; it is a collective responsibility. Hence, the current increase in demand for security guards, bodyguards, executive protection professionals and security gadgets or devices.

As an entrepreneur or investor, you can setup a security guard recruitment or training company, or you can setup an executive protection or bodyguard agency. Also, you can import and retail security products and safety devices.

20. Sewing of Specialized uniforms

There are over 500 schools (*both Crèche, primary and secondary*) in Lagos state alone; and each of these schools have a specific uniform or attire for their students. Okay, let's look beyond educational institutions. *Do you know that other individuals and corporate organizations are in need of uniforms for their security personnel, staff, etc.*? There are also a lot or military (*Army, Air Force, Navy*), paramilitary (*Civil Defence Corps, Police Force*) and non-paramilitary (*Road Safety, Traffic Warden, Kick against Indiscipline, Vigilante groups, etc.*) organizations in Nigeria that make use of uniforms. You can position yourself as a uniform supplier of materials or the finished sewed uniform and make money from it.

21. Construction Company

Nigeria is still a developing country especially in the area of infrastructure but this is set to change in the nearest future. Massive constructions are currently ongoing in Nigeria ranging from bridges, roads, towers and skyscrapers, etc. If you run a construction company oversee, or you have the financial capacity to assemble the needed team and machinery for a construction company; then this is a business you should invest in. though, it requires a lot of money.

22. Call Centre agency

Have you called the customer care service of a telecom network before? Or have you tried sending a message or complaint to a corporate organization before? Do you know that those who take your calls, complaints and respond accordingly are not employees of the companies you patronise; neither do they operate in the premises of the company? If you are hearing this for the first time, then welcome to the world of "*Call centre outsourcing.*"

You can setup a call centre agency and work for big companies on a contract basis. One sweet fact about this business is that you can always start small by becoming a call centre agent from home, as it doesn't require much start-up capital unless you want to scale up by employing more helping hands.

23. Recruitment Agency

The labour market is becoming tougher and there are over five million unemployed youths in Nigeria. Another hard fact is that companies are no longer employing full time in-house staff; they are now using the services of recruitment agencies to employ people based on contract basis. This strategy is aimed at reducing the cost of doing business by avoiding the cost of conducting a recruitment exercise and also avoiding employee claims and benefits. This is the sole reason why banks and other companies are sacking their workers on daily basis.

So rather than fight the trend, why not profit from it by setting up a recruitment agency and connect jobseekers to their dream jobs. You can also be a corporate executive head-hunter and make money poaching competent staff from one company to another. If this is too capital intensive for you, then you can setup a resume writing service from home and profit from the trend.

24. Day-care centre

The demand for quality childcare service is increasing daily. Parents are now working harder just to generate enough income to keep the family going, thus leaving them with less time for the children.

Now to be honest with you, there are a lot of day-care centres existing but only a few are providing exceptional services; and parents that cherish their kids are never comfortable leaving their kids in a child care centre whose environment is dirty. If you can come in with exceptional service and creativity, you will make money from this business. Another thing you must know is that you can start this business from home.

Now for those who lack the capital and experience to setup a full-scale childcare centre, you can still make profit of this niche by starting a small scale babysitting service or Nanny Agency.

25. Plantation Farming

Do you have a fertile vacant land and you know that you won't be developing any structure on it in the nearest future? Then why not start livestock farming, crop cultivation or plantation farming. There are a lot of cash crops you can plant, nurture and forget; and they will keep providing you with steady returns annually. Examples of crops you can start a plantation around are *Orange, Plantain, Kola nut, Oil palm, Cocoa, Cassava, Yam*, etc.

26. Manufacturing

You can also venture into small scale manufacturing of products that are in daily need. You don't need to build a factory or industrial plant; you can start on a small-scale from your room or a rented store or apartment. Products you can start manufacturing include *Toothpicks, Tissue paper and Serviette, board marker production, candle,* sticks, nylons, *cartons, paper bags*, liquid soap etc.

27. Become a Cement Distributor for Dangote or start-up your own Cement company if the means is available.

WHAT YOU NEED TO KNOW ABOUT STARTING A MANUFACTURING BUSINESS AT HOME

Manufacturing your own products is a very smart idea. Millions are spent on different goods yearly and yet, the demand for some goods still outweighs supply. A lot more people need to explore manufacturing options. though capital might seem like a challenge for many but the truth is that you can start small and if you are dedicated and focused, you would build a business empire for yourself before you know it.

However, for a good start-up approach to start your own manufacturing business, you have to know the steps involved in order to help you develop a strategy for your business.

a. Start with an idea-: The first thing you need is an idea. *What is that thing you want to start manufacturing*? It is important to come up with innovative ideas and not just a copycat kind of manufacturing business. I mean, you can copy but it has to be a better version of what already exists. Some of the ways to come up with innovative ideas include-:

- **Choose a niche you like-:** There might be a product you are passionate about; this is a good place to start from.
- **High demand products-:** There are certainly some products whose demand exceeds supply or products that typically have high levels of demand; you can look into any of these products.
- **Fill a gap-:** You could also look for existing gaps in the market that you can fill. For instance, if you live in a place where getting clean, portable

drinking water is a problem, you can consider production of packaged water to fill this gap.
- **Solve a problem**-: Another way to find profitable niches in manufacturing is to find out some of the products that people are dissatisfied with, and then come up with a better version that would be more satisfactory to people.
- **Innovations**-: Nothing stops you from thinking of a product that doesn't already exist in the market.

b. Find Out laws and Regulations-: We are all guided by the laws of the countries we reside in. Before you go further with your manufacturing plan, you should find out what the position of the law is on the item to be produced. You should also find out what licenses and approvals you would need and then comply accordingly.

c. Select a production facility-: You would need a place to use as your production factory. This of course depends on the size of your business. If it's a small manufacturing business, you can start from home provided that there are no zoning laws preventing you from doing so. But if it's a big manufacturing business, you have to look for a production facility. Some factors to consider when selecting a facility include- your needs, funds available, budget and infrastructure suitability.

d. Choose Equipment and Machines for Production-: The next step to take is to find out what equipment's and machines you would need to manufacture the product. When you have found this out, you can now start to think of how to get these machines. Some things to put into consideration include quality of the machines; you don't want to spend money buying a machine that would end up giving you problems. You should also take price into consideration but never at the expense of quality. You can also reduce the costs of purchasing equipment by hiring equipment or buying from suppliers who provide flexible financing options.

e. Decide on your production method-: There are different ways to produce any given product and it's important to find out and adopt the most cost-effective option. Some of the popular production methods include; job production which involves a single person/worker making a product from start to finish, batch production which involves several people working on different stages of the production and assembly line production method. Select the method that is both cost-effective and efficient.

f. Plan your raw materials-: You would also need raw materials to make your product and this must be planned beforehand to ensure that you would always have access to the materials you need at every point in time. You have to determine the quantity of each material you would order for, the size of your order and your re-order level. You can make use of material planning software or economic order quantity formula to do this easily.

g. Find out your production costs-: This is important especially when you need to decide how much capital you would need to start your business. There are different costs in productions. There are fixed costs, direct costs, indirect costs and variable costs. It is important to find out what these costs would be.

h. Decide on Logistics-: *How would you move your raw materials around? What about your finished products, how would you transport them to wholesalers and buyers? Would you have to purchase a vehicle or contract this function out?* It is important to figure this out beforehand.

I. Marketing-: This is very important as well. You need to figure out how you would create awareness for your product and increase patronage. You can hire a marketing consultant to do this for you or find out cheap ways to do it yourself.

j. Funding-: When you have figured out all you need and how you would get them, then you should write your business plan and find out how much you need to start your manufacturing business. Then you can start looking for capital to fund your business.

k. Protect your innovation-: You don't want anyone stealing your ideas hence; you have to protect yourself through patents and copyrights. You should also perform risk assessment and protect yourself through product liability insurance and other necessary insurance coverage that may be needed for the type of your business.

l. Consider Export Options-: A good way to expand your business is by exporting to other countries; find out how to go about this from the export promotion agency in your country.

SESSION 2: TOP PROFITABLE ONLINE BUSINESS IDEAS IN NIGERIA
Over the past years, the business landscape has changed in Nigeria and many parts of Africa. As a result, many Nigerian businesses are going online. With so much business opportunities and start-up business ideas viable in Nigeria and all over Africa, you would be regarded unfortunate if you don't join the entrepreneurs starting an online business in Nigeria today. Instead of asking "what are the best online business ideas in Nigeria?" and searching endlessly for

an answer, here are ten profitable online business ideas you can start in Nigeria today:

1). E-Commerce (Electronic Commerce):

Buying and selling online is getting hotter than ever in Nigeria. With many businesses coming online every month, Nigeria's e-commerce business market is exploding. Many businesses and individuals are generating millions of Naira in revenue every month from running e-commerce start-ups. You too can jump on the band wagon. You can start an e-commerce business from home without owning a single item. Simply resell other people's items like books, clothing, accessories, etc. and over time, you can start stocking your own merchandise.

2). Online Market Place:

This involves selling your products on online marketplaces like Jumia, Konga, Opiid, Amazon, and others. Selling on marketplaces saves you advertisement costs and marketing stress. You can start selling on online marketplaces from your home in Nigeria today.

3). Search Engine Optimization Services (SEO):

Every online business in Nigeria now is racing to get their businesses on the first page of google. Search Engine Optimization (SEO) being a tricky trade has got many scampering around to find professionals that can help them get to the top ten results on google in the shortest time possible. Companies are paying a ton of cash to SEO experts. If you know how to get any web page to rank on the top ten results on the first page of google, then you're in business.

4). Social Media Marketing:

Social media consultants are helping Nigerian companies grow their revenues and get very relevant on social media. They employ strategies ranging from social virility to pure user engagement. Social media consultants help businesses make their customers on social media feel like family. Their services are too vital for the success of any business's image on social media and the internet as a whole.

5). Trading Forex:

Forex trading has over the years proven itself to be a viable source of income for some Nigerians. Many are yet to get involved with trading forex. With the right training, a computer, internet connection and a little start-up capital, you can start growing your revenues from trading forex.

SESSION 3: GENERAL ONLINE BUSINESS YOU CAN START AT HOME
Affiliate marketing

The first venture you can start online is to own your own affiliate store. To become an affiliate marketer means that you will be promoting other people's products and services. Whenever there is a sale, you will get a commission and the most interesting fact here is that you don't even need a dime of your own to start it and you get to partner with some of the biggest companies in the world.

A great advantage of affiliate marketing is that you don't have to spend a dime to set it up. What you do in affiliate marketing is to promote people's products and services from your website or any other means. Every time the link is clicked and a purchase is completed, you'd get paid. So, if you have a large following on twitter, Facebook, or a website with some traffic, you can harness your audience and start your affiliate marketing for any company selling, and start earning revenues with every successful sale. Some companies in Nigeria looking for affiliate marketers are Konga, Jumia, etc.

2. Blogging

If you have a particular subject that interests you and you are passionate about it, then you can start a blog around such topic. Blogging is one of the fastest growing business trends on the web and the sweetest thing is that it is an information-based business. So, no worries about technicalities, programming, etc. You also don't need to invest a dime to get started as there are free platforms you can utilize like Blogger, TypePad, Joomla and WordPress.

This is becoming one of the fastest growing online business ideas in Nigeria. If you have a flair for a particular topic and are a great writer, you can setup a blog and start writing on that topic. Writing to suit your target audience is the most important part of blogging. You must write the way they understand, so they can easily connect with what you're telling them. This will ensure you have a loyal audience that's there to stay.

Blogger to WordPress services

Most blogs are hosted on Google's free blogging platform Blogger; but bloggers are switching over to WordPress because of its usability and features. The only fear of moving from one blogging platform to another is that you may lose your content and page rank.

Most bloggers don't want to go through this nightmare, so the reliance on blogger to WordPress service providers. If you can switch from blogger to WordPress and vice versa without a loss of page rank or content; then you have a profitable business on hand.

Blog Installation

Blogging is the latest craze online. Every Dick and Harry now maintains a blog; and a lot more people desire to own one or two but unfortunately, not many people understand the technicality involved with installing a blog and they are not willing to learn it. If you are good at blog installation; then you can offer it as a service and I bet that you will smile to the bank daily.

3. Auction selling –eBay

This business involves selling or reselling products (using goods, purchase and reselling of wholesale goods, using drop shipping) on an online market place like eBay, Amazon Auction or Craigslist.

4. Online Beading Store

If you love beading, and you have beading skills, you can launch an online business that will not only focus on selling the coolest beads on the web, but also offer video tutorials on how to make beads.

Build your own Blog network

One of the best online businesses you can start today is a blog. The downside of a blog is that it's not a short-term profit maker; but it can bring you fortunes and fame. Owning a blog network is definitely not an easy thing to do, but it can be done. However, it's advisable you start from only one blog. Once your blog or blogs are up and running, you can enjoy steady streams of passive income.

5. E-book Publishing

If you love writing and you possess some marketing skills, then you can venture into information marketing. In this situation, your business will be to identify people's problems and provide a solution in the form of an eBook.

People go online to download thousands of e-books every day in Nigeria. People are also looking for helps on various subjects and topics, while many others just enjoy reading a lot of books. If you're a great writer that's vast in a particular skill people are willing to learn, you can write a detailed e-book on that and have your work published. With the right marketing plan and execution, you'd make money from every purchase of your e-book in Nigeria, Africa, and all over the world.

6. Do It Yourself program

Just as the green revolution is on, the DIY (*Do It Yourself*) movement is also on. As the economy gets tighter, people are spending less and they are learning to do things themselves to save money. You can still take advantage of this situation and position yourself as a DIY expert and start publishing tutorials on how to fix things, install gadgets and make repairs.

7. Advertising Network (Ad Network)

You can also start a company online that connect advertisers to websites who wants to host advertisements. The key responsibility of an Ad Network is the aggregation of Ad space supply from publishers and matching it with advertisers' demand.

The basic concept with Advertising Networks is to feature advertisers' ads on websites that are willing to have the Advertising Network's Ads show on their websites. A perfect example of this online business is Google AdWords. People advertise through google, and it shows on many websites at the same time. If you have the resources, a niche idea, and a wide network of websites to partner with, you can also start an ad network.

8. Website flipping business

You can start buying and selling websites for a profit. To understand this business model, just consider yourself a real estate entrepreneur; who buy houses at a low price, renovates the house and resells at a higher price for a profit. You can begin by checking out websites that are listed on Flippa.com to understand how this business works.

Web hosting reselling business

One thing about a web hosting reselling business is that the market is a bit saturated; but I don't believe a market can be saturated if you can be creative and focus on a specific niche. But the good side of this business is that it can run on autopilot; once you have put in the initial effort and gotten some clients, you are set.

9. You Can Make Money Taking Surveys Online

10. Set up an e-commerce store online

Yes, you can set up an e-commerce or retail store online and you can start this online business from home without even owning a single product. You can sell virtually anything ranging from books, clothes and electronics to household item through wholesale drop shipping or by setting up an affiliate store with Amazon or eBay.

11. Research and sell information online

Yes, you can research on people's problems and needs; then all you have to do is to come up with a solution, package it in an eBook, video or audio format and you are in business. In fact, the overhead start-up cost for this business is so low that anybody can do it. To have an idea on hottest selling information products, I will recommend you visit *Clickbank.com*

LESSON 2: PROFITABLE WEB-BASED SERVICES BUSINESS IDEAS AND OPPORTUNITIES TO START

To build a successful business online around service provision; you need nothing but specialized knowledge or skill and thorough understanding of how the internet works. Your overhead can be kept low by operating your business from home. In fact, providing business services on the internet can be started from home with zero capital. All you need is core expertise and you are good to go. You can get such expertise by attending seminars and workshops, reading books and practicing on your own.

Growing an online service business is quite easy because of the ease of referral; and the automation of several processes. Marketing your business expertise online is quite cheap and can even be done for free; if you know how to go about it.

16. Programming Services

With the growing demand for software, applications and plugins; <u>offering programming services is definitely a business to beat</u> because of the steady demand. But a downside to offering programming service is that it requires specialized knowledge that doesn't come easy. If you are patient enough to learn the ropes of programming; you are sure of a steady supply of contracts. Remember that *Larry Page, Bill Gates, Larry Ellison and Mark Zuckerberg* started out as programmers.

17. Web Copywriting

Web copywriting is a service business you can start today and begin to make money because of insufficient copywriters on ground. Affiliate marketers and info product marketers will be your major clients because they are always on the lookout for possible ways to increase the click through rate, subscription rate and conversion rate of their websites. If you have a passion for playing with words; then <u>you can start a web based business offering web copywriting services</u>.

18. <u>Virtual Assistant</u>

The next web-based service business opportunity you can start today is to provide virtual assistance to web entrepreneurs. Your duty will be to carry out assigned tasks that your client considers cumbersome or not-too-relevant.

19. Web-Design

Web-design is an online service business that has being around for quite long; yet, the market is not saturated. With an ever-growing demand for websites, forums and blogs; the momentum for web-design services will never die down. <u>To get started as a web designer</u>, all you need are some artistic talents, programming knowledge and time. As you design your websites, you must ensure you build your portfolio and look forward to <u>having additional clients through word of mouth</u>.

The most exciting fact about offering web-design services is that you don't need to know how to design a website or blog; all you need to do is to master the automated web-design software made available online and you are in business.

With a lot of Nigerian businesses going online, a lot of people and businesses are seeking the services of professional web designers. Without a great looking website, many customers will not trust what you have to offer on your website.

Because of this, the demand for good web designers is rising, leading to higher fees for the designers. Some earn from as low as 50,000 Naira ($166.67) to as much as 1,200,000 Naira ($4000) for a web project. Web-design is one great business you can start from your home in Nigeria. All you need is a good computer, proper training, and a sample website to get started.

20. Start a Local SEO Company

The battle to be on the first page of Google is getting hotter by the day. Companies are now paying huge sums of money to search engine positioning experts to help increase their page rank. *Do you know how to get a web page to rank in the top ten search results of Google?* If yes, then you have a money minting skill on hand. Aside providing search engine optimization services; you can actually build a successful business around this single service, big time.

21. Social Media Consultancy

As the craze for social media content increases; so also does the competition for social media attention by big company increases, thereby increasing the need for social media marketers. Do you know how to make a content go viral on social media? Can you build a strong brand presence on social media? Have you mastered the intricacies of social networking? Then become a social media consultant and you are in for cool cash.

22. Web Promotion

There are hundreds of millions of websites on the internet; and each of these websites seeks publicity. You can start a business as a web promotion expert and make money online. If you can effectively promote a website without spending much on advertising; you have a good business on hand.

23. eBook Cover Design

eBook publishing is on the rise; so also, is the demand for quality eye catching eBook covers or product covers. The good thing about starting an eBook cover design business is that you don't need to have knowledge of graphic design or Photoshop. The process of creating an eBook cover is now automated with the use of eBook cover design software.

24. Become a Freelance Writer and Make Money Writing Articles Online

One of the most outsourced online business processes is content creation and written content happens to be one of them. In fact, ghost writing as a service business is so broad that you can fill it all. Do you have a passion for writing? Then start a business offering ghost writing services to individuals and companies. You specialize on guest blogging for clients, article writing, eBook writing or freelance writing.

25. Proofreading

Do you have an eye for spotting grammatical errors? If yes, then you can make money online by offering proofreading services to online publishers.

26. Internet Press Release Services

The demand for free publicity will always be on the increase as long as there's competition in business. Imagine getting on the front page or home page of a high traffic media website without spending a dime, that's the power of press releases. If you are good at writing press releases and also submitting them, then you are in business.

27. Website Appraisal

Just as businesses are bought and sold offline, so also are websites bought and sold online. You can become a website valuation expert and offer appraisal services to website developers (virtual real estate developers).

28. Website Critique

Are you good at website optimization? Can you help internet business owners increase their conversion rate simply by overhauling a website? Then you can critique websites for cash. I know several entrepreneurs that have built successful online business by offering landing pages and squeeze page makeovers. You can do the same.

29. Web Development

Web development goes beyond web-design; it encompasses website critique, forum installation, e-commerce site development and specialized website building. This is a profitable business opportunity; though it's capital and time intensive, it's a guaranteed money maker.

30. Joint Venture Brokering

You can start a web business around offering joint venture brokerage services. If you have the capacity to link product creators with marketers in any niche; I don't see anything that stops you from starting a joint venture brokerage business.

31. Lead Generation Services

Do you know how to generate leads online? Then you can help businesses build their mailing lists. Most internet marketers attest to the fact that the money is in the list and they are willing to do anything to have this list. You can start a lead generation business and charge either per lead or on a bulk basis.

32. Niche Research Services

One of the best web-based business services to offer is a niche research service. This is a business that requires you to spot online trends and niches before the rest of the crowd discovers such. It also entails digging deep to discover ignored or overlooked niches. If you are well grounded in online business research; then you can start a business online researching upcoming trends and niches, and selling these business trends to internet entrepreneurs and investors.

33. Software / Script Installation services

The last web-based business service you can offer internet business owners for cash is software / script installation. Most people desire to start a social networking site, forum, bookstore and so on but they don't know how to go about it.

Some of these entrepreneurs have even taken a bold step ahead to purchase the necessary software or script needed to power their desired site; but they don't know how to go about the installation. I have seen several small businesses that charge $97 for installations that don't take more than 20 minutes to implement. If offering script installation service thrills, you; then you can learn the rudiments of script installation.

34. Recruiting and Online Headhunting

If you know your way around the web and you are good at digging up people's profile, then you can become a contract staff agent to some companies. Your duty is to go online and search for the right candidates for specific positions within a company and the company will pay you when the hire is made.

As a final note, I want it to sink into your skill that you can become a successful entrepreneur simply by taking advantage of any of the web-based service business opportunities listed above. All you need is the right knowledge, the right marketing skill and determination. Once these three keys are locked in synergy; the sky will be your starting point.

35. Consultancy-: You can be a consultant to business people online, and your task is to keep informing them of the latest or new developments within their industry.

36. Resume writing service

A resume writing service can make a big internet home business, especially during economic difficult times and in areas where unemployment rate is very high.

37. Desktop publication services

Getting used to software, meeting deadlines, and making yourself popular online are the keys to launching a desktop publication home businesses. While some desktop publishers would like to meet clients in person and serve their local neighbourhood market, a desktop publisher who renders services through the internet will have a much broader market to work on. Additionally, working this business online permits you to show case prospects samples of your work and to publish testimonies from your satisfied clients/customers.

38. Internet marketing services

Assisting people to drive customers to their websites can be an excellent online business with a strong profit potential. Doing business on the web is quite tough because things change so fast online, so it will be your job to help the online entrepreneurs keep up with the ever-changing trend. Example of services you can offer include pay-per-Click (PPC) advertising services, blog marketing services, article marketing services, guest blogging, link building service, etc.

39. Graphic Design

There are lots of graphic designers on the web. So, if you have plan to succeed in this area online, serving a particular target audience will be your best friend. Suppose you are specialized with fashion and you have a good graphic design skill, you can try your hand at launching an online graphic design firm that focuses on graphic design for fashion designers. You can also choose to focus on infographic designing, eBook cover design, etc.

40. Online life coaching

Sometimes, life could be complicating thus requiring a little correction or encouragement for an individual along the way. If this sometimes appeals to you, you can consider launching an online business that tackles just one aspect of life's most common challenges. For instance, if you are naturally born cupid, you can be a dating coach. Or if you know how to get things done, you can be an effective coach to assist others to quit procrastinating.

41. Membership sites

If you are an expert in your industry, then you should definitely think of starting a membership site. A membership website is a site that offer "specific information" to people; all for a monthly recurring fee. A successful membership site can generate income monthly without you lifting a finger.

LESSON 3: MORE INTERNET BASED BUSINESS IDEAS AND OPPORTUNITIES TO START

APP DEVELOPMENT

- Direct sales online
- Transcript service
- Online video editing service
- College Entrance Essay writing
- Baking school online

COMPUTER REPAIR REMOTE

- Social media for Non-profits
- Online custom baby clothes
- Online personal finance coaching

CHALLENGES OF SMALL BUSINESS START-UPS IN URARL AREA BEFORE U SET UP YOUR BUSINESS

1) Client Communication Issues as a result of GSM network in some Specific Locality

2) Language barriers for non-indigenes

3) Lack of inadequate Electricity power

4) Water: majorly affects product-based business

5) Little or no Availability of corporate Funding

6) Lack of proper government funding

7) Ignorance and illiteracy among prospective entrepreneurs on know how

8) Assumed or ignorance of target market and how to get to them

9) Skilled Staff availability for services or specialist areas

10) Government Policy and Environmental factors.

SOLUTIONS TO THIS PROBLEMS

a) Buy generator if it's a product or services-based business with a shop
b) Get a location where Services is most sufficient
c) Create a personal Time to meditate and think about solution to the problems you are facing but more importantly get a feasibility report on how to over this factors and yet experienced factors
d) Build/create a group of think tanks that can help out in solving problems faced on a daily basis

3 STEPS TO REGISTER YOUR BUSINESS IN NIGERIA

Are you thinking of doing business in Nigeria? Register your business with the Corporate Affairs Commission which is the Agency empowered by the Company and Allied Matters Act 1990, Pursuant to section 659. It is the requirement of the law that you should register your business if you want to do legitimate business in Nigeria.

Lagos – The commercial capital of Nigeria

Depending on the magnitude of your business, you can register it all by yourselves without the need of a Lawyer. The categories for business registration in Nigeria are:

(a) Business Name Registration

(b) Private Limited Company (LTD)

(c) Public Limited Company (PLC)

(d) Company Limited by Guarantee (LTD/GTE)

(e) Unlimited Company (ULTD)

(f) Incorporated Trustee

In this section, the first two section to be spoken about is (Business Name, and Private Limited Company) which is the two most popular and most relevant to small and medium scale Entrepreneurs. Apart from the requirement of the law, there are other great benefits of registering your business.

1. It helps you secure your company name before someone else takes it. So early registration helps secure your choice name.

2. Registering your business add seriousness and authenticity to your business. It makes you feel more responsible and work harder towards establishing your business and brand. It will make people to take you as a serious business person and Increases your drive towards success.

3. You will be able to open a corporate account with your business name only if it is registered and of course you know the importance of having a corporate current account – it makes people feel more relaxed to transact business with you. Now that you know the importance of registering your company, how do you proceed to register your business in Nigeria? The steps are simple but sometimes can be very tedious due to our system. Here are the practical steps how you can go about it without much tears!

Step 1 – Proceed to the Corporate Affairs Commission Office nearest to you and submit your business name for Name Search. Just walk into the place and obtain the CAC Form one for N200. Or you go to CAC site pay N500 to search for business names not yet in used just from the comfort of your home

Fill the form correctly in CAPITAL LETTER – There is nothing much to fill, just your name, your address and The Names you intend to register, tick the type of company category you want to register as. You have option one and two – Option one is your first-choice name, while option two is the alternative name in case the first choice isn't available. Make a Photocopy of the filled form before submitting it, the photocopy is what you will bring back to be used to locate your form. Submit the original and go back in three days to check if your name is available. If not, you will have to repeat the process all over again until you find one that is available.

Note: If you go for popular phrases, you have 99% possibility of not having it available. Chose something unique and uncommon.

Step 2 - Once you checked and your name is available, begin the registration process immediately! Obtain the Business Name registration form for N250 (as at February 2013) and fill it. If it is Limited Company you want to register, you will buy the set of Company Incorporation forms for N500 of the detailed requirement for Incorporated Trustees under Part C of CAMA No.1 of 1990.

If you are confused about what to fill in those forms, ask someone there to assist you. For business name, it's really not difficult. For Limited Liability, it can be quite challenging but someone there can just be of help as long as you've provided all the requirements in the PDF downloadable above.

Step 3 – Take your completed form to the Federal High Court or State High Court for attestation. That one cost N250 but if you don't know your way, those guys will short change you – a friend paid ₦800 for his. But hope you know that in 2016 prices have changed. So, when you get there, ask for where you can do attestation. When you are through with that, return back to Corporate Affairs Commission office and submit your completed and attested forms. The first person will view it and sign on it and ask you to pass it to the next person who will type it into the computer and print it out for you to see and make amend if necessary.

Make your final payment for the registration into their UBA Bank account usually attached to all the CAC offices, so you don't need to go elsewhere to make the payment. When all these have being successfully fulfilled, your business will be up for registration and certification.
For Business Name – Go back for your Certificate after 8 working days or thereabout. As for Limited Company, your certificate will be sent to you once it is ready.

Note the price mentioned here is subject to change due to time value of money but the concept is to give you an idea of what to expect.

NIGERIA ONLINE REGISTRATION PROCEDURE FOR REGISTRATION OF COMPANY/BUSINESS NAME/INCORPORATED TRUSTEES ONLINE

Connection to the Company Registration Portal (CRP)
1. Services.cac.gov.ng, or
2. cac.gov.ng

Creation of account
1. Click on create account on the home page of the Portal.
2. Complete the forms displayed

NOTE:
1. ACCREDITED USERS should select "ARE YOU AN ACCREDITED CUSTOMER?" and enter their accreditation number in this format for

individual NBA/IND/12345 or ICAN/IND/12345 or ICSAN/IND/12345, and for firm NBA/FM/12345, or ICAN/FM/12345, or ICSAN/FM/12345.

2. Accredited users must ensure that they enter the e-mail address that was used during their accreditation.
3. Enter the catcher as displayed in the box.
4. Click on submit.

FOR GENERAL USERS, the system will display the pre-entered ''USER NAME'' and the auto generated ''PASSWORD'' immediately. While accredited users will be mailed their ''USER NAME'' and ''PASSWORD'' after approval at the back office.

ACCESSING THE CRP AFTER ACCOUNT CREATION

1. Enter the ''USER NAME'' and ''PASSWORD''.
2. Click on ''LOGIN''
3. Accept terms of use.
4. Change your ''PASSWORD''.

You can thereafter transact business with the commission using your profile without any interruption.

CONDUCT AVAILABILITY

1. Login using your profile details.
2. Select ''NAME SEARCH''.
3. Complete the forms displayed.

NOTE:

1. Always make use of the ''CONTINUE'' button until you get to the end of the form and make payment.
2. For Incorporated Trustee make sure you provide the main object in the column provided.
3. All fields make asterisks and in red are compulsory and must be populated.

TO VIEW AVAILABILITY APPROVAL

1. Login with your profile.

2. Click on "ACTION" button" on the name already reserved.
3. Click on DOWNLOAD OF NAME APPROVAL".
4. The system will download the document at the base of your computer system.
5. Click on the "OPEN" option, the approved availability will be displayed.

NOTE: This is where you see the availability serial number that is required for registration.

REGISTRATION OF COMPANY, BUSINESS NAME, INCORPORATED TRUSTEES

1. Reserve name.
2. Log in with your profile.
3. Select "REGISTRATION"
4. Select the classification that is "BUSINESS NAME, or COMPANY, or INCORPORATED TRUSTEE".
5. Enter the availability serial code.
6. Click on continue.
7. Enter the details of the "PROPRIETOR, DIRECTORS, TRUSTEES, SHAREHOLDERS, SECRETARY (depending on whether you are registering a BUSINESS NAME, COMPANY, or INCORPORATED TRUSTEE).

NOTE:

1. Where the director of the company is also a shareholder select the director that has the dual role enter the number of shares and classification of shares then click on "ADD SELECTED RECORD".
2. For companies and Incorporated Trustees, click on "ADD AN OBJECT" or "ADD OBJECTS" and type in the nature of Business or objects for which the company or Incorporated trustee is registered, then click on "ADD". Continue to add the object until all the objects have being added.
3. For companies, either adopt the "ARTICLE" or edit by adding or removing the content of the Article and replacing the same with your own Articles.
4. Select the "DROP OFF and PICK UP STATE".
5. Click on continue until payment is made.

6. Select "GET STAMP" to stamp the document electronically.
7. Make payment for electronic stamping.
8. The system will automatically affix the electronic stamp duties on the documents (Form CAC1.1, and Memorandum and Article of Association).

TO DOWNLOAD STAMP DOCUMENT
1. Select "REGISTRATION".
2. The system will display all the list of companies registered.
3. Under the "DOCUMENT" click on "DOWNLOAD DOCUMENTS". Or
4. Click on "ACTION" button.
5. Select "DOWNLOAD DOCUMENTS".
6. Print the document.

TO UPLOAD DOCUMENT ON DOCUMENT UPLOAD INTERFACE
1. The documents already printed must be signed by the directors/subscribers
2. Go to the commission's web site "www.cac.gov.ng"
3. At the middle of the page extreme right select "DOCUMENT UPLOAD".
4. Enter the company/Business name/Incorporated Trustee "AVAILABILITY CODE".
5. Select the "ORIGINATING OFFICE" (THIS IS WHERE YOU WILL PICK UP THE CERTIFICATE).
6. Select "I AM NOT A ROBOT" then follow the instruction.
7. Click on "BEGIN".
8. Select the type of document to be attached one after the other and attach each one after properly identifying same.
9. After attaching all the documents click on submit.

AFTER UPLOAD WHAT'S NEXT

1. The Commission will rely on the uploaded documents to treat your application. The certificate will be generated by the Commission and all relevant documents will be certified.

2. You don't have to come to the Commission to follow up on the status of your application, you can check the status of your application on the portal. There is a column that reads "STATUS" on your profile. This will show the state or status of the application, it will show "NOT SUBMITTED, or SUBMITTED, or PENDING APPROVAL, or APPROVED depending on stage the application is.

3. Also note that where the application is approved and certificate generated the Registration number will be displayed on the column for "REGISTRATION NUMBER".

4. When the status reads "APPROVED" and Registration number displayed, then you can approach the office where you had selected as the DROP OFF/PICK UP OFFICE or "ORIGINATING OFFICE" with the original copy of the document that you had earlier printed and uploaded. You should submit the originals in exchange for the certificate and CTC's.

5. **AUTOMATIC TAX IDENTIFICATION NUMBER (TIN) GENERATION:** Immediately a certificate of incorporation is generated in the CRP, a TIN will be issued and sent to customer's e-mail address from the FIRS/JTB through the Integrated Stamp Duty System (ISDS) Portal. This has dispensed with the need for a separate TIN application to the Joint Tax Board.

DOCUMENTS NEEDED BY CORPORATE AFFAIRS COMMISSION FOR BUSINESS NAME REGISTRATION IN NIGERIA

- ✓ **Form1**: Availability Check and Reservation of Name
- ✓ **Form C.A.C 2**: Registration Form
- ✓ **Form C.A.C 3**: Identification (Voters card, international passport or National ID)
- ✓ **Form C.A.C 4**: Payment Receipt

DOCUMENTS NEEDED TO GET TAX CLEARANCE CERTIFICATE FROM FIRS (FEDERAL INLAND REVENUE SERVICE) IN NIGERIA

- ✓ Tax Payer Registration Input Form
- ✓ Completed Firs Questionnaire
- ✓ Copy of Memorandum and Articles of Association
- ✓ Names and Address of Tax Adviser
- ✓ Letter of Appointment of Tax Adviser and Letter of Acceptance
- ✓ The Date Company Commenced Business
- ✓ Names, Addresses and Mobile Numbers of Major Promoters and Chairman of the Company Including Their E-mail Addresses
- ✓ Other Sources of Income of the Chairman and The Promoters of the Company
- ✓ Name and Address of the Principal Officers of the Company Including the Chairman, Managing Director, Legal Adviser and Accountant

DARLINTON OMEH PERSPECTIVE ON HOW TO BECOME A SUCCESSFUL ENTERPRENUR (OMEH)

Every big thing has a small beginning. If you ask the successful entrepreneurs making wave in the industries of the world today, they will tell you that the path to their success was never an easy one. Mastering how to become a successful entrepreneur is very essential if you desire to become one.

But who really is an entrepreneur? By short definition, entrepreneur is an individual who prefer working as an employee. Entrepreneur runs a small business and assume all risks and rewards of a given business venture or service offered for sale. An entrepreneur must have the capacity to develop, manage and organize a business venture with any of its risk in order to make profit.

Avoidance of calculated risk taking is the major reason most people do not become entrepreneur. As a starter you need not get anxious about whether you will fail eventually. Failing is not an option if you follow the rule. The following are just some of the tips that may prove very helpful to you.

The Will to Succeed

Many people remain as paid employer because they are afraid to fail as entrepreneurs. As such, they get contented with crumbs that their employers pass down to them as salaries. Entrepreneurs succeeds because of their willingness to succeed even in the face adversities. They are not scared of challenges and failures; they see opportunities where people see obstacles in fact, they are known to stand in the face of this.

Have a Unique Idea

To succeed as an entrepreneur, you need to take a look at the people in your territory and see what they are truly lacking. The more unique your idea, the more chances of survival you have though in the real world having an idea is not enough but executing it is. Even when the idea of goods or service you want to sell is not a new one, you can still add some flavour of uniqueness in it that will enable you beat your competitors. If the market is big enough, you will make as much as or even more than your competitors. Most companies die from indigestion rather than starvation - in other words, companies suffer from doing too many things at the same time rather than doing few things very well. Stay focused on the mission. An insight of a good business is where an individual create idea or see things in a particular direction in a field of business in a way other do not see it. In a competitive environment, that is the secret of business success.

Draft a Business Plan

Never go into any business venture without a business plan. Even when your idea is a great one, it may not be effective enough unless you put it in writing. It is important that you write a good business plan. There is no hard and fast rule about how this should be done. But ensure that it must include factors like the market you are targeting, what it will cost you to carry out the production or service, how you will get financing for your business and the growth you are projecting. Include details and descriptions, and plan everything out realistically. Take your time to evaluate your product at each section. The section of a good business plan includes Competition.

Stick to Your Plan

There is nothing as worse as losing focus. It is important that you are objective with yourself as you draft plan for your prospective business. Since budget is an integral part of a plan, it will kill your dreams and goals if you later become frivolous with your spending. There is nothing wrong in being flexible however if your original plan is getting unfavourable.

Talk to Entrepreneurs That Are Already Successful

There are entrepreneurs who have made it big from small beginning. Since they did not get to the top by mistake, it is important that you seek their opinions especially when you meet with challenges. Learn from the mistakes they made while investing and avoid repeating similar mistakes. Compare more than one viewpoint especially when investing in capital intensive project. Never start a business because the business looks amazing or boasts high profit margin or returns. Choose what you like to do, what you desire and find easy doing. Business built on basis of your strength and skills have greater chances of success instead of starting on the basis of affection for making money. Talking to other successful entrepreneurs will help you discover what propelled them to business and how they managed crisis.

Acquire Good Leadership Skills

A good leader must have good communication skills and the ability to amass a team of group of people towards achieving a common goal. A good leader must earn trust and respect of his team mates by demonstrating positive works ethics and confidence. Road to success may be so long so it's important to always remember to enjoy the journey. Everyone would teach you to focus on your goals but successful focus on the journey and celebrates the milestones along the way.

Flexibility and Persistence: Every Entrepreneurs has to be agile in order to perform. You have to continually team and adapt as new information is available. At the same time, you have to remain persistent to the cause and mission of your enterprise. Successful Entrepreneur fined the balance between listening to that voice and staying persistent in driving for success.

Imploring Hard Work: We all know there is no such things as overnight success. Behind every overnight success lies years of hard work and sweat. People with luck will tell you there is no easy way to achieve success and that luck comes for those who work hard. Successful entrepreneurs always give 100 percent of their efforts to everything they do. If you know you are giving your best you will never have a cause to regrets. Keep your focus on things you can control.

Be Good at Marketing Your Products and Services

Here you should know how to sell your products and again ask yourself what kind of product do you want to display? Your product marketing, how will the packaging look like? Also, another vital thing is where your product will sell.

Advertisement: This is a stage where u create awareness for your goods and services to the final consumers through media: T. Vs, newspaper, magazines, internet, sharing of hand bills etc. This should be done from time to time. With this, I think you will be on your way to becoming a successful entrepreneur.

CHAPTER 5
12 INSIGHTS TO ENTERPRENURIAL START-UP FOR PROSPECTIVE BUSINESS MEN/WOMEN

INSIGHT 1. TAKE SKILLS AND INTEREST INVENTORY:

"When Opportunities come, you need to inspect them to see what the content is. You need to respect it so that it does not slip of your hand. You need to prospect it even where it does not seem to present itself and every day of your life you need to expect an opportunity" by **Matthew Ashimolowo**

Making a choice from list of businesses to do is a soul-searching process to determine which business is right for you. You'll definitely have an advantage with a business that's a spin-off of your background or experience. You can Also enjoy success in an area where you have strong interest yet lack experience, though you May need to qualify yourself through entrepreneurial training or professional certification programs. Jot down the skills that already exist in your talent bank. What do you like to do with your time? What technical skills have you learnt or developed that can generate money for you? Do you have hobbies or interests that are marketable? It might help to create a personal resume that lists your professional and personal Experiences as well as your expertise. For each job you list, describe the duties you were responsible for and how successful you were at each. Be sure to include professional skills, educational background, hobbies and accomplishments that required expertise or special knowledge. You should also talk with others in businesses similar to the ones you're considering about the traits and temperaments needed to be successful. Find out what they really like about the businesses they're running and also what they don't like. Compare their responses with your own interests and personality to see if there's a fit. Don't stop searching until you find an idea that couples your love for the work with your marketable talents. *Always remember that if you want to start a business, you don't have comparative advantage in then you must leverage on other people expertise if you wish the business to grow. But if you are not willing to, then you must not start a business you don't have adequate skills for or enthusiasm for, because if you do the business might not live to stand the test of time. Start only with the business you know, prepared feasibility study for and also acquired expertise on, if you want to make it in business.*

2. RESEARCH AND EVALUATE IDEAS

Thorough research will help support expectations about a business's success as well as uncover any potholes in your thinking. Ask yourself these questions:

    a. What problem does my product or service solve?

b. Who will buy my product or service?
c. Why will they buy it?
d. Where will they buy it—specialty shops, department stores, mail order, online?
e. What do I need to charge to make a healthy profit and will people actually pay that?
f. What products or services will mine be competing with?

The more narrowly you can define your business and your target market, the better. So, it's crucial that you create a niche for yourself in the marketplace—it's the key to success for even the biggest companies. Wal-Mart and Tiffany's are both retailers, but they have very different niches: Wal-Mart caters to bargain-minded shoppers, while Tiffany's appeals to upscale jewellery customers. To find out if your business idea has a chance of succeeding in the marketplace and to help you create an effective marketing plan, you'll need to do more than just answer the questions listed above. You'll also need to conduct more formal market research. **Generally, you'll need to collect information on three crucial aspects of your business: industry information, target market and your competition.**

WAYS OF DEVELOPING NEW BUSINESS IDEA (VISION)

1. For a potential business, conduct a market survey on products or service that are essential to people
2. Find out what motivates peoples' need
3. *Physiological needs* – food, water, shelter, etc. e.g. water business, real estate business, fast food business. Think outside the box
4. *Safety needs* – safety, protection e.g. security business, intelligence business, NGOs. Don't limit your mind
5. *Social needs*- affection, friendship, events (canopies, chairs, pots, cakes, balloons, parties, decorations, etc.) e.g. match making business, rental business, event management business (ceremony business). Explore possible options
6. *Ego needs* – success, prestige, self-respect (exotic cars from friends abroad for sale, nursery/ primary schools, jamb/WAEC business) e.g. Seminar business, training business. Don't judge the idea first without first running a viability test first for the business.
7. *Self-actualization-* self-fulfilment (professional examinations, adult education, vocational education, skill acquisition, computer literacy

programme, etc.) e.g. e-centres. Don't restrict yourself without first understanding your potentials.

OTHER WAYS OF GENERATING IDEAS

1. Because of the nature of needs, people will pay you if you can do the following for them better or do things differently than anyone else
2. Find a need and fill it
3. Find a problem and solve it. Good solution to peoples' problem could change your life
4. Example- peoples' problem that can save them money
5. Save them time with your services
6. Consider peoples' needs that can supply them with food, shelter or clothing
7. Provide them with security, safety or comfort
8. Offer them leisure or entertainment, affection, fun, friendship or social interactions
9. Give them status, prestige or self-respect
10. Add value to their lives
11. Many businesses do some of these and make fortunes
12. Therefore, ask yourself if you can offer better, quicker, cheaper, more durable or higher quality product or service than people in that line of business
13. If the answer is yes, then business opportunity has emerged

THE MANAGER AS THE VISIONARY

1) Get to understand what your customers are looking for
2) Set your goals for your business and review them often
3) Identify the key factors needed for your business to succeed
4) Focus on strategic thinking not just on planning
5) Access your business strength and weakness

SESSION 0.11: DESCRIPTION

Figure 4: Performance management system

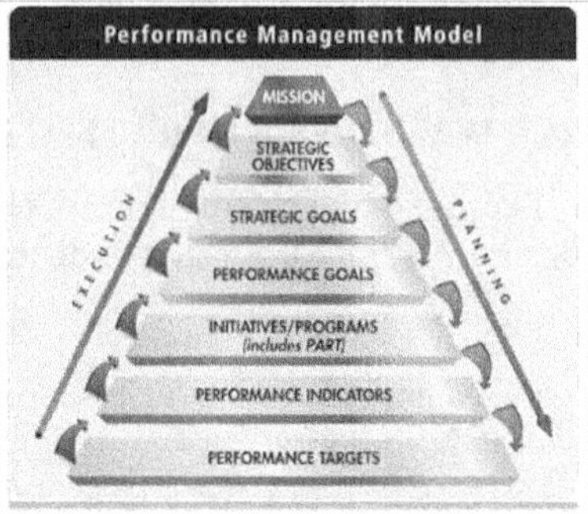

Figure 5: Performance management model

1. Be Passionate About the *Mission*.

To get a start-up off the ground, you must be willing to work about 80 hours a week with little pay. Doing that is impossible without deeply felt passion, in summary you must have a clear sense of your daily or monthly task you wish to achieve that will lead to the overall attainment of your goals and target for that year, if you are not enthusiastic about the task ahead and how you intend to accomplish it with practical working steps. The end result might turn out unfavourable and not the kind of result you would have loved to have.

2. Make sure people will actually buy what you sell.

A product nobody will buy is not worth selling; as a matter of fact, it's a waste of money and investment. If you want to sell a product make sure you know who your potential customers are before you even start selling, who are your target market? But more importantly the way you package and brand what you are selling matters a lot; it will go a long way for you the seller. Also, whatever product you are selling ask yourself if you were a customer and you see your product will you buy it? Whatever answer you get gives a clue of the kind of fate that awaits you.

STEP 2: CONDUCT NEED AND COST ANALYSIS AND VERIFY PROSPECTIVE BUSINESS NAME ON NIGERIA CORPORATE AFFAIRS COMMISSION

COST ANALYSIS

It's critical to determine how much cash you'll need to open and operate your business before you hang out your shingle. To keep your business running smoothly in its start-up phase, you'll need enough capital to cover all expenses until you reach the breakeven point. Many experts recommend new companies start out with enough money to cover projected expenses for at least six months. It's foolhardy to expect to generate revenue immediately—it's best to play it safe and plan for all contingencies.

Create a checklist of expenditures. These suggested tips will help you get started:

a. List the equipment, furniture, supplies and people needed to operate your business.

b. Itemize start-up costs for inventory, signage, sales and marketing literature or tools,

c. Research and product development, licenses, permits, operating capital, and legal or professional fees.

d. Calculate your monthly overhead for rent, supplies, utilities, business and health insurance,

e. Taxes, Internet access, shipping and other services.

f. Factor in your salary and employee or contractor wages.

g. Refer to industry-specific start-up books and resources for additional costs that may apply to

h. Your respective business types. As for determining accurate cost estimates, a good rule of thumb is to assume everything will cost more than you expect, so pad your numbers in order to create a safety net.

NEED ANALYSIS

Is the business idea meeting the need of the people, if yes what are those needs? Are they: Economical need, Psychological need, Physical need, Basic need,

Emotional Need or Business environment need? What kind of need/problem are you solving?

INSIGHT 3: WHAT YOU NEED TO KNOW BEFORE YOU WRITE YOUR BUSINESS PLAN

You gain an advantage by building your business on paper first. A business plan's value goes beyond its ability to help secure a loan package for you. It's a working document that helps you Prepare for opportunities as well as difficulties. There are three primary parts to a business plan. The first is the business concept, where you discuss the industry, your business structure, your product or service and how you plan to make your business a success. The second is the marketplace section, in which you describe and analyse potential customers: who and where they are, what makes them buy and so on. You'll also describe your competition and how you'll position yourself to beat it. Finally, financial section contains your income and cash flow statement, balance sheet and other financial ratios, such as breakeven analysis. This part may require help from your accountant and a good spreadsheet software program. Breaking these three major sections down further, a business plan consists of six major components:

- ✓ Executive summary
- ✓ Management
- ✓ Product or service
- ✓ Marketing
- ✓ Operations
- ✓ Financial data

Mental Success *System:* Reasoning, Thinking, meditation

General and accepted definition by **Microsoft® Encarta thinking, planning, pursuit**:

1) Reasoning:

Reasoning is the Principal raw material for effective Planning.

logical thinking: the use of logical thinking in order to find results or draw conclusions.

Reasoning is a very potent and necessary tool to avoid making hasty decisions and unwise responses to situations that arises. Someone once said its either you are part of a new evolving revolution or you are flushed away with the old revolution. Productive and critical thinking is what would pave the way for you in today's world. Always remember that when you make your brain sweat concerning your business it will produce money as the result. Therefore, start working and reasoning your way to financial fortune.

THINKING

a) forming of thoughts: use of the mind to form thoughts

There's *a lot of thinking to do before we make that decision.*

b). judgement: opinions or conclusions arrived at

What's *your thinking on the political situation?*

A wise man once said you cannot feature in a future you cannot picture, meaning that the essence of thought formation is to brain storm on how you can practically execute your idea into success. Why else would you think employers would be willing to pay so much money for thinkers, it is simple, thinkers are seen as idea tanks meaning one idea is more than enough to transform any business into financial giant. So as a young entrepreneur you must be ready and willing to engage in productive and knowledge base thinking with a business target focus which is a very useful tool for growing any business.

ii) **Meditation:**

a. **emptying or concentration of mind:** the emptying of the mind of thoughts, or the concentration of the mind on one thing, in order to aid mental or spiritual development, contemplation, or relaxation.

b. **pondering of something:** the act of thinking about something carefully, calmly, seriously, and for some time, or an instance of such thinking.

Now one thing you should know is that meditation is the foundation upon which understanding is established in relation to any subject of concern. How do I mean? Isaac Newton discovered the law of gravity through meditation and reasoning of why the apple fell from the tree. Now I know that Isaac Newton was not the first man to see an apple fall from an apple tree but he was the first man to ask why it fell? Reason for its falling? Forces responsible? And so on. Now the good news was the more he thought about it in terms of reasoning and deep meditation the more answers he got for his supposed scientific hypothesis and theory. What do I mean? If you want to grow a small business into fortune, then you must create a conducive environment around you where you can think your way out to financial freedom and prosperity. This particular choice is completely yours to make so engage it or not?

16) **PLANNING**
There are couple of definitions to the word planning but a few of these summarized definitions are as stated below:
   a) Planning gives value to your time and resources and ultimately to your pursuits
   b) Planning is the application of logical, rational and analytical thinking to your objective.
   c) Planning deals with facts that will make your work resourceful and result oriented
   d) Planning is the arrangement of facts to achieve your set of objectives.
   e) Planning is the application of logical rational and analytical thinking to your objective. It can be simply seen as approaching your set objective with appropriate counsel.
   a) Planning strategy: this can be simply expressed as business plan

b) **Information:** The information you get and know is what adds value to your planning, and makes it resourceful and result oriented. You must be well-informed about the business subject matter.

3) **PURSUIT**

a) Purpose discovery: This involves knowing the very reason why your business is existing? What is it created to do? What problem is it solving? What need is it meeting? These and many more are what I call business discovery of purpose

b) **Discretion in business execution**. This involves using your instinct or a rule of thumb in solving problems or making decisions or carrying out a planned line of action of which might not produce optimal result but at least produces an accepted result.

STRATEGY: CREATE A SOLID BUSINESS PLAN

After you've determined the know-how of your business idea alongside an insightful knowledge of what it is all about then you will need to lay down the basics of the business before executing it. A few questions to ask yourself:

- **What are my financial goals?**
- **How can I keep costs low?**
- **How do I build a solid customer base?**
- **How can I ensure success?**

If you're going into business with a partner, find someone who has complementary skill to what you are doing or intend to start-up. Owning half of a start-up with a person who doesn't have the business sense to make you both successful will only bring you down in the long run and cripple the business in terms of management and decision making.

WRITING YOUR BUSINESS PLAN
SESSION1: REFERENCEFORBUSINESS.COM APPROACH TO BUSINESS PLAN WRITING

A company's business plan is one of its most important documents. It can be used by managers and executives for internal planning. It can be used as the basis for loan applications from banks and other lenders. It can be used to persuade investors that a company is a good investment. For start-up ventures, the process of preparing a business plan serves as a road map to the future by making entrepreneurs and business owners think through their strategies, evaluate their basic business concepts, recognize their business's limitations, and avoid a variety of mistakes.

Virtually every business needs a business plan. Lack of proper planning is one of the most often cited reasons for business failures. Business plans help companies identify their goals and objectives and provide them with tactics and strategies to reach those goals. They are not historical documents; rather, they embody a set of management decisions about necessary steps for the business to reach its objectives and perform in accordance with its capabilities.

"By its very definition, a business plan is a plan for the business, clarifying why it exists, who it exists for, what products and services it provides these client groups, how it intends to develop and deliver these products and services, and where it is headed," Rebecca Jones wrote in *Information Outlook*. "A business plan is a roadmap for the organization, showing the destination it seeks, the path it will follow to get there, and the supplies and wherewithal required to complete the journey."

1. SITUATIONS THAT REQUIRE A BUSINESS PLAN

Business plans have several major uses. These include internal planning and forecasting, obtaining funding for ongoing operations or expansion, planned divestiture and spin-offs, and restructuring or reorganizing. While business plans have elements common to all uses, most business plans are tailored according to their specific use and intended audience.

When used for internal planning, business plans can provide a blueprint for the operation of an entire company. A company's performance and progress can be measured against planned goals involving sales, expenditures, time frame, and strategic direction. Business plans also help an entrepreneur or business manager identify and focus on potential problem areas, both inside and outside the company. Once potentially troublesome areas have been identified, proposed solutions and contingency plans can be incorporated into the business plan.

Business plans also cover such areas as marketing opportunities and future financing requirements that require management attention. In some instances—such as scenarios in which an entrepreneur decides to turn a favorite hobby into a home-based business enterprise—the business plan can be a simple document of one or two pages. A business proposal of significant complexity and financial importance, however, should include a far more comprehensive plan. A tool and die manufacturer looking for investors to expand production capacity, for example, will in all likelihood need to compose a business plan of greater depth and detail than will a computer enthusiast who decides to launch a desktop publishing business out of his/her home.

Ideally, everyone in the company will use the information contained in the company's business plan, whether to set performance targets, guide decision-making with regard to ongoing operations, or assess personnel performance in terms of their ability to meet objectives set forth in the business plan. In addition, workers who are informed about the business plan can evaluate and adjust their own performance in terms of company objectives and expectations.

Business plans can also be used in the restructuring or reorganization of a business. In such cases, business plans describe actions that need to be taken in order to restore profitability or reach other goals. Necessary operational changes are identified in the plan, along with corresponding reductions in expenses. Desired performance and operational objectives are delineated, often with corresponding changes in production equipment, work force, and certain products and/or services.

Banks and other lenders use business plans to evaluate a company's ability to handle more debt and, in some cases, equity financing. The business plan documents the company's cash flow requirements and provides a detailed description of its assets, capitalization, and projected financial performance. It provides potential lenders and investors with verifiable facts about a company's performance so that risks can be accurately identified and evaluated.

Finally, the business plan is the primary source of information for potential purchasers of a company or one of its divisions or product lines. As with outside lenders and investors, business plans prepared for potential buyers provide them with verifiable facts and projections about the company's performance. The business plan must communicate the basic business premise or concept of the company, present its strengths as well as weaknesses, and provide indications of the company's long-term viability. When a company is attempting to sell off a division or product line, the business plan defines the new business entity.

2. PREPARING THE BUSINESS PLAN

The process of preparing and developing a business plan is an interactive one that involves every functional area of a company. Successful business plans are usually the result of team effort, in which all employees provide input based on their special areas of expertise and technical skill. Business owners and managers provide overall support for the planning process as well as general guidelines and feedback on the plan as it is being developed.

Some companies make the planning process an ongoing one. In other cases, such as for a business acquisition, it may be necessary to prepare a business plan on short notice. The process can be expedited by determining what information is needed from each area of a company. Participants can then meet to complete only those plan components that are needed immediately. During the planning process, it is usually desirable to encourage teamwork, especially across functional lines. When people work together to collect and analyze data, they are far more likely to be able to arrive at objectives that are consistent with one another.

A few basic steps can be identified in the planning process. The first step is to organize the process by identifying who will be involved, determining the basic scope of the plan, and establishing a time frame within which the plan is to be completed. Company leaders not only communicate their support for the planning process, they also define the responsibilities of each party involved. Work plans that supplement the general timetable are helpful in meeting deadlines associated with the planning process.

Once the planning process has been fully organized, participants can begin the process of assessment. Internal evaluations include identification of strengths and weaknesses of all areas of the business. In addition, it is generally useful to assess and evaluate such external factors as the general economy, competition, relevant technologies, trends, and other circumstances outside the control of the company that can affect its performance or fundamental health.

Setting goals and defining strategies are the next key steps in the planning process. Using the assessment and evaluation of internal and external factors, fundamental goals for the business are developed. Pertinent areas to be studied include the company's competitive philosophy, its market focus, and its customer service philosophy. Specific performance and operational strategies are then established, based on these goals.

After strategies and goals have been defined, they are translated into specific plans and programs. These plans and programs determine how a company's resources will be managed in order to implement its strategies and achieve its goals. Specific areas that require their own plans and programs include the overall organization of the company, sales and marketing, products and production, and finance. Finally, these specific plans are assembled into the completed business plan.

3. UNDERSTAND THE ELEMENTS OF A BUSINESS PLAN

Business plans must include authoritative, factual data, usually obtained from a wide range of sources. The plans must be written in a consistent and realistic manner. Contradictions or inconsistencies within a business plan create doubts in the minds of its readers. Problems and risks associated with the business should be described rather than avoided, then used as the basis for presenting thoughtful solutions and contingency plans. Business plans can be tailored to the needs and interests of specific audiences by emphasizing or presenting differently certain categories of information in different versions of the plan.

Business plans contain a number of specific elements as well as certain general characteristics. These include a general description of the company and its products or services, an executive summary, management and organizational charts, sales and marketing plans, financial plans, and production plans. They describe the general direction of a company in terms of its underlying philosophy, goals, and objectives. Business plans explain specific steps and actions that will be taken as well as their rationale. That is, they not only tell how a company will achieve its strategic objectives, they also tell why specific decisions have been made. Anticipated problems and the company's response to them are usually included. In effect, business plans are a set of management decisions about how the company will proceed along a specified course of action, with justifications for those decisions. Listed below are brief descriptions of the major elements found in business plans.

A) EXECUTIVE SUMMARY This is usually a two-to five-page summary of the entire business plan. It is an important part of the plan; in that it is designed to capture the reader's attention and create an interest in the company. It usually includes the company's mission statement and summarizes its competitive advantages, sales and profit projections, financial requirements, plans to repay lenders or investors, and the amount of financing requested.

B) DESCRIPTION OF BUSINESS The business description includes not only a profile of the company, but also a picture of the industry in which the company operates. Every business operates within a specific context that affects its growth potential. The description of a company's operating environment may cover new products and developments in the industry, trends and outlook for the industry, and overall economic trends.

The intent of the company profile, meanwhile, is to provide readers with a description of unique features that give the company an edge in the environment in which it competes. A brief company history reveals how specific products and services were developed, while descriptions of pertinent contracts and agreements should also be mentioned (information on contracts and legal agreements may also be included in an appendix to the business plan). Other topics covered include operational procedures and research and development.

C) DESCRIPTION OF PRODUCTS AND/OR SERVICES The goal of this section is to differentiate a company's products or services from those of the competition. It describes specific customer needs that are uniquely met by the firm's products or services. Product features are translated into customer benefits. Product life cycles and their effects on sales and marketing can be described. The company's plans for a new generation of products or services may also be included in this section.

D) DESCRIPTION OF MANAGEMENT AND ORGANIZATIONAL STRUCTURE The quality of a company's management team can be the most important aspect of a business plan. This section presents the strengths of the company's management team by highlighting relevant experience, achievements, and past performance. Key areas include management's ability to provide planning, organizational skills, and leadership. This section also contains information about the company's ownership and work force. It may present an existing or planned organizational structure that will accomplish the goals set forth in the business plan. Specific management and control systems are often described as well.

E) MARKET ANALYSIS A thorough market analysis serves as the basis for a company's sales and marketing plans. The analysis generally covers the company's competition, customers, products, and market acceptance. The competitive analysis details the competition's strengths and weaknesses, providing a basis for discovering market opportunities. A customer analysis provides a picture of who buys and uses the company's products or services. This section of the business plan highlights how the company's products or services satisfy previously unfulfilled market needs. It also includes evidence of market acceptance of the company's unique products or services.

F) SALES AND MARKETING PLAN The marketing plan delineates the methods and activities that will be employed to reach the company's revenue goals. This section describes the company's customer base, products or services, and marketing and sales programs. The latter is supported by conclusions drawn from the market analysis. Different revenue outcomes may be presented to allow for contingency planning in the areas of finance and production.

G) PRODUCTION PLAN A production plan is usually included if the business is involved in manufacturing a product. Based on the sales and marketing plan, the production plan covers production options that are available to produce a desired mix of products. The production plan contains information that allows for budgeting for such costs as labor and materials. In non-manufacturing companies, this section would cover new service development.

H) FINANCIAL PLAN This section covers the financing and cash flow requirements implicit in other areas of the business plan. It contains projections of income, expenses, and cash flow, as well as descriptions of budgeting and financial controls. Financial projections must be supported by verifiable facts, such as sales figures or market research. Monthly figures are generally given for the first two years, followed by annual figures for the next three to eight years. If the business plan is written for investors or lenders, the amount of financing required may be included here or in a separate section.

I) IMPLEMENTATION SCHEDULE This section provides key dates pertaining to finance, marketing, and production. It indicates when specific financing is needed, when specific aspects of a particular marketing campaign will take place, and delivery dates based on production schedules.

J) CONTINGENCY PLANS This section defines problems and challenges that the company may face and outlines contingency plans for overcoming obstacles that might arise. Specific topics that may be explored are competitive responses, areas of weakness or vulnerability, legal constraints, staffing, and continuity of leadership.

K) OTHER DETAILS Most business plans include a table of contents and a cover sheet containing basic information about the company. An appendix may include a variety of documentation that supports different sections of the business plan. Among the items that may be found in an appendix are footnotes from the main plan, biographies, graphs and charts, copies of contracts and agreements, and references.

4. TAILORING THE BUSINESS PLAN TO SPECIFIC AUDIENCES

Business plans are organized to address major concerns and interests of their intended audience. They are commonly tailored to a specific audience by emphasizing aspects that directly relate to the interests of the reader. For example, a business plan written to obtain a loan for ongoing operations would address the major concerns of potential lenders.

5. BANKS, INVESTORS, AND OTHER SOURCES OF FUNDING

Business plans are frequently written to obtain additional funding. Start-up capital may be needed for a new venture, or the company may require additional working capital for ongoing operations. New capital may be needed to acquire assets for expansion, or equity financing may be needed to support a company's long-range growth.

Potential lenders of debt or equity financing are usually concerned with minimizing their risks and maximizing the return on their investment. It is important, then, when composing a business plan to this audience, to make a strong financial presentation and provide adequate documentation of projected revenue and costs. Areas to be stressed in the business plan include the predictability of the company's cash flow, how well cash flow will cover debt servicing, the reasons additional funding is needed, strengths of the company's financial management, assets used to collateralize debt, and the capital and ownership structure of the company. In addition, business plans written to obtain funding for expansion provide details on the overall scope of the market and profit potential. Such plans typically enumerate the return on investment for equity investors.

6. POTENTIAL BUYERS Potential buyers are generally interested in such factors as the basic business concept underlying the company, its long-term viability, and its strategic position within its industry. They also look for strengths and weaknesses in the company's basic functional components and its management team. Business plans written for this audience stress the company's strengths and include contingency plans designed to overcome weaknesses, challenges, and other possible developments.

Other factors that might be emphasized in a business plan written for potential buyers are the company's ability to improve profitability and market share, the company's competitive edge, the company's potential to take advantage of opportunities in related industries, managerial and technical skills within the company, and the company's financial capacity.

7. PARTIES INTERESTED IN REORGANIZATION OR RESTRUCTURING Business plans written for a company reorganization may be tailored for a variety of readers, including internal management, outside creditors, or new owners. Such a plan sets forth the necessary action designed to reorganize or restructure the company to achieve greater profitability or production capacity. The business plan identifies operational changes that need to be made in different functional areas of the company. It also establishes performance and operational measures against which the functional areas of the company are evaluated.

The audience for this type of business plan is interested in such factors as the timing and sequence of specific changes, and the operational and financial impact of restructuring efforts. The business plan provides details on the new functional organization, as well as key personnel and their responsibilities. Transitional plans are typically furnished, and operating and financial goals are defined.

8. INTERNAL USERS Business plans written primarily for use within the company generally stress the benefits that will result from implementation of the plan. These may include improved and more consistent performance, improved coordination and consistency among various segments of the company, greater ability to measure performance, empowerment of the work force, and a better motivated and educated work force. The plan provides a comprehensive framework and direction for ongoing operations.

Business plans written for internal use typically identify the company's strengths and weaknesses, potential problems, and emerging issues. They set forth performance standards on which expectations will be based, and clearly delineate goals and objectives to allow for coordination and better communication between all company areas.

BUSINESS PLANS AS PLANNING DOCUMENTS

Business plans are not historical documents about a company's past performance. Rather, they are planning documents that provide information to decision-makers who can help the company achieve its goals and objectives. These decision-makers may be the company's own managers and executives, or they may be sources of capital or potential buyers. Regardless of the intended audience, all business plans address the fundamental strategic issues facing a business. They provide verifiable data and projections covering marketing and sales; production, service, and quality; product development; organization and management structure; and financial requirements.

SESSION1.2: CREATING A BUSINESS PLAN FOR A NEW OR EXISTING BUSINESS ACCORDING TO BUSINESSTOWN.COM
From the business plan summary to the exit strategy, Bob Adams takes you through a complete business plan and explains each step.

Business Plan Objective

THROUGHOUT THE PROCESS of creating a business plan, you need to keep in mind its objective. Why are you writing the plan? Is it to manage the business? Or is it to raise money?

A business plan may be an annual plan for managing your business. Or a business plan may be primarily developed for attracting capital. There are exceptions, and often the difference between annual plans and business plans becomes muddled. Banks and other lenders or investors may require a copy of each year's annual plan. Management may use the start-up business plan as a basis for operating the business.

When creating your business plan, keep your objectives in mind.

Keeping a clear distinction between annual plans and business plans is not important. What is important is keeping the primary objective of and the primary audience for the plan clear. As a rule of thumb, if the plan will be used to attract investors or lenders, this is the primary objective and outsiders are the primary audience. If the plan will help manage the business, this is the primary objective and insiders are the primary audience.

What follows is a discussion of key parts of a relatively simple business plan.

Summary

Summaries should be short and concise—one page is ideal. It should cover the following points:

A) Strategy overview: Start with a brief overview of your business strategy. If your business will be based, at least initially, on a product or service, describe it in the introductory paragraph.

B) Strategy logic: In the next paragraph or two explain why your strategy makes sense or why your product or service has promise. Are you entering a fast- growing market or providing a unique product or service that distinguishes your business from existing businesses?

C) Business development: Next, you should describe the stage your business is in.

Is it already generating sales?

Have you done test marketing?

Has a prototype been developed?

Has market research been performed?

D) The team: Name the key people in your organization and describe, briefly, what special talents, expertise, or connections they will bring to the business.

E) Financial objectives: If your plan is being developed to raise capital, be clear about the amount of capital you are seeking and how you plan to use investor or lender funding.

F) Business organization: Describe the form of business organization you will take and where the company will be located.

Your business plan summary should short and easy to understand.

Remember to keep your summary short and easy to understand. Avoid technical jargon and details. Don't try to summarize all of the different major elements of your plan. Just focus on the key elements that you think will be of most interest to your audience. Skip the pie-in-the-sky profit projections and outlook generalizations.

Concept

The concept is a clear explanation of your business strategy. It is not a definition of the business or a summary of its markets but, instead, a quick summary of the one or two key factors that set your business apart from the competition.

G) Product description: New business strategies are often closely tied to a specific product or service. If this is your situation, include a clear and substantive description of your principal product or service. Follow this with a focused discussion of what will make your product or service stand out from any similar offerings in the marketplace. Focus in depth on just a few of the most competitive attributes of your product or service.

Impact factors: You should also describe any other aspect of your business that is fundamental to your strategy. Areas that might have significant impact on your strategy are marketing, research and development, or strategic alliances with other firms. For example, if everyone else in your industry is selling his or her products through retail channels but you feel that you can develop a strong competitive advantage by selling via direct mail, then you should discuss this in the concept section. Market conditions and the competition should be included as points of reference only when necessary. An in-depth analysis of these factors will be included later in the plan.

H) Current Situation

This section is most appropriate for plans being used to seek financing. Within this section you will describe what stage of development your company is in and what the sought-after financing will be used for.

If you are seeking financing, this section of your business plan is particularly important.

There are three basic reasons for seeking outside financing: start-up financing, expansion financing, and work-out financing.

Start-up financing: If you are seeking start-up financing, you will need to list specific milestones that have been achieved and emphasize all positive developments without being misleading. You should anticipate the questions your lenders or investors may ask.

a) Has the market research been done?

b) Has a prototype product been developed?

c) Have facilities been leased?

d) Is the management team in place?

e) Has manufacturing been contracted?

Are marketing plans finalized?

Whether or not you receive financing and the terms of that financing will depend upon the stage of development your company is in. The more fully developed your company is, the better your financial arrangements will be.

I) Expansion financing: If your business is already up and running and you are seeking expansion financing, you need to give clear evidence that you are not, in reality, seeking financing as a way to solve existing problems, or to cover losses or extraordinary expenses such as might be experienced during a start-up.

Work-out financing: Many investors and lenders do not like to offer work-out financing. Those who are willing to consider it will want to see a plan that clearly identifies the reasons for current or previous problems and provides a strong plan for corrective action.

No matter what type of financing you are seeking, financiers like to be apprised of the source and amount of any capital that has already been secured. They will expect key executives to have made substantial personal equity investments in the business. They will feel even more comfortable if they recognize any other investors who may have participated in earlier stages of the financing process.

J) The Market

Here you want to address questions such as:

a) How large is the potential market?

b) How many people or businesses are currently using a competitor's product that is the same or like the one you are offering or plan to offer?

c) How many prospects potentially have any possible use for the product?

d) Is the market growing, flattening, or shrinking?

K) Market Segmentation

Almost every market has some major and distinctive segments. Even if it is not currently segmented, the probability that it could or will be is great. This is particularly true if the marketplace for your product or service is multiregional or national. If this is the case, segmentation is almost necessary, especially for a small firm, if you hope to be competitive.

You will need to discuss segmentation within your business category and how you intend to cope with any positive or negative effects it may have on your business. Almost all markets are segmented by price and quality issues. Generally, however, price and quality do not provide the most clear or definitive market segmentation. Much stronger segmentation can usually be found through an evaluation of product or service uses and their importance to various consumers.

L) Consumer Analysis

In your business plan you will need to evaluate the typical end users within the market segments you are targeting. There are countless variables to consider when analyzing consumer behavior. Try to focus on behavioral possibilities that will best determine how viable your product will be in your target markets. Look at:

a) Which features will most appeal to consumers or end users?

b) How are choices made between competing products?

c) Which marketing promotions or media avenues seem to offer the best vehicles for reaching the consumer base?

d) How much disposable income do target consumers have to spend on this product?

e) How do your target consumers make purchasing decisions?

f) Are consumers presold on a particular brand before they visit a store or do they buy on impulse?

g) What characteristics influence the purchase of one product or service over a competing one?

M) Competition

Include an overview of the firms and their products and/or services that you will be in direct competition with. Identify the market leader and define what makes it successful. Emphasize the characteristics of the firm or offerings that are different than yours.

Don't dismiss this section just because you don't have any current competition. If there isn't a product or service like yours on the market, identity firms that provide products or services that perform essentially the same function. You should also try to identify any firms that are likely to enter the market or are in the process of developing products or services that will be competitive with those you are offering.

Product Features and Benefits

You briefly described the key features of your product or service in the concept section of the plan. In this section you should explore features and benefits in depth. It is essential not only to be clear about the distinguishing features of your product or service but also to delineate any strong consumer benefits. What makes your product or service significantly better than competitive offerings?

N) Competitive Analysis

In this section you need to do an in-depth analysis of the competitive advantages and weaknesses of your firm. When exploring weaknesses, you should include information that will help allay any concerns that may arise as to their ability to significantly hinder your success.

This section is important, especially if your company is a start-up, because you will, typically, be competing with established companies that have inherent advantages, such as financial strength, name recognition, and established distribution channels.

O) Positioning

Positioning can be thought of as a marketing strategy for your product or service. Positioning defines how you are going to portray your product to your target market.

Your first step is deciding who your target market will be. It will consist of potential customers toward whom you will direct most of your marketing efforts. Often this group will not be the sole or even the largest market for your product, but it will be the market that, based on competitive factors and product benefits, you feel you can most effectively reach.

Start-ups are more likely to be successful if they focus on a highly specific, very narrow target market. Large, well-established firms usually dominate general markets.

Small businesses should focus on highly specific niches to avoid competing against large, well established companies.

Once you have determined who your target market is, you need to decide how you want consumers to perceive your product.

a) Is it the premium quality leader?

b) Is it a low-cost substitute?

c) Is it a full-service alternative?

If you have a one-product or -service company, your marketing strategy may coincide with your overall business strategy. This doesn't necessarily have to be the case, but it is extremely important, in all cases, that your product strategy be in sync with your overall business strategy.

P) Advertising and Promotion

Use this section to provide an overview of your general promotional plan. Give a break-out of what methods and media you intend to use and why. If you have developed an advertising slogan or unique selling proposition you may mention it, but it isn't strictly necessary. (I offer a specific presentation on unique selling propositions.)

a) You should outline the proposed mix of your advertising media, use of publicity, and/or other promotional programs.

b) Explain how your choice of marketing vehicles will allow you to reach your target market.

c) Explain how they will enable you to best convey your product features and benefits.

d) Make sure that your advertising, publicity, and promotional programs sound realistic based on your proposed marketing budget. Effective advertising, generally, relies on message repetition in order to motivate consumers to make a purchase. If you are on a limited budget, it is better to reach fewer, more likely prospects, more often, than too many people occasionally.

Sales

Your sales strategy needs to be in harmony with your business strategy, your marketing strategy, and your company's strengths and weaknesses. For example, if your start-up company is planning on selling products to other businesses in a highly competitive marketplace, your market entry will be easier if you rely on wholesalers or commissioned sales representatives who already have an established presence and reputation in the marketplace. If your business will be selling high-tech products with a range of customized options, your sales force needs to be extremely knowledgeable and personable.

Q) Research and Development

A discussion of research and development is, obviously, not germane to all companies. If it applies, though, financiers are going to want to know that research and development projects are aimed at specific, realistic objectives. And they will want to be assured that an undue portion of the company's resources will not be plowed into this area. Remember that banks generally lend money to businesses on a short-term basis, and venture capitalists and other first-round investors generally want to cash out in just a few years.

R) Operations

"Operations" is a catchall term for any important aspects of the business not described elsewhere. If the start-up is a manufacturing concern, discuss critical elements of the manufacturing process. For retail businesses, discuss store operations. Wholesalers should discuss warehouse operations.

In addition to discussing areas that are critical to operations, briefly summarize how major business functions will be carried out and how certain functions may run more effectively than those of your competitors. But don't get into long descriptions of any business or operational practice that will not sell your business plan to financiers.

S) People

The focus here is key people and positions. Primary attention should be on key people who have already committed to joining the firm. Elaborate on their relevant past experience and successes and explain what areas of responsibility they will have in the new company. Resumes should be included here as part of an appendix or exhibits addendum at the end of the plan.

Don't neglect this part. Many investors will reject your plan if the management team is incomplete.

If there are any important positions that have not been filled, describe position responsibilities and the type of employment/experience background necessary to the position.

If there is a board of directors, present each member, and summarize that person's background. If members will have an active role in running the business, elaborate that role here.

If consultants have been engaged for key responsibilities, include a description of their backgrounds and functions.

Fill as many of your key positions as possible before you seek funding. Many financiers reject plans if the management team is incomplete.

T) Payback and Exit Plan

Both debt and equity lenders will want to know how they can expect to receive their investment back and realize interest or profit from the company.

Most private investors and venture capitalists will want to be able to exercise a cash-out option within five years. They will be concerned that, even if the company becomes highly profitable, it may be difficult for them to sell out their share at an attractive price. This concern is particularly true in the case of minority stakeholders. Therefore, you must provide an exit strategy for investors.

Ideally, investors hope a firm will become so successful that it will be able to go public within five years and their shares will become highly liquid investments, trading at a hefty multiple of earnings. But, often, a more realistic goal is to make the company large and successful enough to sell to a larger firm. State what your exit plan is and make sure it seems realistic.

U) Financials

In this section you need to show projected (also called "pro forma") income statements, balance sheets, and cash flow. Existing businesses should also show historical financial statements. How far into the future you need to project and the number of possible scenarios you can anticipate depend on the complexity of the business. Three to five years for financial projections and three scenarios are typical for a start-up business seeking angel investors.

Scenarios should be based on the most likely course your business will take, a weak scenario with sales coming in well under expectation, and a good scenario with projected sales well over expectation.

Pro forma income statements should show sales, cost of operations, and profits on both a monthly and an annual basis for each plan year. For all but the largest businesses, annual pro forma balance sheets are all that are necessary. Cash flow pro formas should be presented in both monthly and annual form. If your business is already established, past annual balance sheets and income statements should also be included.

Include information that will assist potential lenders in understanding your projections. Lenders will give as much credence to the assumptions your projections are based on as they will to the numbers themselves.

Goals and Objectives

- ✓ Tell your prospective investors what you want (e.g. a business loan for a specific amount to Purchase equipment).
- ✓ State your sales, production and profit goals. Be specific in amount and time Line.
- ✓ If this is for a bank loan, comment on goals such as anticipated time to achieve
- ✓ A positive cash flow and the ability to service debt. (Note you cannot complete this section until the rest of the plan is complete.)

Market Research: Professionals define market research as a systematic collection and analysis of information relating to the market for your business. It is designed to give basic information about your industries, trends and outlooks as well as information concerning the location and size of your market.

If there are not enough customers for your product, you won't be in business for long.

Providing an overview of the industry sector such as industry trends, major players in the industry and estimated industry sales. An examination of the primary target market for your product or service should be provided including geographic location, demography your target markets needs and how these needs are being met currently. Also, an investigation of your direct and indirect competitors should be included with an assessment of their competitive advantage and an analysis of how you will overcome any entry barriers to your chosen market. Research will give you an insight of people that will give you money for what you have to sell to them. All of this information will influence your choices, including the kind of location you will be looking for.

THINGS TO CONSIDER WHEN WRITING ANALYSIS OF THE MARKET
a) What segment of the market are you in?
b) What is the potential size and current size of the market?
c) Is the market growing, declining or static or dependent on another industry or market? Does this offer sign of opportunity?
d) What are the seasonal trends in your market?
e) How is the market made up?
f) Why is the market emerging and what will it look like in some distinct future?

THINGS TO CONSIDER WHEN WRITING YOUR CUSTOMER RESEARCH
1. Who are your potential customers?
2. Any special characteristics from the class/group of customers that will attract them to your product or services?
3. The estimated size of the group of potential customers, the location of individuals within the group. it's important you restrict the geographical horizons of your business to the physical area to which you can cope and can give an indication of future expansion potential?
4. Trends from the group of potential customers/customers such as buying habits, customer preferences, overall group size changes, technological developments and outside influences which might affect the group?

Management Team: Provide the names and short biography of the people you will use to fill the key positions in the business. A job description of yourself in jobs is required, what skills are you bringing into the venture? Stating whether you have been in any business in the past? Describe their success and failures. Include a short biography of yourself.

Management Ownership
- ✓ Briefly describe the technical qualifications of each principal in this enterprise.
- ✓ Briefly describe the business qualifications of each principal in this enterprise.
- ✓ Tell the prospective investor your business structure (i.e. proprietorship, partnership, or Incorporation).
- ✓ Provide a fact sheet with contact information such as name, address, telephone, E-mail, etc.

Ownership: This section explains to your prospective investor two important elements. First is the form of business organization you are establishing. An investor or banker must know this because each form has certain legal and tax implications. The typical forms are: Sole Proprietor, Partnership, Limited Liability Company and corporation.

1) **Location Start-up Plan:** Tell when and where you plan to start the business and why you chose the time frame and location.

2) **Operational Plan/Product Description:** Describe, in details how your business will operate. Include diagrams of production or service areas if appropriate.

3) **Marketing Plan**: describe, in detail, how you will attract customers or clients and how you will deliver your product or service to them.

4) **S.W.O.T Analysis:** *this stands for strength, opportunity, weakness, threat.* **Strength:** This involves what gives one business competitive advantage over the competition in the same industry. This is something you have got now which can be an asset or key operational resources that makes your business to better compete; this might be a new invention or a great sales force or the fact that nobody else is doing what you want to do yet.

Some of the examples of organizational strengths are as follows:

1. Abundant financial resources
2. Established brand name
3. Economies of scale
4. Lower production costs
5. Superior management
6. Excellent marketing skills

7. Good supply chain distribution
8. Great Employee commitment

Weakness: these are things you know about now which you would like to improve on. Acknowledge this honestly but also think about how serious your weaknesses are. How you can either fix them or work your way around them. They might include lack of funding or lack of one particular management skills or vacancy.

Weaknesses such as:

- Characteristics that place the organization at a disadvantage relative to others.
- Detract the organization from its ability to attain the core goal and influence its growth.
- Factors which do not meet the standards set in the organization.

Some of the examples of organizational

Example of Weaknesses Such as Follows:

1. Limited financial resources
2. Low R & D Budget
3. Narrow product line
4. Weak supply chain distribution
5. Higher production costs
6. Obsolete or Out-of-date products/technology
7. Poor market image
8. Poor marketing skills
9. Weak management skills
10. Under-trained employees

Opportunities are:
1. Chances to make greater profits in the environment.
2. External attractive factors that represent the reason for an organization to exist and develop.
3. Condition of the environment that benefits the organization in planning and executing strategies that enable it to become more profitable. Organization

should be careful and recognise the opportunities and grasp them whenever they arise. Opportunities may arise from market, competition, industry/government, and technology.

Some of the examples of opportunities for an organization are as follows:

a) Rapid market growth
b) Complacent rival firms
c) Changing customer needs/tastes
d) New uses discovered for existing product
e) Economic boom,
f) Government deregulation
g) Decline in demand for a substitute product

Threats are:

a) External elements in the environment that could cause trouble for the
b) business.
c) External factors, beyond an organization's control, which could place the organization's mission or operation at risk.
d) Conditions in external environment that jeopardize the reliability and profitability of the organization's business.
e) Threats compound the vulnerability when they relate to the weaknesses. Threats are uncontrollable. When a threat comes, the stability and survival can be at stake.

Some of the examples of threats for an organization are as follows:

a) Entry of foreign competitors
b) Introduction of new substitute products
c) Decline in product life cycle
d) Changing customer needs/tastes
e) New strategies adopted by rival firms
f) Increased government regulation
g) Economic slowdown

Financial Plan: Provide a detailed financial plan, including a cash flow projection, which accounts for the money you will need (borrow) and the repayment Plan not plan and return on investment to investors.

<u>Note</u>: Some persons must have asked the question What Does Market Analysis mean? While others might have had misconception of what market analysis really mean, well you are not too far from its meaning:

SESSION3: AREAS INVESTORS ARE LOOKING FOR IN YOUR BUSINESS PLAN

KEY AREAS INVESTORS ARE MOSTLY INTERESTED IN AS BUSINESS PLAN IS CONCERNED

a) **Management:** Investors are mainly concerned with good management not just ideas, it is very important you express your knowledge, Passion and dedication to your business as best as you can. The competence of your team along with their experience levels and commitment levels are also factors that investors research before making their investment decisions.

b) **Customers:** Here you should include a definitive description of your customers and market size. It is important to communicate to the investors that you understand the needs and requirements of your customers.

c) **Product/service Description:** A complete description of the product and/or the services offered by you should be outlined in details. It is essential to include a description of the overall market for your product and/or service along with details of your customer base. The investors need to know the reach and kind of customers your product/service is targeted at.

d) **Marketing Plan**: A marketing plan will outline your sustainable competitive advantage to your investors. In this section you should include market growth prospects. Trends and sales potential per product/service category. This is where the pricing strategies are outlined and how they can directly influence the growth

e) Potential of each product/service. It is also crucial to include the future growth, market share and trend influences. Make your marketing strategy crystal clear within your marketing Plan.

CONCEPTS

Market Analysis: This is a documented investigation of a market that is used to form a firm's planning activities, particularly around decisions of inventory, purchase, work force expansion /contraction, facility expansion and purchases of capital equipment, promotional activities and many other aspects of a company.

THERE ARE VARIOUS ASPECTS/DIMENSIONS OF MARKET ANALYSIS

1) **Market Size (current and future):** The market size is defined through the market volume and the market potential. The market volume exhibits the totality of all realized sales volume of a special market. The relation of market volume to market potential provides information about the chances of market growth. Examples of information sources for determining market size:
   a) Government data
   a) Trade association data
   b) Financial data from major players from your preferred industrial sector
   c) Customer surveys.

2) **Market Trends**: examples include changes in economic, social, regulatory, legal and political conditions and in available technology, price sensitivity, demand for variety and level of emphasis on service and support.

3) **Market Growth rate**: A better approach here is to study market trends and sales growth in complementary products. Such drivers serve as leading indicators that are more accurate than simply extrapolating historical data.

4) **Market profitability**: Factors that influence market profitability are;
   g) Buyers' power

h) Supplier's power
i) Barriers to entry
j) Threat of substitute products
k) Rivalry among firms in the industry

5) **Success factors**: these are elements necessary in order for the firm to achieve its marketing objectives such as;
a) Access to essential unique resources
b) Ability to achieve economies of scale
c) Access to distribution channels
d) Technological progress

SESSION7: ELEMENTS OF FINANCIAL PLANNING

Financial Plan is a series of steps used by an individual or business, to accomplish a financial goal or a set of circumstances example: elimination of debt, retirement preparedness and soon. Budget is often included or referred to as financial planning but you should know that budget is just a "subset" of financial planning. Meaning its more than just budget.

Budget organizes an individual's finances and sometimes includes a series of steps or specific goals for spending and saving future income. Financial Plan is sometimes referred to as an investment plan.

OBJECTIVES OF FINANCIAL PLANNING

a) **Determining capital requirements:** This will depend upon factors like cost of current and fixed assets, promotional expenses and long-range planning. Capital requirements can be reviewed with both short- and long-term requirements.
b) **Determining capital structure**: The capital structure is the composition of capital that is the relative kind and proportion of capital required in the business. This includes decisions of debt equity ratio both short and long-term.
c) Framing financial policies with regards to cash control, lending, borrowings
d) A finance manager ensures that the scarce financial resources are maximally utilized in the best possible manner at least cost in order to get maximum returns on investment.

BASIC FINANCIAL PLAN STATEMENT

a) **Balanced sheet:** This reports a business's financial position at a particular point in times. Which include the following:
I) The amount of businesses assets (what the business owns)

ii) The amount of the business's liabilities (what the business owes to creditors).
iii) The amount of capital contributed by its owners and generated by the business (what the business owes to the owners).

b) **Profit and Loss statement for the next 3 years**: This statement summarizes the changes in profitability that has occurred over a period of time between one balance sheet and another. This shows:
I) the total revenue of the business for a period (example, from sales made or services rendered by the business).
ii) The expenses of the business for the same period.

c) **Cash flow statement:** Showing the timing of cash receipts and payments; it describes where the cash comes from, where it goes, and when and how much extra cash will be needed from outside sources for the business to remain solvent.

d) **Financial ratios:** These are used to analyse and interpret financial statements. They are very effective control technique and can identify financial problems before they become serious.

MATERIAL RESOURCES FOR BUSINESS START-UP

Make a list of the one-off equipment and periodic or regular materials, estimate quantities of items when the business is just starting Think about transport to your business location. If any of the items, you need are too expensive how will you overcome this difficulty?

9 Tools That Will Give You Enterprise-Grade Technology at Affordable Prices.

1. GetResponse's Marketing Automation.
2. AdRoll's Retargeting.
3. Leadfeeder's Site Tracking.
4. Rebot.me's Chatbots.
5. InsightSquared's Sales Forecasting.
6. Hubspot's CRM.
7. Searchmetrics's SEO Tracking.
8. Segment's Consolidated Metrics.

5 Marketing Technology Must-Haves for the Modern Marketer

1. Website Content Management System (CMS) A CMS is no longer a nice-to-have for most marketers but an essential tool in the arsenal.
2. A Blog.
3. Customer Relationship Management (CRM) e.g. Bitrix24, Hubspot CRM, Zoho CRM etc.
4. Marketing Automation.
5. Web Analytics.

CHAPTER 6
BEYOND THE PLANNING AND WRITE-UP PHASE

SESSION 1.1: WHAT ANY ORGANIZATION NEEDS TO SURVIVE AND SUCCEED

Essentially five things or factors are needed by any organization wanting to succeed:

1. **People** – those who make up the organization
2. **Purpose** – the reason for organizing and working together
3. **Processes** – activities which the people undertake to fulfil their purpose
4. **Physical Resources** – a place to work, the right equipment, money to pay the bills and the people who work there
5. **Customers** – people outside the organization who are willing to pay money in return for the products and services the organization provides; for government organizations taxpayers are the customers; many non-profits depend on contributions from donors who believe in the value of what the organization is doing.

But it's not just the existence of these five basic factors that enables success -it's what you do with them. In the same manner, just having a body will not make you a successful athlete – you have to train, learn the skills, practice, eat right, sleep enough, and much more. So now let's translate the five basic factors into what we call "The five Key Success Factors – A Powerful System for Total Business Success".

SESSION 1.2: THE FIVE KEY SUCCESS FACTORS OF BUSINESS

1) Managing and developing people - People today want some direction and structure, but they also want freedom and encouragement to develop their skills and knowledge. Effectively managing people requires balancing constraining forces (providing direction, structure, organization, some rules) with liberating forces (encourage personal growth, development and creativity). If you as manager/leader err too much in one direction or the other, your organization will be either too rigid or too chaotic. To make it more complicated, each person has a different set of needs for structure vs freedom, order vs opportunity, logic vs personal values, factual information vs meaning and connections, and so on. Effective managers do not manage all people the same, except for some basic rules. They manage each person according to what he or she needs, what motivates them to do their best. This can be complicated but is necessary for success.

(2) **Strategic focus** - In today's 21st century, it's not just enough to have a purpose for existing. Leaders have to focus the organization's resources on the greatest opportunities, which shift with each new day. Just run through your mind what has happened in the world or your organization in the past year or two, and you'll understand what we mean by the reality of constant change. Doors open and doors close. Major customers or income sources can change or even go out of business at any time. So, it's necessary for leaders to keep focused on the desired end results such as increased sales and profits, or more satisfied customers, while constantly steering the organization across the stormy waters of the marketplace. As the illustration shows, the job of focused leaders is to connect and align all the Success Factors for optimum performance.

(3) **Operations, or what people do all day** - What the people in your organization do day in and day out to create value for customers, to earn or justify income, strongly determines whether you succeed or fail. Like the other Top 5 Success Factors, you can't separate operations from strategic focus which gives direction, people who do the work, customers who pay the money and physical resources to do the work. Effective operations ensure that customers get exactly what they want at the right time, the right price and the right quality. Thus, effective operations management focuses on what is called cycle time (producing a product or service from start to finish), cost control, and quality control (which requires some form of measurement). Strategic focus is largely externally oriented, operations largely internally oriented. Both need to be totally in sync with each other – not something that happens automatically but rather requiring constant effort. This is why communication is the true lifeblood of a successful organization – a high flow of information so everyone and everything is connected. Easy to say, hard to do.

(4) **Physical resources** - Finances, facilities and equipment are the big three physical resources. If you don't have enough money, you can't start or sustain any organization. And one of the biggest expenses is providing adequate facilities and equipment for people to work with. Experienced managers know that cash flow is the "lifeblood" of any business. It doesn't matter how much customers owe you, it's when their money enters your bank account, you can use it to sustain the organization, then you are in business. Failing to manage cash flow is the Number 1 reason for business failure. Too many business owners leave the money up to someone else and can easily get blind-sided when suddenly the money isn't there to keep the doors open. And in a few rare, unfortunate cases, the person tracking the money embezzles or cooks the books, then you really are in trouble. Likewise, nice facilities can be energizing, something to feel proud about, but also very expensive. The economy is always

cyclical, and if you buy or lease really nice facilities when times are good, paying for them can be difficult or impossible in a downturn.

(5) **Customer relations** - Customers are where the money comes from, so in many ways this is the most important success factor. As the famous business guru Peter Drucker said years ago, the purpose of a business is to get and keep customers. Getting customers involves marketing – indeed this success factor includes all kinds of marketing and sales. The key to successful customer relations is to give them what they need, not just what you want to sell. Effective sales and marketing begin with asking existing and potential customers what they need, what problem they want solved or deficiency filled. By keeping in touch with customers and asking these questions often, you'll do a better job of developing customer loyalty and keeping competitors away. In the broadest sense customer relations can be considered the organization's relationships with the external world. It involves tracking competitor actions, analysing changes in the market environment, and adapting according. This is closely linked to Strategic Focus.

SESSION 1.3: ESSENTIAL BUSINESS VITAMINS FOR GROWING BUSINESSES
Vitamins A- Action

Your actions determine everything, it is the seat of progress and Failure, there is a saying that your attitude determines your altitude but I see the back bone of your altitude in business is your actions tied to your attitude, no actions = no attitude = no altitude.

Vitamin B – Belief

In the world of business either you believe me or not your belief has a key role to play in your flight journey in accomplishing your attitude. If you believe that you will make it no matter what, all you just need is to think enough, act enough, talk to the right people and meet the right people. Believe me there is no height that is too small for you to scale through. But once you make up your mind with the belief that you can't make it and nothing will work even if you try even though you have not tried then at that point nothing will ever work.

Figure 6: Quote by strategic profits

Vitamin C – Confidence

Majority of the time, if you are selling a product or services with no confidence to show for, the client or potential customer will in most cases turn you down and tell you things like "sorry I am not interested" because people believe that it is safer to buy a product that they don't know before when the seller is confident about it than to buy from a person that is not sure of what he is selling, so if you want to increase sales then work on your self-confidence. For only then can customers have confidence on your product after your product has given then quality of usage?

Vitamin D – Determination

Even when it seems like nothing is working, keep doing what you are doing, don't give up, just keep trying and trying even if it does not work, keep changing the methods, styles and how you do what you do until you get a method that works then keep doing it and you will see yourself smiling and enjoying the benefit in the end.

Vitamin E – Enthusiasm

Your passion is everything, when you are passionate about your business, the word "I can't do it" does not just seem to exist rather the only thing you see is how can I make this burning fire burning inside of me a living reality, how can I go about it to make money out of it. In the world of business any passion you cannot convert into money and fulfilment is a waste of investment and energy of the carrier. Do you want to know why? Because you might burn with fire now but in the nearest future frustration would set in and reduce that fire to "ashes" and in the end you find yourself settling for something outside what you ever thought you would ever settle for, because you did not channel your passion into the right channel and in the right way, but if your passion has not being reduced to ashes or frustration yet then you are in the right place but if you have lost it you can still regain it.

In majority cases, start-up success or failure is all about knowing, the know how and what action comes next, and always being clear about which step to take next.

1. **Offer what people want to buy**, not just what you want to sell. Too often, people jump into a business built around a product or service they think will be successful, rather than one that is already proven to have a market.

How do I mean?

Instead of creating and selling a new sports shoe with the latest trendy design and materials, you'd be much better off from a business perspective to focus on shoe category generally (a proven category because which people buy shoes every day) and then focus more specifically on the niche of high-performance sports shoes, (which you may even sell in a section of a shoe retail outlet). Better to have a small slice of a large category than a large slice of no market at all.

2. **Get cash flowing ASAP**. Cash flow is the lifeblood of any business, and is absolutely essential to feed bottom line profits. So, you need to find ways to jump start cash flow immediately.

How do you do that? In a professional services business, you can ask for deposits on work up front, with balances due on delivery. You can do the same in retail, especially on high-ticket or specialty item and position it as an added value and a way to insure delivery by a specific date. You can also add value to generic items by creating private labels, and develop continuity programs where customers pay an upfront monthly fee to ensure delivery or availability of items they will buy on a repeat basis. Of course, the key is to make sure there is little or no gap between when you pay for labour, stock inventory and when you actually get paid. Ideally, you'll find ways to get money up front, and your cash gap will never be an issue.

3. **Always find new ways to keep costs low**. All the cash flow in the world is worthless if it's not a positive cash flow, means you have to bring in more cash than is paid-out. To do this, you need to keep your costs and expenses low. The main idea is look up possible options on either to go for new or used items/equipment/equipment, and look up for used or gently used items to furnish your office or your retail space. Paying vendors up front also gives you leverage for negotiating better prices. Especially in advance economic environment, where credit is at a premium, vendors are more willing than ever to find creative ways to finance transactions, and that is a trend will likely continue over time. So, do some extra work and research now to discover how owners and vendors are finding ways to work out deals, and you just may hit on whole new ways of doing business.

4. **When planning, always overestimate expenses and underestimate revenues**: The Reason for this is for shock absorber just in case unforeseen expenses come crashing in, now due to previous over estimation you could take out what is left and pay for little and unforeseen expenses. The reason why sometimes you underestimate revenues is just making back up plans for worst case scenarios if things didn't turn out the way you planned it. Especially when it comes to money, because you should know that every business has good days and not so good days. Good days are days where sales are at its peak. While not so good days are days where sales and returns are quite low or very low so under estimating allows you to plan for the worst with the hope of achieving and getting excellent results on sales.

5. **Focus on sales and marketing**. In business, nothing happens until a sale is made. From the jump, you'll need to find a good way to get leads, convert leads into sales, and make sure you keep getting repeat sales from your customers. The way to do this is to find or create a marketing and sales funnel system that you can work, test, measure; one that anyone in your company can utilize. Too

many entrepreneurs focus on getting their brand right before they start to generate leads. That is exactly the wrong way to go about business. Leads are always more important than your brand, so don't waste money getting your brand right at the expense of spending that same money to buy new customers. Soon, you'll discover you can build your brand from the ground up, versus spending years and hundreds of thousands of dollars or naira on building it from the top down. Don't presume you'll even survive that long, because without leads, you won't!

6. **Find ways to exponentially increase profits.** Seeking ways to increase profit should not be mistaken as a cheap way of cheating others of their money, to increase sales, read on to previous session, you will get a good hint on how to generate funds for your business. But the common way of profit making is the extra money outside the cost price for any item being sold. Whatever you do never make your customers or potential customers feel you have cheated them one of the best ways is by product and service branding and packaging.

7. **Test and measure everything.** You can't change what you don't measure, and you can't tell if a program or strategy is working if you are not faithfully testing, measuring and tracking your results. Another way to look at this is to think in terms of doctors. Most like to get baseline stats of your heart rate, blood pressure and breathing before they delve into identifying symptoms or recommending corrective courses of action. The same is true in your business. Why keep literally throwing money away on an ad campaign that costs thousands of dollars/naira but doesn't bring anybody through the door?

8. **Accept that learning more equals earning more**. If you've never run a million-dollar business, you don't know how to start a business--simple as that. But you can learn to run one, even if it is your million-dollar business you are building from the ground up. However, you need to accept right now that learning always comes before "earning" (except in the dictionary). You'll need to be committed to learning as much as you can about sales and marketing and operations if you want to have a truly successful business. Once you do that, however, the sky is the starting point. Knowing and applying those simple fundamentals in a highly leveraged way is one of the reasons many top executives and entrepreneurs earn so much. Identify those areas and you then can decide to learn it yourself or hire an expert and learn as much as you can from that person--because you never know when you can run across a distinction in thinking or a strategy that can really take you and your business to a new level of success.

9. **Don't discount, add value.** Whenever you discount, you are taking money directly out of your pocket and directly from your bottom-line profit. So, don't do it except for sales promotion and for increasing customer base and attracting more customers. But rather, create added value propositions all the way up and

down your product or service line. Whatever the industry is, look to hold your price points, increase your margins with the low-cost or no cost extras and any kind of freemium offerings. In the end, those little things won't cost you a lot, but will build up tremendous goodwill and word-of-mouth with your customers and customer base.

10. **Get a coach.** Even if you don't get a business coach at first to help you and guide you in your planning and operation, get someone who is objective and outside of your business you can rely on for nitty gritty business advice and to hold you accountable to getting results.

Too often, we think we have all the answers and are the only people who can really get things done. The reality is that another set of eyes can work wonders for how you operate both on and in your business. An outsider can also make sure you are getting the numbers you need both on the top line and the bottom line to survive. I hope this initial checklist will be valuable in helping you clarify your thinking and helping you prioritize some activities in your planning and start-up mode. I like to say there are no mysteries in business or in life, there's just information you don't know yet. So, prepare as well as you can, knowing you will need to make changes and corrections. But armed with the right strategies up front, you can cut the time it will take you successfully get to your ultimate destination--wherever it is that may be for you and your business.

INSIGHT 4: IDENTIFY SOURCES OF START-UP FINANCING
The Most Common Criteria for a Business Loan

a. Business Financial Statements

b. Business Tax Returns

c. Business Plan with Budget or Projection

d. Personal Financial Statements

e. Personal Tax Returns

Places to Obtain Loan

1. Small and Medium Scale Enterprise (S.M.E)

2. Microfinance Banks

3. Banks

4. Personal and Family Savings Fund

5. Business Plan Competitions from Private Companies

HOW AND WHERE TO RAISE FINANCE FOR YOUR SMALL TO MEDIUM SCALE BUSINESS IN NIGERIA.

1. Nowadays, securing project financing loan for a business involves the use of little known, unusual and carefully planned method and technique to raise, borrow or obtain funds.
2. Funding, irrespective of its source of acquisition, is the single most important factor required for the continued growth and development of a business and at one stage or the other, an entrepreneur maybe be faced with the challenge of securing a loan for his/her business if he or she doesn't know where to look.
3. It is important first that we define the concept of loan. Loan is the fund that an organization such as bank borrows a business for a business start-up or expansion within a specified period of time.
4. To apply for a loan means you are using Other People's Money {OPM} and to be successful with this method, the basic principle is that you operate on the highest ethical standard of integrity, trust, loyalty and consent. A dishonest man is not entitled to credit/loan.
5. Banks are in business to loan money and the more money they loan to honest borrowers; the more profit they make. The best time to obtain a loan is on the basis of facts and need and not for show off. When there is no much pressure for the need of the funds is the best time for some but the pressure for funding is the best time for others. Just look out for the one that works best for you.

Some of the sources for loan include:

1. Commercial banks
2. Credit Unions
3. Co-operative society
4. Federal Government grant for SMEs
5. Bank of Industry
6. Pension funds
7. Venture capitalist
8. Private lenders

9. State Government grants Like Lagos state business grant

Below are the different types of other kinds of loans available

a. Signature loan

b. Consigners loan

c. Loan of collateral security

d. Co-operative loan

6. **Signature Loan:** This is a loan you get based on signing a promissory note to repay the lender as at when due. You do not need to give collateral to get a signature loan.

7. **Co-signer Loan:** You can also use a co-signer to secure a loan. A co-signer is a living collateral with the lender. It is usually an agreement between the lender and the consignee to provide collateral for the purpose of securing a loan. To get a co-signer, the lender needs to convince the co-signer that you are a good credit risk, and the co-signer may demand a certain percent of the profit in a situation of little or no collateral.

8. **Loan of Collateral Security:** A collateral loan is one in which the borrower puts down an asset that would stand as the security for the loan he/she is applying for. The types of collateral loan available includes

    Paper Collateral [which includes stocks, bonds, certificate of deposits, any contract with guarantee of payment and promissory notes]

    a. Fixed deposits in banks

    b. A fixed asset such as real estate and machinery

    c. Rented Collateral

    d. Personal property like boat, cars, airplanes, jewels etc.

9. **Co-operative Loan:** As the name implies, this is a loan gotten from co-operative society. You need to be a member before you can access loan facilities from co-operative bodies and they are usually given without collateral.

10. If you desire to raise money by borrowing, you must know how to prepare a winning package to borrow from any lender. If you want to borrow your way to riches, you must study the technique of successful borrowing of fund for investment. You must know how to prepare a winning package.

11. A package is simply a collection of documents providing important details about a proposal loan. The content of the package depends on whether the borrower is seeking for funds for expansion of an existing business or for start-up.
12. If the borrower is borrowing to expand an already existing business, below would be the content of the package

    1. A loan application letter stating how much you and the purpose of seeking for the fund

    2. A profit and loss statement account of the business for the past three {3} years

    3. An appraisal of your business / property

    4. Description of the assets of the company

    5. Insurance on the assets/ property if any

    6. Deed, title and mortgage information if any

If, however the borrower is seeking for funds in order to establish a new business, a sound business plan would be needed and below are some of the contents of a sound business plan

    1. Executive summary

    2. Market analysis of the project

    3. Financial analysis of the project

    4. SWOT analysis of the project

    5. Risk and mitigation strategies of the project

    6. Socio- economic analysis of the project

13. Loan packages must be well-prepared, detailed and not cumbersome to understand. A winning package does not need to be bulky. It should not be more than ten {10} pages in your first loan request to the lender. Short packages are usually a winning package.

INSIGHT 4.0: FINANCE GENERATING APPROACHES FOR SMALL BUSINESSES IN NIGERIA

CONTENT PARTNER FOR THE SME TOOLKIT
OBJECTIVE OF BUSINESS FINANCES: Money makes your business go, and usually banks make loans only to businesses with operating histories. You

will learn how to locate, negotiate for, and maintain sources of money to help you start and expand your business.

First Things First

Money makes your business grow. But don't try going to a bank to get it when you've just started in business. Banks normally make loans only to businesses with operating histories. This section will give you some alternatives, some strategies and some things to think about as you go about finding the money to make your business work. Our first reminder is that personal savings should be considered the primary source of funds for starting a business. If you haven't started already, start now to begin accumulating cash through Personal savings. Also, don't overlook the Small Business Administration (SBA) loan guarantee Programs available for start-up businesses. With an SBA guarantee program in hand, your bank Will be happy to talk with you! Refer to the Resources section to get more information.

How Much Money Do You Need?

Or, how much can you reasonably expect to get? Don't get too excited just yet - this is not your chance to Ask for a million Naira when you only need NGN50,000. Refer back to your business plans. If you don't have one create one, Answer the question, let's go step-by-Step. What do you need it for?
- Buying supplies and inventory while waiting to get paid
- Paying payroll and rent
- Buying equipment and fixtures
- Getting a computer
  OR
- Buying the business

Prioritize those areas where your options are limited to paying in cash, and review your alternatives where there may be another way. For example, it is not necessary to pay all cash for a delivery truck when you can rent or lease one. Next review what might serve as collateral for your loans. Some credit is granted on an unsecured basis, such as credit cards, but most small business loans are secured by the assets of your business or your personal assets or both. Unsecured means that there is no collateral granted for the loan. Examples of unsecured are:
- Credit cards
- Unsecured lines of credit (like you get in the mail)
- Friends or relatives

Secured loans mean that there are assets pledged to secure the payment in the event you are not Able to pay. Examples of this are:

- Computer lease
- Home mortgage
- Car loan or lease
- Small Business Administration loan

Common types of collateral are equity in your home, accounts receivable, inventory of the business and equipment. Lenders go through an evaluation of the collateral to determine How much they can Lend. Some key variables as to what kind of loan terms you can get are:

- **Number of years in business** - This is your track record and is very important. Banks Usually Require three years while others are less stringent.
- **Size of your company and the amount needed** - Financing institutions vary in the Way They Service the public. For example, you would probably not get a car loan and a large Corporate loan at the same place. Do your research. Ask around. Get to the Right spot.

Loans (Debt) vs. Investment (Equity)

You are most likely familiar with a straight loan (debt) where the lender gets an interest rate and fees. Equity is where the money raised gives the investor an ownership interest. This is common in the sale of stock to a limited number of investors or participation by venture capitalists. The sale of stock is highly Regulated by state and federal agencies and you will need the help of a corporate lawyer. Normally the initial sale of stock to the public (initial public offering or IPO) is deferred until an earnings history is Established. Sometimes such a discussion arises with friends and family who want to be your partner. Consider this Carefully because they will then participate in the increased value of the business and have voting rights. It is well beyond the Scope of this discussion to cover all the aspects of debt and Equity. Just be careful! Your lawyer and accountant would be appropriate sources for more Information on this subject.

Where to Get the Money

The chart below will show some differences between some of the types of lenders. Terms will vary considerably from lender to lender; the summaries in the chart are only meant to be representative and give you an idea of what to expect when seeking money from different Sources. Important issues to consider:

1. Cost

2. Payback program
3. Loan size

Some of the pros and cons of the different lenders are briefly listed below. There will likely be one Common characteristic among them all. As an entrepreneur, you will be legally obligated to have individual responsibility for the credit obligation of your business. Regardless of legal Organization lenders will have documentation to circumvent the Organizational structure. This is usually called a personal guarantee. Don't panic! It is very Common.

The Art of Getting the Money

This starts by knowing what your lender wants. A common way is to simply ask. A better way is to ask a friend or business adviser such as your business mentors/friends for a business loan, the most common things are:
1. Business financial statements
2. Business tax returns
3. Business Plan with budget or projection
4. Personal financial statements
5. Personal tax returns

Step two is to be ready to answer questions about your business, and be ready to highlight your financial Performance both in the past and in the future. You will be more impressive if you have carefully thought-out and become familiar with your plan. Bring your accountant if you need help. Be prepared to tell them why you need the money. "I just need the money," does not inspire confidence or the fact that you have thought it through. Earlier in this session you studied a number of different Purposes. Give them some detail.

Propose a repayment plan. Examples of different structures are:
1. A line of credit, payable at your discretion but subject to renewal annually by the bank Term loan payable monthly over ___ years starting on ____ date. Most places have some flexibility. Potential lenders appreciate that you are thinking about paying them back instead of just getting the money.

Other tips to keep in mind:
1. Needless to say, being well dressed and neat in appearance at bank meetings will reflect positively.
2. Most lenders (including the SBA) will want to see your business plan.
3. Keep your lenders informed on the status of your business: the good and the bad. If you are unable to make a loan payment on time, call your lender in advance, advise Him/her of the problem and request the extension you need. Explain the sources of Repayment. Virtually all

lenders will do a personal savings and corporate credit check through a Company called TRW or other means. Be prepared to discuss any prior credit issues /problems. The best access to a lender is by a referral. Lending is a people business. Have your lawyer or attorney or friend introduce you to a lender. The first thing that will spook lenders or investors is the fear you are "puff" rather than "Substance." Avoid giving the impression of being an over optimistic, "pie-in-the-sky" operator.
4. Most start-up businesses don't find a place for expensive entertaining. Your lenders will be more Interested in knowing how their money is being used to grow your business.
5. Do not depend on a bank to loan you money to start a business. Most small businesses are funded by personal savings.
6. Make a shrewd appraisal to minimize your risks and to limit losses to a pre-determined Limit.
7. Your suppliers and vendors can be sources of financing. For example, if you need an illuminated sign for your store front, the company you contract with to make the sign may provide financing so you can make monthly payments rather than pay cash. (They want your business.)

Examples:
1. Longer payment terms
2. Advertising and marketing assistance
3. Furnishing or financing of equipment, signs or inventory.
4. Advertising and promotional programs
5. Bartering, which is to trade by exchange one commodity for another, can provide a Source of financing. For example, your advertisements in the local newspaper might be Paid for by the bagels you make!

INSIGHT 4.2: OTHER WAYS OF GENERATING CASH: SUCH AS BUSINESS PLAN COMPETITION (AFRICA A. S., 2015)
Apply for Total Startupper Challenge for African Entrepreneurs – Up to $30,000

Brief description: Do you aspire to start your own business and build a brighter future?
Startupper of the year by Total is a unique opportunity for Start-Ups and entrepreneurs' in Africa to get coaching and financial support (Up to $30,000) to grow their ideas and business.

Eligible Projects: All projects are eligible regardless of the type of business or activity, as long as they share the characteristics common to creative start-ups: innovation, competitiveness, growth Boosting and job creation.

About the Challenge
In Africa as elsewhere, many young people aspire to start their own business and build a brighter future, which is why Total created the **Startupper of the year** challenge. If you're currently preparing a business plan or are in the early stages of creating your own business, you're eligible to enter this challenge! What challenges need to be tackled where you live? How will your innovative project address them? After you show how, Total will support those of you who will inspire, create, invest, hire and produce, all to transform "your" world

Offered Since: 2016
Contest Type: Challenge for African Entrepreneurs

Eligibility
- Are you under 35 years old?
- Do you want to create a business or develop one that is less than two years old?
- Are you a citizen of one of these 34 African countries: Algeria, Angola, Burkina Faso? Cameroon, Chad, Côte d'Ivoire, Democratic Republic of the Congo, Egypt, Equatorial Guinea, Ethiopia, Gabon, Ghana, Kenya, Madagascar, Malawi, Mali, Mauritania, Mauritius, Morocco, Mozambique, Namibia, Niger, Nigeria, Republic of Guinea, Republic of the Congo, Reunion, Senegal, South Africa, Tanzania, Togo, Tunisia, Uganda, Zambia or Zimbabwe? If so, this challenge is for you! Only one application by contestant is admitted.

Selection Criteria
Be clear, concise and efficient. Demonstrate your thoroughness, precision, knowledge and
desire to Be an entrepreneur. In each of the 34 countries, **"Startupper of the year by
Total** "jury will evaluate the innovativeness, boldness and originality of your project,
along with its social and economic impact, Feasibility, sustainability and potential in terms
of growth, development and employment. To boost your Score, don't overlook anything.

Number of Winners: up to three winners per country
Value of Award: Each winner will receive a customized coaching to help him/her to create and/or Develop its business. Its content and duration will be defined by the jury in accordance with the needs of the winner that it will have

identified during the selection process. Total will provide financial support up to $30,000 (in winners' local currency)

Duration of Program: will be defined by the jury based on the needs of the winner
Eligible Countries: see list above
To be taken at (country): The contestant must be a citizen of the country where its Application is submitted in order to create or develop its project there.

Application Deadline: Find out the recent deadline!
Challenge schedule
- Next month after closing date – Notification of preselected finalists
- Then another month – Finalists oral presentations before the jury
- The final month – Announcement of the winners

Offered annually? Not specified
How to Enter
To enter, create your profile and provide the required information online. To support, justify and illustrate your project, you can attach as many documents as you wish to your
application, including:
- *your résumé*,
- your business plan,
- your financing plan,
- your partnership strategy,
- an executive summary,
- a marketing brochure,
- your logo,
- your graphic standards,
- And/or a photo or video presentation, etc.

Each country has specific rules for the application process. Go to startuppers.total.com/en/challenges/ And download the rules for your country (PDF). On completion of the pre-selection stage, the jury in Each of the 34 countries will select up to ten finalists of the best projects submitted. The finalists will Then be invited to present their project orally to the jury, which will select up to three winners.

ULTIMATE LIST: *40+ BUSINESS FUNDING OPPORTUNITIES and AWARDS FOR AFRICAN ENTREPRENEURS* (Ikenna, 2016)
From students, start-ups, young and social entrepreneurs to small and medium and successful businesses, African and global organizations open business plan

competitions and awards annually to support and Encourage budding and successful entrepreneurs' in Africa. Whether you need funding to bring your bright idea to limelight or have made innovative progress as an entrepreneur in Africa and need a Platform to demonstrate your achievements, there are opportunities out there. Below is Afterschool Africa list of 40 plus, business plan competitions and awards for African entrepreneurs. Most of these programs are offered annually. Look out for the next application. **With Emphasis on Women Entrepreneurs**

BMCE Bank of Africa – African Entrepreneurship Award – USD$1 Million for Women (and Men) Entrepreneurs:
Are you dreaming of launching or growing your business idea in your community? Join the thousands of women (and men) entrepreneurs creating jobs all over Africa and submit your idea for a chance to share in the $1 million award.

She Leads Africa is a social enterprise dedicated to supporting young African women and Their journey Towards professional success. The SLA Accelerator is a 3-month program designed to identify, support and fund the next generation of Nigeria's brightest female entrepreneurs and offers. The winner of a Demo Day will receive **a N 2mn investment** from She Leads Africa Fund.

Ashden International Award World's leading green energy awards, seeks pioneering enterprises and programmes demonstrating achievement in any of the following areas:
Increasing energy access for homes or businesses, Sustainable buildings, developing innovative financial mechanisms or business models for delivering sustainable energy, Sustainable travel, improving the lives of women and girls Through sustainable energy, Sustainable energy and water. **Prize money of £20,000; one International Gold Award of £30,000**

SESSION 1: STUDENT ENTREPRENEURSHIP
Note: click on the name of the interested school with an internet connection to follow: **The African Innovation Prize** (AIP) is a UK based non-profit organization founded by Cambridge University Graduates to spur student innovation and entrepreneurship in Africa. Through university-based business planning competitions, AIP aims to encourage students to dream, design, and Dedicate themselves to their business ideas. AIP also develops connections between students and the local enterprise community through seeding

entrepreneurship clubs within universities, and brokering Mentorship between students and local business leaders.

The **Dell Social Innovation Challenge** identifies and supports promising young social innovators who dedicate themselves to solving the world's most pressing problems with their transformative ideas. The program provides university students with world-class teaching and training, as well as with start-up capital and access to a network of mentors and advisers.

INDIAFRICA: A Shared Future features a series of multi-disciplinary contests across top Campuses in Africa and India. The contests are aimed at offering students and professionals from both geographies a common platform for future collaborations in business, design and culture.

The Cola-Cola Africa Foundation Entrepreneurship programs provide students with the too ls needed to prosper as a young adult. The main objective is to help today's youth understand the importance of self-reliance and the impact they all have on the future of the economy by addressing the issue of unemployment in Africa and helping to create a culture of entrepreneurship. The Coca-Cola Africa Foundation has invested **$3.1 million** in programs that promote entrepreneurship among the Youth in twelve countries.

Allan Gray Entrepreneurship Fellowship for South Africa, Namibia, Botswana and Swaziland Students:
The Allan Gray Orbis Foundation offers the exceptional Allan Gray Fellowship to Southern Africa's Pioneering bright young students. This initiative aims to develop students, known as Allan Gray Candidate Fellows into Southern Africa's future high impact responsible entrepreneurs.

The **School Enterprise Challenge** is a global business planning awards programme run by the educational charity 'Teach A Man to Fish.' It aims to create globally aware, socially responsible, young entrepreneurs. The School Enterprise Challenge is an international awards programme for schools around the world with **up to $50,000 in prizes** available for the most entrepreneurial schools, teachers and students.

The **Skoll Scholarships in Social Entrepreneurship for International Students, UK**
provides funding and exclusive opportunities to meet with world-renowned entrepreneurs, thought leaders and investors. The Skoll Scholarship provides tuition for entrepreneurs who have set up or have being working in entrepreneurial ventures with a social purpose, and who wish to improve their

knowledge of market-oriented practices so they can be more effective in their subsequent social change pursuits. The Skoll Scholarship covers full costs of Said Business School tuition and college fees. The Scholarship also covers partial living expenses based on need, up to an additional **£8,000**.

Google Hash Code Programming Competition for Students and Professionals in Africa, Europe and Middle East is a team-based programming competition organized by Google for students and industry professionals (18+) across Europe, the Middle East and Africa. You pick your team and programming language, Google picks a real-life engineering problem to solve.

How will you change the world with US$1 million? Apply for 2015 Hult Prize – Social Enterprise Challenge: thousands of universities students' worldwide team up to create start-ups aimed at solving an issue faced by billions in need. More than 10,000 applicants will begin the journey, and only 300 start-ups from around the world will move on to pitch their start-up ideas at one of five global locations, including: Boston, San Francisco, London, Dubai and Shanghai.

The **Google RISE Awards** is an annual grant program for informal education organizations around the world that promote computer science for K-12/pre-university age youth. It aspires for students to be creators not just consumers of tomorrow's technology, and that Includes students from all backgrounds. This is why its efforts emphasize participation from **girls**, youth in low-income communities, and minorities who have historically being Underrepresented in the field of computer science.

SESSION 2: ASPIRING AND START-UP ENTREPRENEURS
Is DB Business Plan Competition for Sub-Saharan Countries? The Islamic Development Bank Business Plan Competition is a recently introduced initiative of the Is DB Group. In this competition, candidates come together to develop and further refine their business plans to launch their start-ups or grow ventures, while competing for the cash prizes! As at 2014 Cash prizes ($25,000 for the 1st Place Winner, $15,000 for the 2nd Place Winner, $10,000 for the 3rd Place Winner for each track of the competition); Mentorship; Networking Opportunities. (not offered in 2015).

BID Network: Are you an aspiring entrepreneur from Rwanda or Uganda with a finance Need between USD 10,000 and USD 500,000? Entrepreneurs can register on one or more of the online portals and submit their business plan for assessment by our advisers. Bid Network introduces a unique offering of one-on- one, tailor-made Business Development Support (BDS) to help Ugandan entrepreneurs to professionalize their operations, accelerate growth and obtain finance. Benefit includes sourcing, business development support, coaching and matchmaking.

Development Innovation Ventures aims to find and support breakthrough solutions to the world's most important development challenges interventions with the power to change millions of lives at a fraction of the usual cost. Through its grant program DIV invests in these game-changing ideas, rigorously tests them using cutting-edge analytical methods, and scales solutions that prove they work. The Argidius Foundation and the Aspen Network of Development Entrepreneurs (ANDE) have announced the **Argidius-ANDE Finance Challenge (AAFC)**, a new competition designed to support innovative ways to provide capital to small businesses in emerging markets that require $20,000 - $250,000 in early stage capital. The goal of the challenge is to accelerate the development of innovative and sustainable solutions in a number of emerging markets, ideally establishing models that can be replicated.

In 2011, the United States Agency for International Development (USAID) and Western Union launched the second **African Diaspora Marketplace**(ADM II). ADM II encourages sustainable economic growth and employment by supporting U.S.-based African Diaspora and other entrepreneurs through grant funding and technical assistance facilities. ADM II Awardees are individuals with demonstrable connections to or experience in Africa, who have innovative and high impact start-ups and established businesses on the continent. Each business venture can receive matching partnership grants up to $50,000 and other forms of technical assistance.

Launched in 2009, the **MENA 100 Business Plan Competition** is co-organized by the MENA-OECD Investment Programme, aims to promote entrepreneurship and small- and medium-sized enterprises (SMEs) in the Middle East and North Africa, by mentoring entrepreneurs with innovative ideas to come up with the perfect business plan for them Start-up or expanding their young enterprises.

First prize US$ 25 000, Second prize US$ 10 000 and **Third prize US$ 5 000** Nigerian billionaire investor and philanthropist Tony Elumelu has committed **$100 million** to create 10,000 entrepreneurs across Africa over the next 10 years.

Tony Elumelu Entrepreneurship Programme TEEP, a Pan-African entrepreneurship initiative of the Tony Elumelu Foundation, is a multi-year programme of training, funding, and mentoring, designed to empower the next generation of African entrepreneurs.

In Africa as elsewhere, many young people aspire to start their own business and build a brighter future, which is why **Total created the Startupper of the year challenge**. If you're currently preparing a business plan or are in the early stages of creating your own business, you're eligible to enter this Challenge! Each winner will receive a customized coaching to help him/her to create and/or develop its business. Total will provide financial support **up to $30,000** (in winners' local currency).

Seedstars World offers exclusive and global start-up competition to promote, connect and invest up to **$1.5mn for Entrepreneurs** in emerging market in over 65 countries across Asia, Africa, LatAm, CEE and MENA. Companies less than two years old, MVP ready, thinking global and with less than $500k raised so far can apply to become Global Winners!

Diamond Bank's **BET – Building Entrepreneurs Today** – business grant marks another great opportunity for entrepreneurs all over Nigeria in the following industries (fashion and lifestyle, agriculture, information and communication technology) to present them businesses and innovation and have the opportunity of being selected as one of the top 50 businesses that will be provided with extensive training, mentoring and advisory by the Enterprise Development Centre with the top 5 businesses winning **3 Million naira each.**

Shell Live WIRE is a social investment programme that aims to help young Nigerians explore the option of starting their own business as a real and viable career option. It provides support, access to training, guidance, and business mentorship to young entrepreneurs and potential entrepreneurs between the ages of 18 and 35. The programme operates mainly in the Niger Delta region and aims to inspire, encourage and support young people aged 18-35 to start-up their own businesses through the provision of finance and training for young entrepreneurs.

Ashoka Africa: Ashoka is the world's largest network of change makers and social innovators with more than 3,000 social entrepreneurs in 70 countries, and has being working in Africa for over 20 years. Ashoka believes that building a critical mass of leading social entrepreneurs with ground-breaking ideas is an important INSIGHT towards creating a vibrant, prosperous African continent. Ashoka Fellows in Africa are empowering people to create their own economic and civic opportunities, addressing the pandemic of HIV/AIDS and other devastating health concerns, implementing transformative education systems, protecting their environments and natural resources, and introducing effective methods of conflict Resolution.

Since 1976, Rolex has honoured extraordinary individuals who possess the courage and conviction to Take on major challenges. Each **Rolex Award for Enterprise** is given for a new or ongoing project anywhere in the world – one that deserves support for its capacity to improve lives, or protect the World's natural and cultural heritage. These projects have touched all aspects of humanity by expanding Knowledge or improving life on the planet.

The Youth Citizen Entrepreneurship Competition is a global programme and an online platform, which supports the implementation of the **17 Sustainable Development Goals (SDGs)**. Young people from around the world are invited to submit their innovative ideas and projects with a societal impact, which champion and implement one or more of the 17 Sustainable Development Goals. The 17 SDGs address the most important social, economic, environmental, health and governance challenges of our time.

The N10 billion **Youth Entrepreneurship Support (YES) programme** is an ambitious programme by the Bank of Industry (BOI) aimed at addressing youth unemployment in Nigeria which is currently over 50%.

The SOCAP Scholarship for Social Entrepreneurs is a world-renowned conference series dedicated to increasing the flow of capital towards social good. Social entrepreneurs are the heart of SOCAP. They identify new solutions to pressing issues, balancing true impact with sustainable business models. We prioritize support for inspiring entrepreneurs, as they are the future of the social capital markets.

The Saville Foundation Pan-African Awards for Entrepreneurship in Education is a Competition initiated by Teach a Man to Fish and generously sponsored by the organization Educating Africa. The competition is open to all organizations based in Africa working in education, from primary through to tertiary, as well as in non-formal and adult education. As well as a **First Prize of $10,000** and two Runners-Up Prizes of **$5,000**, there are up to **50 Awards of $1,000** available for the best entry from every country on the continent.

SESSION 3: BREAKTHROUGH ENTREPRENEURS AND SMALL BUSINESSES

The **Anzisha Prize** seeks to award young entrepreneurs who have developed and implemented innovative solutions to social challenges or started successful businesses with in their communities.12 finalists from across Africa will win an all-expenses paid trip to South Africa to be a part of a week-long entrepreneurship workshop and conference at the African Leadership Academy campus on the outskirts of Johannesburg. The grand prize winners, selected from these finalists, will share prizes worth $75,000 USD.

The **Innovation Prize for Africa (IPA)** IPA honours and encourages innovative achievements that contribute towards developing new products, increasing efficiency or saving cost in Africa. Specifically, the award targets technological breakthroughs in five main areas: manufacturing and service industry, health and well-being, agriculture and agribusiness, environment, energy and water and ICTs. By providing **USD 150,000** to winners who deliver market-oriented solutions for African-led development, the IPA acknowledges and encourages the endeavour of innovators and entrepreneurs and works to raise them profiles on the development agenda. **USD 100,000 for the winner** with the best innovation, **USD 25,000 for the Second Prize** and **USD 25,000** for the Special Prize.

The **Facebook Internet.org Innovation Challenge in Africa** supports Internet.org's vision of a Connected world. To this end, the goal of the Challenge is to recognise individuals and organizations that are working on internet-based solutions to promote education and economic empowerment in countries throughout Africa. Up to $150,000 awarded. The African Media Initiative (AMI), the continent's largest association of media owners and operators, has announced a **$1 million** fund to spur innovation in the news industry.

The **African News Innovation Challenge (ANIC)** is designed to encourage experimentation in digital technologies and support the best innovations that strengthen African news organizations.

The **Zayed Future Energy Prize** invite entries from companies, individuals, organizations and high schools to submit applications, for a chance to win part of the **US$4 million prize fund**. The scope of the Prize has also been broadened to include five distinct categories: Large Corporations, Small and Medium Enterprises (SMEs), Non-Governmental Organizations (NGOs), Lifetime Achievement, and the newly instituted Global High School Prize.

The **Sustainable Energy Fund for Africa (SEFA)** is a bilateral trust fund administered by the African Development Bank – anchored in a generous commitment of **USD 60 million** by the Government of Denmark and the United States – to support small and medium clean energy and energy efficiency projects in Africa.

The **Africa Prize for Engineering Innovation** aims to stimulate and reward engineering entrepreneurship in sub-Saharan Africa. The Africa Prize will encourage ambitious and talented sub-Saharan African engineers from all disciplines to apply their skills to develop scalable solutions to local challenges, highlighting the importance of engineering as an enabler of improved quality of life and economic development. Finalists will be invited to present at an event held in Africa and a winner will be selected to receive **£25,000** along with runners-up, who will **each be awarded £10,000.**

Successful Entrepreneurs and Business leaders
Ernst and Young's **Entrepreneur of the Year** awards are the world's most prestigious business awards for entrepreneurs. The award encourages entrepreneurial activity among those with potential and recognizes the contribution of people who inspire others with their vision, leadership and achievement. The African Leadership Network celebrates entrepreneurs by hosting the

Africa Awards for Entrepreneurs, the most distinguished business and entrepreneurship awards Programme in Africa, which considers candidates from African Nations. The award recognizes and award exceptional entrepreneurial leaders who serve as role models to Africa's aspiring entrepreneurs and demonstrate business excellence, innovation and profitability.

African Leadership Network – ALN has hosted the **Africa Awards for Entrepreneurship (AAE),** dubbed the 'Oscars of Entrepreneurship in Africa', since 2012. AAE was established in 2007 by the Legatum Group to recognize business leaders who demonstrate innovation, profitability, and business Excellence while serving as role models to inspire Africa's next generation of entrepreneurs in Africa.

African Achievers Awards is a set of annual awards bestowed on Africa's most accomplished politicians, diplomacy and entrepreneurship. Now in its fourth year, the African Achievers Awards recognizes individuals and organizations that selflessly devote their time and talents towards Improving Africa's international profile and building stronger, integrated communities in Africa.

After You Get the Money

Getting the money is only the first step. You should strive to be a good customer so you can get Cooperation if you need help later. A good customer sticks to his/her agreement. Make sure you Understand the requirements and perform to them as much as possible. In a business relationship, Lenders will ask for regular financial statements, which you should produce on time. There may be Covenants. A covenant is a written agreement in which you promise to meet specified obligations such as submitting the aging's of your accounts receivable. The "aging's" report will show the lenders if your credit customers are paying on time or not. Be proactive. Contact them if there is a problem. Be sure to stay in touch even if nothing new is going on. Get to the next highest level within the organization.

Activities

Sources of financing can surface from unexpected sources: List at least five of them:

A. _____
B. _____
C. _____
D. _____
E. _____

Some possible answers are:

- **Suppliers:** Ask for longer terms of payment.
- **Your landlord:** Ask the landlord to provide you with tenant improvements.
- **Your customers:** Ask for either cash or prompt payment.
- **Your capital investments:** Ask the suppliers of your fixtures, equipment and signs to Finance your purchases. They will be interested in doing so in order to get your business.

10 Do's and Don'ts to note when it involves Business Finances

Do's

1. Live frugally and begin saving up money now to start your own business.
2. Use your cash flow projection as your key tool to determine financing required.
3. Complete a business plan for meetings with potential lenders or investors.
4. Has your business plan critiqued by appropriately informed people? Revise as necessary.
5. Maintain a current financial information packet including financial statements and recent tax returns.
6. Consider bartering services if appropriate.
7. Use your accountant or attorney as referrals to lenders.
8. Keep your lenders informed of your progress and any potentially adverse events.
9. If you need a loan for 6 months, ask for 12 months to be on the safe side.

Don'ts
1. Expect a bank to help finance your new business.
2. Ask for a loan without a detailed repayment plan in hand.
3. Overlook vendors and landlords (for tenant improvements) as sources of financing.
4. Avoid being the bearer of bad news to your lender.
5. Ask for less than enough to meet your realistic needs.
6. Exaggerate. (Instead, be conservative in your presentations to lenders.)
7. Write a check without adequate funds in your bank account.
8. Risk losing your home by taking a "Home Equity" loan unless you are certain of your ability to repay.
9. Sign personal guarantees unless absolutely necessary.
10. Budget or spend money on expensive entertaining of potential lenders.

WHAT ARE SOME INVESTORS/LENDERS ARE LOOKING FOR?

What are lenders really looking for when they pore over your loan application? Lenders (particularly bankers) typically base their decisions on four criteria, often called the "Four C's of Credit":

1. **Credit:** The lender will examine your personal credit history to see how well you've managed your past obligations. If you have some black marks on your record, the lender will want to hear details.

2. **Character:** Character is hard to measure, but lenders will use your credit history to assess this as well. They take lawsuits, tax liens and

bankruptcies pretty seriously. They'll also do a background check and evaluate your previous work experience.

3. **Capacity:** What happens if your business slumps? Do you have the capacity to convert other assets to cash, either by selling them or borrowing against them? Your secondary repayment sources may include real estate, stocks and other savings. The lender will look at your business balance sheet and your personal financial statement to determine your capacity to repay the loan.

4. **Collateral:** As a start-up, you'll probably be seeking a secured loan. This means you must put up collateral—either personal assets, such as certificates of deposit or stocks, or business assets like real estate, inventory or equipment.

Type	Cost	Payback Terms	Sizes	For	Against
personal savings	no cost	none		easy, cheap	risk of loss
friends and family	usually good rate or none	very flexible		flexible, best value	can create friction
home mortgages - traditional or seconds	7-9% 8-14% on equity loans	very long and flexible	80-100% + of home equity value	cheapest, longest term	your house is at risk in the event of non-payment
credit cards	16-23%	40-60 months	3,000-10,000	easy qualifying, no collateral	small amounts
suppliers	free	30 days +/-		inexpensive, unsecured	short-term
landlord	adds to rent cost	over term of lease		preserves cash for assets you can't take with you	hard to get; assets acquired are usually only good at one

						location; difficult to move
venture capital	25-40%	5-7 years	N500,000+		can get large amounts	very hard to get; share ownership
commercial mortgage	7-9%	25-year payment; all due in 10 years	ngn300,000+; 75% of appraisal			
specialized lenders (industry expertise, auto, business brokers, high tech, specialized equipment, computers, phones, etc.)	12-18%	5-7 years	varies		accessible through dealer, who is motivated to make sale of equipment or business; payback terms more favourable than bank	debt service can be high
leasing companies	12-18%	5-7 years	varies		same as above; also 100% financing	
sba	7-9%	7-20 years	N50,000-1,000,000		longest payback for other than real estate loan	can be a complex process
finance companies	14-30%	1-3 years	N100,000+		an alternative when you don't have many	expensive; picky about collateral
banks	6-9%	1-5 years	N50,000+		generally, least expensive	generally hardest to qualify for

INSIGHT 5: CHOOSE A BUSINESS NAME AND REGISTER IT WITH THE APPROPRIATE AUTHORITIES

One of all the decisions you make when starting a business, probably one of the most important is the type of legal structure you select for your company. Your structure can make a big difference in how you pay taxes (how much and how often), raise money, handle lawsuits, or dissolve or pass on the business. Will you operate as a sole proprietorship, partnership, corporation, S corporation or limited liability company? Because each business form comes with different tax consequences, you'll want to want to make your selection wisely and choose the structure that most closely matches your business's needs. If you're not a tax or legal expert, you should seek advice from a professional on how to pick the structure that'll best manage your liabilities. Also important in the success of your business is the right name for your new venture: The right name can make your company the talk of the town; the wrong one can doom it to obscurity and failure. If you're smart, you'll put just as much effort into naming your business as you did into coming up with your idea and writing your business plan.

PREDICTING HOW MUCH YOU WILL NEED

Cash Received:

a) Payment from customer who bought on credit
- d) Cash sales
- e) Advance payment from customers
- f) VAT refunds
- g) Bank Loan
- h) New share capital
- i) Cash received from the sales of other business assets

HOW MUCH WILL THE BUSINESS SPEND?

- a) Payment to suppliers
- b) Wages and salary
- c) Rent, rates and service charge
- d) Payment of acquisition of new assets such as cars, equipment and business stationaries.
- e) Loan repayments

CALCULATING MONTHLY COMPANY INCOME

Net cash flow = total expenditure – total income/money generated

If the net cash flow is negative it means the business is paying more money than it is receiving. Balance at the start of a month + net cash flow for the month to get closing balance for that month. This closing balance is the opening balance for next month. What you need to spot in your business is how much money in total the business will need before it starts to make positive net cash flows every month. This will be a combination of the amount it takes to setup in the first place, the amount it takes to run the business before it becomes profitable and the cost of funding the business as it grows, even after it is profitable.

Grants and Investment in the Region/City/Town of Start-Up: There are countries who give out grants and loans to small-scale business and places very little tax on them as a result giving such business the atmosphere to strive, grow and expand. You have to make your findings if where you have in mind for your business possesses this attribute before jumping into any city to start business.

Tax Policy: you must understand the tax policy of the economy you wish to set up your business in, before you start your business so as to avoid making mistakes in involving yourself in wrong investment because there might never be second chance which is all dependent on your fighting spirit to get a second chance for your business, that's where perseverance comes in. a good example is a country/city I know charging as much as 50% tax meaning that if you are paid 400,000 dollars on a salary job, you will only get to take 200,000 dollars home. Imagine losing so much more just to tax while in some other country, the tax rate is considerably low even to the point that even after deduction you won't even notice its deduction from income or salary paid to workers.

OFFICE PREMISES

Premises and Location

Selecting the right option for accommodating your business is one of the most important decisions when getting started. A great location can help improve sales and productivity, attract the right kind of clients and good employees. The location you choose will depend on the nature of your business, for example: retail, manufacturing, or professional services. It will also depend on your target market and consumer demographics such as age, gender, income, lifestyle and whether you need to see clients or customers at your premises.

You should already have an idea of who your customers are from conducting market research. This research will help you locate your business in an area where you are likely to attract the most customers.

Generally, you have four options for accommodating your business:

1. Home-based
2. Business incubator
3. Leasing commercial premises
4. Buying commercial premises

It is strongly recommended that you seek advice from your accountant or financial adviser about the viability of each option for your business in relation to your personal financial circumstances, and obtain legal advice before entering into any agreement to lease or buy commercial premises.

Locating your business at home

If you are starting out, it may be possible to operate your business from home until you become more established, especially if you provide a service.

You need to consider what facilities you require for your home-based office. This will depend on whether you operate your business *from* home or *at* home.

Business incubators

If you are starting a new business, or have outgrown your home office, you may find all the space and flexibility you need in a business incubator unit. Tenants in business incubators also have easy access to free assistance and support services provided by the Small Business Centre or incubator manager.

Leasing commercial premises

Leasing commercial premises does not require the large capital investment necessary for buying premises. Once the lease expires you can leave the premises without any further financial commitment. If you decide to end or relocate your business before the lease expires, you may have the option to sublet or assign the lease.

However, security of occupancy extends only until the lease expires and your business may suffer losses from business disruption and loss of client base that often result if you need to relocate. Generally, leases commit the tenant to increases in rent despite how well their business is doing. Also, if you don't have an investment in the property you don't benefit from capital gains.

Buying commercial premises

In some cases, it could be more cost-effective for a small business owner to purchase a commercial property instead of leasing it. Buying commercial premises is a major financial investment. However, depending on your individual financial and personal circumstances, you may be able to make such an investment.

Furnished Large Office Space Including basic Office Equipment: Furnished offices can be a great way of saving cost of buying furniture and basic office equipment all over again rather its already done for you, all you have to do is move in with your workers. This type of office place is only necessary for already existing business who had grown in staff and in size and need a bigger room to accommodate all its staff. I would not recommend a young entrepreneur who is just coming into business to go for this kind of office size because it will lead to inability to maintain the rates, it will equally lead to waste of space making the office look empty, it would send wrong impression of your business to customers and potential customers which is terrible for your business. Because if care is not taken it can lead to frustration and might lead to the end of such business. Take on office spaces according to your company growth per time.

Empty small Spaces: This is basically for business owners who intend to create their own office equipment and furnish it themselves based on personal taste and fashion style that they find suitable. These is good in a way of getting your own office but is quite expensive to get and furnish up to what you would call required standard. If you have the money to do this and even quoted in your business plan why not? You can get it done but remember that office setup is not advised to be grouped in start-up capital (product production). But should be grouped as total business setup cost so as to be able to make adequate plans for it.

Leases, Buying and Renting Office space: For office acquisition is either done through Leasing, renting or buying for any kind of office space. Whatever choice you are making you should consider the type of space needed for your business. But I recommend you go for a rented office first, once your business have grown and there is a need for a bigger space then you can consider buying an office rather than renting or getting a lease.

SESSION3: POST OFFICE ACQUISITION

Equipping your home office: Now as a young and new entrepreneur, you can use your home most especially if the kind of businesses you are offering is services but some say product-based businesses sell best than services business. Well, I say how much sales you make or job offered to you is completely based on your awareness creation and marketing strategies to bring people and potential customers into knowing what you do and following up on anyone that shows interest on what you do and needs your services or product. To equip your home just require you purchasing the equipment, gadgets and tools you need to allow you effectively do your job as a business person but whatever kind of business try to find out the legal implication of your business so as to avoid being sued or jailed or fined for not having legal backing for your business.

Legal and insurance issues: This involves getting insurance for equipment or devices you can't afford to replace if stolen or damaged. This equally comes in handing when dealing with export and import business because if there is a ship wreck, the goods would all go down the drain without a penny refund to you if it's not insured. Now this is something you can't afford to lose if unforeseen circumstances befall you. Don't take risk or play Mr stingy and get your goods and equipment issued.

SESSION 1: INSIGHT INTO NAFDAC REGISTRATION PROCESS FOR PRODUCT BASED BUSINESS

Mrs. Christiana Obiazikwore is the Chief Public Relations Officer, NAFDAC as at 2016. She says because the product registration process of NAFDAC is stringent, persons who require to go through it often view the process as very tasking and may complain of frustration.

Overview of NAFDAC

Obiazikwor says from an interview that NAFDAC is mandated to regulate and control the importation and exportation, manufacture, advertisement, sales and use of food, drugs, cosmetics, chemical, medical devices and packaged water.

Registration Categories

Obiazikwor says, "Currently, NAFDAC registers products in two categories: drugs and food. Drugs include medical devices, vaccines, chemicals and pesticides, veterinary products, nutraceuticals and supplements, herbal preparations and cosmetics."

Procurement of Samples Requirement – Imported Products

the registration process will require samples of the product. NAFDAC therefore grants special authorization to import such samples. Simply apply to NAFDAC for a written authorization to import samples. Also ensure that other documents required for clearing and taking delivery of samples are obtained, particularly

Certificate of Analysis issued by the manufacturer and Certificate of Manufacture and Free Sale issued by the appropriate regulatory authority in the country of origin. Samples must also conform to stipulated product labelling regulations.

Requirements for Application for Full Registration of Product – Imported or Locally Manufactured Product

this starts with the procurement of the relevant registration application form for each product – NAFDAC approval is granted for each specific product. This simply means that two products from the same source will still require different approvals and numbers. In fact, two different packages of the same products are processed as different products. The application form is also available at NAFDAC's offices or online at NAFDAC's website. The completed form is to be submitted to the registration division of the agency.

You fill the application form and write an application letter. Your application letter must contain the name of the manufacturer and brand name of the product.

The completed application form with the application letter for each product should be returned to **NAFDAC** registration department with the following items:

Five copies of written report for the product

1. Sample of the products. Three packets. (drugs, food or cosmetics)
2. Name and copies of the current license of your company's superintendent/production chemist or pharmacists.
3. The registration license obtained from Pharmacists Council of Nigeria (PCN) that permits you to use your factory for drug production or a license obtained from relevant professional body.

You will need to pay an amount of money as registration fee at **NAFDAC** designated bank. The amount paid for registration differs with respect to each product. You will find below the registration fees paid for each product class as at 2016.

- Pharmaceutical drugs produced in Nigeria cost —- N25, 000 to N70, 000.
1. Herbal drugs cost ———————————————- N10, 000 to N20, 000
2. Packaged Foods cost ——————————————— N40, 000
3. Bottled Water cost ————————————————— N50, 000
4. Sachet Water cost ————————————————— N30, 000
5. Cosmetics cost ——————————————————— N40, 000
6. Pesticides/Chemicals cost —————————————— N40, 000

Finally, if you want your products to be approved quickly by **NAFDAC**, you will need to fix a date and invite them to inspect your factory and production facilities.

Key Requirements (For Drugs)
1. Application is on single product basis
2. Written application stating name of manufacturer and name (and brand, if applicable) of product
3. Completed NAFDAC registration application form (Form D-REG/001)
4. Certificate of Incorporation with the Corporate Affairs Commission, if it is a company
5. Five (5) copies of the product dossier
6. Three (3) packs of the products samples
7. Notarised original copy of the duly executed Power of Attorney from the product manufacturer (imported product)
8. Certificate of Manufacture issued by the competent health or regulatory authority in country of origin and authenticated by the Nigerian Mission in that country (if foreign import). Where there is no Nigerian mission, The British High Commission or an ECOWAS country Mission will authenticate.
9. If contract-manufactured, Contract Manufacturing Agreement, properly executed and notarised by a Notary Public in the country of manufacture.
10. Current World Health Organisation Good Manufacturing Practice Certificate for the manufacturer, authenticated by the Nigerian Mission.

11. Certificate of Pharmaceutical Products (COPP) duly issued and authenticated
12. Current Superintendent Pharmacists license to practice issued by the Pharmaceutical Council of Nigeria
13. Premises Registration License from Pharmacists Council of Nigeria (PCN)
14. Certificate of Registration of brand name with trademark registry in the Ministry of Commerce here in Nigeria
15. Letter of invitation from manufacturer to inspect factory abroad, stating full name and location of plant
16. The applicable fee payable only if documents are confirmed to be satisfactory. Nutraceuticals, medical devices and other regulated drug products have similar requirements, with minor variations.

Foods
The requirements are generally similar

Food – packaged water
any company in Nigeria that wants to sell bottled or sachet water displaying an approved NAFDAC registration number must apply to the agency. The company needs to submit samples of its products for testing and agree to display an expiry date on its packaging. Once it has a NAFDAC number it can market its sachet product as 'pure water'.

Requirements
In order to qualify for NAFDAC registration, the company must be formally incorporated, and its water product must have a trademark registration. It must have a business premises for water production that conforms to generally acceptable manufacturing practices. The company is also required to retain a water analyst to oversee its production process.

Testing
NAFDAC labs will test the water samples provided by the company for purity. The agency carries out tests to establish the alkalinity of the water, and also to check for the presence of any elements harmful to human health.

Criticism

The packaged water industry in Nigeria has being subject to significant criticism over its safety. NAFDAC itself has also come under fire for failing to adequately police the industry. Some companies are known to submit fake samples in order to pass NAFDAC tests and gain a registration number, but then sell untreated tap water labelled as pure. Other companies merely imprint an entirely fake NAFDAC number on their packaging.

SESSION 2: *PRICE*- A CASE STUDY OF PRODUCT REGISTRATION WITH NAFDAC NIGERIA (CHIBUZO, 2016)

Registration Categories and General Requirements

Currently, NAFDAC registers products in two categories: drugs and food. Drugs include medical devices, vaccines, chemicals and pesticides, veterinary products, nutraceuticals and supplements, herbal preparations and cosmetics. Products may be manufactured locally or imported. However, an application for registration can only be initiated by the Nigerian manufacturer, for a locally manufactured food or drug product. In the case of a product manufactured outside Nigeria, application must be by a Nigerian representative of the foreign manufacturer and this must be a registered company or an individual. In effect, the applicant must be based in Nigeria and is expected to possess the capacity to control the circulation of the product. The representative of a foreign manufacturer must however have a duly executed Power of Attorney from the manufacturer (signed by company MD, GM, Chairman or President) appointing and authorizing him/it to act in that capacity and specifying the name(s) of the product(s).

Two-Stage Registration Process

Though the specific documentations vary for different drugs and food categories, the general procedure is similar and, broadly, is a two-stage process:

1. Application for approval to bring in samples - not applicable if locally manufactured

2. Application for full registration of product - applies whether locally manufactured or imported

Sample of Guidelines for obtaining permit to import feed supplement, feed concentrates, feed additive, premixes, fish meal (NAFDAC/VMAP/001/13)

ITEM	OLD FEES	RECENT FEES
Tariff for New Import Permit	N64,000 per product	N102,000 per product
Renewal of import permit	N37,750	N62,000
Application Form permit (1st 25 items) inspection	(Breakdown) N1,000 N25,000 + 5% VAT N10,000 + 5% VAT	(Breakdown) N1,000 N40,000 N20,000 + 5% VAT
Additional page for new import permit	No old fees	N25,000
Additional page for renewal import permit	No old fees	N25,000
Re-inspection fee (after 2 years)	N10,500	N21,000

A few changes in fees: The total fees for obtaining a new import permit increased from N64,000 to N102,000. The renewal fees also increased from N37,750 to N62,000

Requirements - Stage one (Procurement of samples)
The registration process will require samples of the product. NAFDAC therefore grants special authorization to import such samples. Simply apply to NAFDAC for a written authorization to import samples. Also ensure that other documents required for clearing and taking delivery of samples are obtained, particularly Certificate of Analysis issued by the manufacturer and Certificate of Manufacture and Free Sale issued by the appropriate regulatory authority in the country of origin. Samples must also conform to stipulated product labelling regulations.

Requirements - Stage two (Application for full registration of product)
This starts with the procurement of an application form for each product - NAFDAC approval is granted for each specific product. This simply means that two products from the same source will still require different approvals and numbers. In fact, two different packages of the same products are processed as different products. The application form is also available at NAFDAC's offices or online at NAFDAC's website. The completed form is to be submitted to the registration division of the agency.

Guidelines Sample for Registration of Locally Manufactured Animal feed, Pet Food and Premixes (NAFDAC/VMAP/004/13)

ITEM	OLD FEES	RECENT FEES
Registration Form	N500 per product	N500 per product
Registration fee	N50,000 + 5% VAT per product	N51,000 per product
(Breakdown) Inspection fee Laboratory Analysis Issuance Certificate	(Breakdown) N10,000+ 5% VAT N20,000 + 5% VAT N20,000 + 5% VAT	(Breakdown) N10,000 + 5% VAT N20,000 + 5% VAT N20,000
Renewal Fee	60% of the total cost	60% of the total cost

Key Requirements
The key requirements are as follows:

(a) DRUGS

1. Application is on single product basis
2. Written application stating name of manufacturer and name (and brand, if applicable) of product.
3. Completed NAFDAC application form (Form D-REG/001)
4. Certificate of Incorporation with the Corporate Affairs Commission, if a company
5. Five (5) copies of the product dossier
6. Three (3) packs of the products samples
7. Notarised original copy of the duly executed Power of Attorney from the product manufacturer (imported product)
8. Certificate of Manufacture issued by the competent health or regulatory authority in country of origin and authenticated by the Nigerian Mission in that country (if foreign import). Where there is no Nigerian mission, The British High Commission or an ECOWAS country Mission will authenticate.

9. If contract-manufactured, Contract Manufacturing Agreement, properly executed and notarised by a Notary Public in the country of manufacture.
10. Current World Health Organisation Goods Manufacturing Practice Certificate for the manufacturer, authenticated by the Nigerian Mission.
11. Certificate of Pharmaceutical Products (COPP) duly issued and authenticated
12. Current Superintendent Pharmacists license to practice issued by the Pharmaceutical Council of Nigeria
13. Premises Registration License from Pharmacists Council of Nigeria (PCN)
14. Certificate of Registration of brand name with trademark registry in the Ministry of Commerce here in Nigeria
15. Letter of invitation from manufacturer to inspect factory abroad, stating full name and location of plant.
16. The applicable fee payable only if documents are confirmed to be satisfactory.

Guidelines Sample for Manufacturers of Pesticides, Agrochemicals and Fertilizers in Nigeria

ITEM	OLD FEES	RECENT FEE
Tariff for New import Permit	N64,000 per product	N102,000 per product
(Breakdown) Application form Permit (1st 25 items) Inspection	(Breakdown) N1,000 N25,000 + 5% VAT N10,000 + 5% VAT	(Breakdown) N1,000 N40,000 N20,000 + 5% VAT
Additional page for new import permit	No old fees	N30,000
Additional page for renewal import permit	No old fees	N25,000
Reinspection fee (After 2 years)	N10,500	N21,000

SESSION 3: IMPORTANT QUESTIONS AND ANSWERS SECTION
How long does it take to get NAFDAC registration?
Obiazikwor says, "I can say it will take three months, if all requirements are met as and when due. Getting your product registration certificate takes a maximum of six (6) months after the date of approval to be ready. You can also register your product yourself without knowing anybody in NAFDAC or going through an agent."

WHERE IS THE NAFDAC REGISTRATION OFFICE?
In Lagos, with the following addresses.
(a) NAFDAC Central Laboratory Complex
3/4 Oshodi/Apapa Expressway, Oshodi, Lagos.
(For Registration and Regulatory Affairs Directorate, Legal Unit, Establishment Inspection Directorate, Food Laboratory, Narcotics and Controlled Substances Directorate).
(b) NAFDAC Central Drug and Vaccines Laboratory (CDVL)
Edmund Crescent, Yaba, Lagos (for Drug Laboratory and Ports Inspection Directorate).
(c) NAFDAC Enforcement Directorate. Ahmadu Bello Way (Behind Nigerian Air Force Camp by Legico B/stop), Victoria Island – Lagos.

What is NAFDAC's website and e-mail address?
Website: www.NAFDAC.gov.ng
E-mail: NAFDAC@NAFDAC.gov.ng

Can I do test marketing of my product before registration?
No, test marketing of food products is not permitted.

How do I know that the name I want to use for registration of my product will be accepted by NAFDAC?
Write formally to NAFDAC for *clearance of name* which can hold for 2 weeks only.

When is the product likely to come out of the laboratory?
Six — Eight weeks

FOR A SMALL-SCALE BUSINESS, WHEN IS THE RIGHT TIME OR STAGE TO START PROCESSING YOUR REGISTRATION?

Obiaziakwor says, "If I may say this, there are ample benefits in starting with NAFDAC, even at the conceptualization stage, but people are fond of running away from us and they have tagged us as an unfriendly organisation. NAFDAC can put you through your business."

WHAT IS THE PENALTY FOR THOSE WHO FLOUT NAFDAC LAWS?

Obiazikwor says, "For example, more than N20 billion worth of counterfeit drugs, unwholesome foods and other substandard regulated products have been confiscated and destroyed since Dr. Paul Orhii assumed office.

"For the first time in the history of Nigeria and even worldwide, NAFDAC recently got the Federal High Court in Lagos to pass 14 years' jail term on each of the two-production staff of Barewa Pharmaceutical Company, which had manufactured the deadly 'My Pikin' Teething Mixture (Drug) that killed 84 Nigerian children in 2008 shortly before Dr. Paul Orhii assumed office.

"NAFDAC has secured five other major convictions of fake drug offenders, while more than 124 cases are currently pending in court. More than 70 other counterfeit product offenders are currently under investigation.

"Anybody who has lived in Nigeria or monitored the events here in recent years will definitely know that NAFDAC is one government agency that has shown full commitment to executing its mandate without fear or favour. NAFDAC is empowered by the relevant laws to ensure that no processed food shall be manufactured in, imported into, exported from, or advertised, sold or distributed in Nigeria, without NAFDAC's approval.

"To do so will be in breach of the law and NAFDAC has shown it has no sympathy for such offenders. The prescribed penalties are stiff, including forfeiture of the goods. As NAFDAC has continually demonstrated, applying the full weight of the law is not an option it shies away from. If you are serious about the business you propose to engage in, the sensible way is to fully comply with the regulatory requirements.

WHY OUR PRODUCT WHICH IS AN INTERNATIONAL PRODUCT CAN'T BE ACCEPTED AS SOLD ALL OVER THE WORLD.

Because products must comply with the labelling regulations developed to meet the needs of Nigeria.

HOW AND WHERE ARE CLINICAL TRIALS CONDUCTED?

Clinical trials are conducted in accordance with good clinical practice (GCP) and are conducted in research institutions.

WHAT ARE THE REQUIREMENTS TO CONDUCT CLINICAL TRIALS IN NIGERIA?

The requirements for clinical trials can be obtained from our website: www.nafdacnigeria.gov.ng.

- **ARE CLINICAL TRIALS DIRECTLY SUPERVISED BY NAFDAC?**
  Yes.

  DO FOREIGN DRUGS GET SUBJECTED TO CLINICAL TRIALS BEFORE THEY ARE ALLOWED FOR USE IN THE COUNTRY?
  Yes. Particularly if the drug does not have adequate and well documented use in black population or it has some race specific properties or its efficacy, safety and usefulness need to be proven in our population.

  DO NAFDAC CHOOSE INVESTIGATORS TO CONDUCT CLINICAL TRIALS?
  No. Sponsors and applicants are responsible for the choice of their trial investigators.

  HOW MANY STUDY SITES ARE CLINICAL TRIALS ARE SUPPOSED TO BE CONDUCTED? At least two centres.

HOW LONG DOES IT TAKE TO CONDUCT CLINICAL TRIALS?
It depends on t a number of factors, some of which are:

a) The design of the trial.

b) The nature of the investigational product.

c) The investigational product.

d) The rate of recruitment of trial participants, etc.

HOW MANY PEOPLE ARE SUPPOSED TO PARTICIPATE IN CLINICAL TRIALS?
The number of participants to be involved in a study depends on the phase of the study (I, II, III or IV) and the trial design.

HOW MUCH DOES IT TAKE TO CONDUCT CLINICAL TRIAL IN NIGERIA?
The applicant needs to pay NAFDAC N200, 000.00 plus 5% VAT for imported products and N50, 000.00 plus 5%VAT for local and herbal products. Other monetary expenses related to the conduct of the trial are handled between the sponsors and the investigators.

HOW MANY DRUGS ARE CURRENTLY UNDERGOING CLINICAL TRIALS NOW?
Five products.

LIST OF BANNED FOOD COLOURS AND / OR ADDITIVES.
This is in accordance with Codex, EU, and FDA list of Banned Colours and / or food additives. This is usually downloaded on www.codexalimentarius.net, www.fda.gov , and www.eu.net .

CODEX LIST OF FOOD CONTAMINANTS AND MAXIMUM LIMIT IN DIFFERENT CATEGORIES OF FOODS
This is in accordance with Codex, EU, and USFDA position on maximum limit of contaminants in foods. However, in some cases it depends on country's position as some external factors can contribute to high values of contaminants in foods. These values can be downloaded on the websites given above.

INSIGHT 6: IMPLEMENTATION OF BUSINESS STRATEGIES IN PROMOTING YOUR BUSINESS

a) **Develop a unique selling plan:** your next step is to develop a culture for your business that will differentiate you from your competitors. It is an effective marketing strategy to position yourself as the best choice in the industry which is known as unique selling preposition (USP) or essential selling advantage (ESA). It gives you a place in the industry and tells potential clients why they must patronise you and not others.

b) **Create database for your clients and potential customers:** creating a database will give you a competitive edge over others. The database contains names, phone number and addresses of clients and potential customers, with your database you can keep in touch with them and create long lasting relationship.

c) **Provide quality product and services:** For you to sustain and increase your present profit, your product and service must meet the expectation of customers. Once they know and have tried your quality product they will always come back for more. Just by that, they would start recommending you to friends and family in no time.

d) **Study the activities of your competitors:** For example, you must take note and learn from what they are doing right and what they are doing wrong. Once you know this then you can strive to do it better than they are doing it.

e) **Packaging:** The truth of the matter is packaging is everything in today's world, if you can careful and adequately package your products to meet the taste of the consumers, they will buy it even if it is scrapes as long as it is well presented people will buy.

Processes: **To prove the business model, raise cash without selling equity.**

When you are trying to see whether you can turn your passion into a business, avoid selling equity at all costs. Raise cash through other means - such as using your savings, borrowing against your home or credit card, winning business plan competitions, or participating in crowd funding sites in which you exchange a promise to deliver your product in exchange for cash. You might be asking yourself this question; what equity means well I will tell you.

EQUITY:

FINANCE **part of value paid:** the value of a piece of property over and above any mortgage or other liabilities relating to it or can be defined as

STOCK EXCHANGE **stock entitling holder to profits:** shares of stock in a corporation that pays the holder some of its profits

Now you know what equity means under this context of usage.

Forbes says 80 percent of businesses close down within the first year. Don't become statistics; start your business off right with these tips.

b. Do your research

Are you planning to open a fast food joint among a street full of five-star restaurants? Not sure if you should price an original product at $15 each or $25 each from online shopping? When considering your idea, think about the logistics. You need to provide something people need or show them how your product will enrich their lives. Check out locations, competitors' prices, and marketing techniques that other businesses similar to yours use. Get inspiration from them, but forge your own path and be unique.

INSIGHT 6.2: PRE-START-UP INSIGHTS TO CONSIDER FOR YOUR BUSINESS

1. Business plan must be established 3 to 4 months in advance of their implementation
2. Decide on what kind of business you want to go into
3. Determine the regulations guiding the establishment of the business
4. Analyse your strengths and weaknesses
5. Select a product or service
6. Conduct feasibility study of the business
7. Assess your potential share of the market
8. Select a location for your business
9. Borrow money or pool funds from savings or loans to begin
10. Establish goals and objectives of the business
11. Establish figures for short-term, middle-term and long-term targets)
12. Gather information or data relating the proposed goals and objectives

13. Determine the best strategy possible to achieve these goals
14. Develop specific tasks to accomplish each goal
15. Achievement of each task must be evaluated and alternative courses of action may have to be implemented if the results are not satisfactory.

INSIGHT 6.3: WEB SITE BASICS YOU NEED TO KNOW FOR START-UP BUSINESSES

Now you're ready for designing and building your web site. What makes a good web site? Before getting enmeshed in design details, get the big picture by writing a site outline. It's a misconception that you have to throw big dollars at an e-commerce solution. You just have to be a careful shopper for vendors. Having a detailed outline makes the process more efficient. A site outline should include five key areas.

1) **Content:** The key to a successful Web site is content. Give your site visitors lots of interesting information, incentives to visit and buy, and ways to contact you. Once your company's site is up and running, continually update and add fresh content to keep potential and existing customers coming back for more.

2) **Structure:** Next, structure your site. Decide how many pages to have and how they will be linked to each other. Choose graphics and icons that enhance the content. Now organize the content into a script. Your script is the numbered pages that outline the site's content and how pages' flow from one to the next. Page one is your home page, the first page that site visitors will see when they type in your URL. Arrange the icons depicting major content areas in the order you want them. Pages two through whatever correspond to each icon on your home page.

3) **Design:** Site design comes next. Whether you're using an outside designer or doing it yourself, concentrate on simplicity, readability and consistency. Give your Web site's visitors cues using graphics, colour and fonts schemes that make sense to you. For example, if your site offers pet products, should all of the cat-related text and icons items contain blue while dog items are displayed using red? Should all food text and graphics be green, toys red and accessories yellow?

4) **Navigation:** Make it easy and enjoyable for visitors to browse the site. Use no more than two or three links to major areas, never leave visitors at a dead end, and don't make them back up three or four links to get from

one content area to another. Design programs such as Microsoft's FrontPage Express make it easy to create links to other sites. For example, if you have a web site for convention planners, make it easy for visitors to link to city sites where they can find information on recreation and activities in the area.

5) **Credibility:** Your site should look professional and give potential customers the same feeling of confidence that a phone call or face to face visit with you would. In addition, be sure to remind your visitors that you don't exist only in cyberspace. Your company's full contact information should appear on your "Contact us" page.

HANDY TOOLS
There is a wide variety of tools available to help you improve your web site's appearance. If you're able to master HTML and write a script by yourself or get a professional to do that for you, else consider use a WordPress website. Another excellent resource is the large online services, which all have free online tools for web page authoring and site design. Also check out design tools from Tripod (www.tripod.com), with design utilities that allow you to use FrontPage for free; and Angel fire (http://angelfire.com), a service with Web-design tools, including a large graphics library. But that old maxim is true: You get what you pay for, and many sites designed from basic templates are slow and humdrum. Services like BigStep.com, Elated. com, Netfirms.com and WebNow.com offer templates that make their free Web site design programs easy to use with professional-looking results.

HOST WITH THE WEB
Now how does your Web site get on the net? You get online 24/7 by leasing space on someone else's server or host service. A server is simply a computer that is permanently connected to the internet. You connect to a host via the Net using your existing Net provider, then upload your HTML files and graphics in the rented space. From there, anyone can visit your site anytime. There are tons of hosts, so many that you need a strategy to sort through them. CNet's Web site (www.cnet.com) makes comparison shopping easy. It offers ISP fact sheets that compare hosts on a number of variables, starting with price (most begin at about $25 per month). Other variables are: amount of disk space allocated to you, availability of access logs, number of e-mail auto responders (automatic e-mail responses to anyone who has e-mailed you) and forward (e-mails automatically forwarded to a specified address) allowed, customer support availability, database access, uptime (the percentage of time that the service is accessible to visitors), setup and monthly fees. Exactly how much disk space do you need to store your Website? Generally, 1MB can hold several hundred text

pages, or fewer pages when images are included. Web hosts typically offer anywhere from 500MB to several gigabytes of free storage with a contract.

6 BLOGGING TIPS, TECHNIQUES AND STRATEGY

To run a successful blog, there is always one or more technique to be employed. Even in Nigeria, blogging is a highly pure professional career people make a living out of, it requires clever tactics, insights, strategy and much more.

APPLYING THE FOLLOWING STRATEGIES:

Create quality content: good content is unique, entertaining or informative. It discusses things that people want to know in ways they have never heard before. Basically, if it satisfies their search appetite, they are most likely to share it with others if the need arises. Your write-up should be enticing to readers. Try as much as possible to solve people's problem

Consistency and persistence: If you can't build a successful blog if you are not consistent in generating more contents, if you create good content regularly you will attract more followers more than those that do theirs once a week. To build followers create good content on a consistent basis.

Figure out a perfect promotion plan

Promotion plan is one of the quickest ways to attract visitors to your blog. When there is a blog worth promoting and a promotion worth following, your blog starts growing dramatically. You have to know what platforms you want to run your promotion and devise means on how to get visitors/customers or clients.

Leverage on social media platforms

The social media is an attractive tool when it involves blogging. You have a lot of functionalities and flexibility to run promotions suitable for your target market. To build up social media accounts; be informative, not promotional; use images; use hashtags correctly and engage people.

You can use tools such as Hootsuite to get your posts out at the right time, always track when the best time to post on the various social platforms. Figure out which posts are getting you the most traction and emulate those styles.

Use multimedia

Using multimedia should be part of your content creation tactics. Readers like images, infographics, webinars, videos and everything else that stimulates the eyes and ears. Make your blog appealing and eye catching, people will want to see what is going on your blog. Use infographics to capture your most important points in a way that is easy to show off on social media and is more likely to get people interested.

Engage in social forum
The more involved you are with people, the better. When you have a relationship with them, they are more likely to care about the things you have to say. If you want people to engage with them. Apply the following tactics:
- Talk about things that people want to discuss
- Get yourself into conversations
- If people comment on your blog, comment back.
- Re-tweet other people
- Comment on other blogs
- Share another people's content

INSIGHT 6.4: BUSINESS LOCATION AND FEASIBILITY CHECK
GENERAL OVERVIEW

The Country Region, City or town to start your business: The country you set up your business as a small business owner is very important to the success or failure of your business how do I mean? I will tell you; in United States there are some states that have high tax on businesses but lesser tax in some other states, same applies to U.K and every other country on the map of the globe. So, you have to do your research properly before you make that important decision that will be a decider of the future of your business in success or failure. You have to understand the environment you wish to go into and find out what is the government policy on what you want to do? Is your choice business highly appreciated or not? How much of customer base can you build? Remember that your customers are the king of your business if they all leave you, that automatically means no business for you which affects any business including big businesses with big brand names. But on the other hand, big businesses can afford to lose money to get all its customers back but a small business cannot afford such setback for it can close down such business or set them up for cash bankruptcy if not properly handled. You can use already existing business in the country/region/city you wish to do business and see what is the acceptance rate for their products when compared to other cities/towns or countries housing such businesses?

Cost of living: The cost of living in a country can be as important as the growth and expansion of your business though there is an exception to these. There are small businesses that have grown into empire in an economy with high tax rate, and there are some that have grown into empire in regions with very low standard of living or even bad economic situation. Every single business circumstance shared is a product of need. If your product or services are in its highest demand in your locality you can grow such business into big businesses just with a good amount of management skills and packaging. But you really should consider these because setting up a company in a country where tax and cost of living is expensive would most likely affect that business in the long run which can lead the young entrepreneur into frustration and might also lead to the end of the business prematurely.

Labour Availability and Start-Up Cost: This involves what kind of workforce do you want to hire in your business; Are you interested in Automated Labour? or in manual or human Labour? If human Labour, what class of labourers is your company interested in? Availability of human workers for the job in the region or locality the business is currently residing in? if its Automated work line; how readily available are the equipment? Cost for maintenance and repair of such equipment? Cost for initial purchase for such level of workers and cost of replacement or upgrade when necessary? What kind of automated work line are you searching for, is its human working side by side and with your automated process or just having strictly automated machines running the processes? You need to make your cost analysis and productivity implication before making any choice.

Status of already existing Competitor if any for what you want to do: Although I know that we have yet unexplored areas and fields but the truth is, there is no kind of business you want to do right now that somebody else is not doing already or has already done somewhere. All you have to do is look around, ask questions, only then you will find the answers you seek. Find out how they started, as an outsider observing the business is it a small business? Medium scale business or big business? Research on the economic policy and legal involvement concerning that same business? What is the customer base for such kind of business? This and many more questions you need to ask before plunging into the same business. Note the fact that a business is in existence as at the time you carried out your research does not necessarily mean the business is profitable or would stand the test of time. So be careful

Availability of raw materials: This is completely dependent on what kind of business you are setting up? If it's a servicing company, then you need not worry about this but if your business is product based then you need to pay close attention to this. First and foremost, you have to consider how available are the resources for your product? Are they common or scarce? If you can commonly find them around easily then you are safe, if they are hard to come by, I really suggest you reconsider searching for alternative source for raw materials or change your product line completely. Secondly is cost; how much is each of the individual raw materials? How close and reachable are these raw materials to u in terms of Cost? Who are the suppliers involved in the business? Are its seasonal raw materials or some regular raw materials you can find in any dealer shop? How much will it cost to produce in mass production/batches or in samples? Thirdly The already existing business in the line of business you wish to go into what is the distance between the company location and the raw materials/suppliers? What kind of product brand do you want to establish? Finally, how potent/effective is your product? What is the life cycle of your product? Is it perishable or non-perishable? How do you protect the health of your potential customers? What is the risk involved in preserving the product if it's a perishable good would it reduce the quality of the product? What kind of self-preservative do you intend to use? What is the content of this preservative? For product effectiveness/efficiency what are the environmental factors involved? When is the product life cycle best used? Creating awareness to your potential customers concerning how long it can be used? When it should be used? When it shouldn't be taken or used anymore?

Accessibility to suppliers and clients: Transportation cost in moving your raw materials from its source to your company location should be highly considered. Because if you have high transportation cost for your raw materials minus the cost for each individual material, I will automatically affect the price of the product you are selling to your customers. For example, if you are supposed to sell a can drink for 100 naira due to high production cost, transportation cost and cost of raw materials its price tag can go as much as 500 naira reducing your potential customers to only a selected portion of the population instead of selling to an entire population. So, when setting up a location for your company you have to sit down and make a good analysis about how profitable such location will be to your business. Never make hasty decision in choosing a place or making a choice out of impulse because that might just lead to the end of the business in the long run. Or might become an endless hole where most of your money would go to and might not give you the kind of profit you would be expecting.

INSIGHT 7: PUBLIC RELATIONS AND TELLING THE WORLD ABOUT YOUR BUSINESS

JUST WHAT is public relations? And how does it differ from advertising? When you advertise, you pay to have your message placed in a newspaper, on TV or on the radio. In public relations, the article featuring your company is not paid. The print or broadcast reporter writes about or films your company as a result of information he or she received and researched. Publicity is more efficient than advertising for several reasons. First, publicity is far more cost-effective. Even if it isn't free, your only expenses are generally phone calls and mailings to the media.

Secondly, publicity has greater longevity than advertising. An article about your business will be remembered longer than an ad. Publicity also reaches a much wider audience than advertising generally does. Sometimes, your story might be picked up by the national media, spreading the word about your business all over the country.

Finally, and most important, publicity has greater credibility with the public than advertising. Prospective investors feel that if an objective third party—the magazine, radio or newspaper reporter—is featuring your company, you must be doing something worthwhile. Why do some companies succeed in generating publicity while others don't? It has been proved time and time again that no matter how large or small your business, the key to securing publicity is identifying your target market and developing a well-planned public relations campaign. To get your company noticed, follow these steps.

1) **Write your positioning statement.** This sums up in a few sentences what makes your business different from the competition.
2) **List your objectives.** What do you hope to achieve for your company through the publicity plan you put into action? List your top five goals in order of priority. Be specific and always set deadlines.
3) **Identify your target customers.** For example, are they male or female? What is their age range? What are their lifestyles, incomes and buying habits? Where do they live?
4) **Identify your target media.** List newspapers and TV and radio programs that would be appropriate outlets. Make a complete list of the media you want to target, then call them and ask who you should contact regarding your area of business. Identify the specific reporter or producer covering your area so you can contact him or her directly. Your local library has media reference books that list contact names and numbers. Make your own media directory listing names, addresses and phone and fax numbers. Separate TV, radio and print sources. Know the beats covered

by different reporters so you can be sure to pitch your ideas to the appropriate person.

5) **Develop story angles** you'd want to read in the newspaper or see on television. Keeping in mind the media you are approaching; make a list of ideas you can pitch to them. If you own a clothing store, for example, you could alert the local media to a fashion trend in your area. What's flying out of your store so fast you can't keep it in stock? If its shirts featuring the American flag, you could talk to the media about the return of patriotism. Then arrange for a reporter to speak with some of your customers about why they purchased that particular shirt. Suggest the newspaper send a photographer to take picture of your customers wearing the shirts.

6) **Make the pitch.** Put your thoughts on paper and send a "pitch letter" to the reporter. Start with a question or an interesting fact relating your business to the target medium's audience. For instance, if you were writing for a magazine aimed at older people, you could start off with: "Did you know over half of women age 50 and older have not begun saving for retirement?" Then lead into your pitch: "As a certified financial planner, I can offer your prospective investors twenty tips to start them on the road to a financially comfortable retirement." Make sure your letter is no longer than one page, and include your telephone number so the reporter can contact you. If appropriate, include a press release with your letter (see "Meet the Press" on page 11). Be sure to include your positioning statement in any correspondence or press releases you sent.

7) **Follow up.** Following up is the key to securing coverage. Wait four to six days after you've sent the information, then follow up your pitch letter with a telephone call. If you leave a message on voice mail and the reporter does not call you back, call again until you get him or her on the phone. Do not leave a second message within five days of the first. If the reporter requests additional information, send it immediately and follow up to confirm receipt.

SESSION1: HOW TO PROMOTE PRODUCTS WITH SOCIAL MEDIA: 4 PRACTICAL EXAMPLES

✓ Do you want to promote your product online?
✓ Are you looking for ways to use social media to increase your sales?
✓ Both well-known and start-up companies are mixing social media and e-commerce to garner more sales.

Combine Social Media and E-Commerce

Companies have tried to mesh social media and e-commerce before, most notably in 2012 when everyone from Gap to GameStop to JC Penney ended up shuttering their social media stores. Audiences weren't ready to buy from Facebook or other platforms.

Pioneering companies are bringing social e-commerce back by integrating sites like Instagram with websites that look similar to the social sites users are familiar with (e.g., Pinterest). Blurring the lines among social media, websites and e-commerce means these important marketing methods are no longer stand-alone components. Instead, they're one large, fully branded push to increase sales.

1: Link Product Photos with Product Pages

Nordstrom's Instagram fans (all 530,000 of them) are looking for a quick fix of the latest trends and products. When fans find a product they can't live without, it's not uncommon for them to leave a comment asking how and where to buy it. While Nordstrom continues to respond to those comments on Instagram, they're starting to send people to their new Pinterest site that pulls in their Instagram product photos and links them directly to product pages.

Nordstrom created the site with Like2Buy (by Curalate) to partner e-commerce with their significant Instagram engagement. The result is an easier way for fans to buy the products they love right then and there.

How You Can Do It Too

If you're ready to invest, you can **try out Like2Buy** yourself or **look at** Olapic. let's you republish user-generated photos within your site in various ways. However, both options are expensive. If you're looking for a more reasonably priced option, you can **start by creating your own Pinterest-themed website for your e-commerce merchandise**. There are plenty of templates available and Pinterest user Robin Good has handpicked a few of the best for WordPress.

2: Create a Familiar Space

Whether you're working with your website or your social media profiles, as a marketer your question is always going to be "how can we make money here?"

For example, Pinterest is a popular site for sure. The site makes it easy to find new ideas and organize your own. Its feed is filled with attractive pictures and the site is easy to use. In short, people love it. But you may not be making money there.

Social commerce site Wanelo is addressing that problem. They've created a "social shopping site that resembles a well-designed window display." In other words, it provides the familiar feel of Pinterest.

Similar to Pinterest, Wanelo visitors can find items they love, tag them and categorize them into neat little collections. When users browse and eventually buy from a store, that store in turn sends a portion of each sale back to Wanelo.

How You Can Do It Too

There are plenty of photography collage-style themes out there that let you **create individual galleries**. You can use them to **mix and match various products to create a whole set and link to your e-commerce shop**.

The popular Sentinel theme allows for the same type of gallery function, but also holds YouTube and Vimeo clips if you'd like to incorporate video.

3: Use Customers' Feedback

Like the Wanelos and Polyvores out there, Fancy lets users find, collect and buy items from various companies. To set itself apart, it also offers a monthly box subscription (Fancy Boxes) that delivers gourmet food. So where does the social element come in? Fancy's 2 million+ members help curate (via voting) the foods that show up in each month's box. Encouraging this kind of customer input further reinforces that Fancy truly cares about customers and values their feedback. It's a great way to build brand loyalty and turn a profit at the same time.

How You Can Do It Too

The logistics of setting up a subscription goodie delivery service is far too involved to cover in just one article, but you can still benefit from the curation aspect. **Use your website and social media profiles to ask customers what they'd like to see** in next month's box.

The Ultimate Modern Magazine theme for WordPress lets you **curate and spotlight those products** and allows users to review and rate products. Of course, if you'd rather, you can **advertise your products on a curation site** and take advantage of their technology and traffic!

4: Include Customer Images on Product Pages

BlackMilk, a company dedicated to making women's leggings more than just a fashion accessory, asks customers to take pictures of themselves wearing the products and tag the pictures when they share them to Instagram or Facebook.

The company figures if you're going to take a selfie wearing their products, why not share it with other customers? The site even includes instructions on how to tag the photos using Facebook and Instagram.

BlackMilk pulls the hash tagged pictures into their product pages so other customers can see how the clothing fits and looks on others and see how fun it is to wear. Bringing social proof to product pages is one more way to encourage visitors to buy.

To give product pages this look-book functionality, BlackMilk uses the Show. See. Sold add-on that works with the Shopify platform. The add-on lets users zoom, rotate, spin and filter products to see exactly what they want, as well as buy directly.

How You Can Do It Too

BlackMilk has a lot of enviable functionality that other e-commerce stores would be wise to notice and possibly implement. To add this kind of tech to your own site, there are plenty of Instagram plugins for WordPress (and stand-alone sites) that will **show your tagged photos, as well as other users' photos, in the** sidebar of your website.

Over to You

You already have people shopping your site, finding your products on Instagram and hash tagging pictures of themselves using or wearing your products. Take advantage of that social interaction and make it easier for people to buy in the moment.

Recreating a familiar, Pinterest-like site with similar intuitive navigation makes visitors feel at ease. Pulling in your Instagram product feed and linking it directly to product pages makes it easier for fans and customers to buy on the spot—without having to click away to search for the product, click to the site and buy the product.

Expect to see even greater interactivity as sites begin to fully explore what's possible when websites, social media and e-commerce collide.

INSIGHT 8: HIRE A SUPPORT TEAM (RECURIT EMPLOYEES)

Even if you think of yourself as a one-person operation, you'll need a team of support people to help you create a successful business. From contractors and suppliers to advisory board members and employees, each of these individuals can help make or break your new business. Start networking—with friends, family, business associates, and the professionals in your life— to widen your network and choose the best people for your team. Your advisory board can include a mix of professional peers, legal or financial advisers, or mentors. You need to develop a network of advisers whose talents, knowledge, resources and skills Can be used to help you handle the demands of your business. Besides providing you with Sound advice, the collaborative talents of your team can also help you obtain larger projects and grow with your clients' needs. Meet with them a few times a year to solicit their professional feedback. If you need to hire employees, consider interns, students or part-timers as your first time hires. If you think you won't need permanent employees in the beginning, you can also look into temporary services and independent contractors. If you're planning to hire someone on full time, however, remember that the employees you hire can make or break your business. While you may be tempted to hire the first person who walks in the door "just to get it over with," doing so can be a fatal error. A small company just can't afford to carry deadwood on its staff, so start smart by taking time to figure out your staff needs before you begin looking for job candidates.

Training of staff and Payment: How successful your business will be, it will completely rest on the team you are working with, for work with a team that shares in your vision, believes in your vision and are willing to give you their best and see how fast your business will grow from struggling to profitable then into big business in little or no time. That's why business management body without a team is like an aircraft without an engine. So, what that means is that you have to consciously interview your potential staff, then train them on the job to not only understand customer but to know how to bring customers into buying from the company. Some other fellows believe its expensive training workers so they are basically looking for the already trained workers that would work them well that is good and has its merits too but if that worker does not share in the company dreams, vision and goal of the company it's as good as a wasted investment. So, whatever it is you are doing, it's your responsibility to train your staff and induce into them team spirit and working together with the company to build it which goes with monthly reward and incentives. That alone can spring passion and loyalty into them if followed up with motivation and inspiration in self-growth. For whatever you do, giving your workers a good and liveable pay is another great way of motivating them but you as a person must first build the business up to the point where a need for extra hand(staff) is needed so as to have a foundational resource to hire your staff.

HIRING STAFF

1) Recruitment

2) Training

3) Motivation/inspiration

4) Keeping them focus

5) Building Loyalty

Employing People

Your staff are one of your greatest business assets, so it's vital that you hire the right people for the job. Once you've found good staff it's important to look after them to create a vibrant business. Staff can bring exciting, dynamic ideas and possibilities but you will also have a number of legal obligations to think about.

In this section we'll look at some of the most common questions small business owners have about managing their staff. It can be a complicated and confusing area, so don't hesitate to ask for help.

Employee or contractor?

It's important that you know the difference between an employee and a contractor, as you will have different obligations for each.).

Types of employment

Types of employment can range from full time, through to piece-work and casual and everything else in between. You need to know the options, so your final staffing combination is one that best suits the needs of your business. There are a variety of employment types that you can offer staff including full time, part-time, casual, fixed term employment, traineeships and apprenticeship.

Recruitment and selection

Your staff are instrumental to the success of your business so you want to make sure that you recruit the right person for the right job. The 'right' person will vary from business to business and will be determined by a number of factors. Throughout your recruitment process keep in mind that you want to attract a small group of suitable candidates not a large group of unsuitable candidates.

Generally, there are five steps to successfully selecting and recruiting staff:

- **Step 1:** Define the job, and know what you're looking for
- **Step 2:** Attract candidates
- **Step 3:** Managing applications
- **Step 4:** Conducting interviews
- **Step 5**: Award the job

Obligations to employees

In Australia as a case study, there are a range of obligations that all employers must adhere to by law. These include provision for:

- insurance;
- tax and superannuation;
- employment records;
- staff health and safety
- legal obligations; and
- paid parental leave.

Employment records

In both the state and national system, all time and wages records must be kept for at least seven years, and records relating to calculation of long service leave should be kept for at least 10 years.

Terminating an employee's employment

Terminating an employee's employment should be done carefully. When you terminate a worker's contract you must provide them with appropriate notice, any leave and termination entitlements comply with any relevant award or agreement and depending whether you are in the state or national system, comply with other termination requirements.

CHAPTER 7
BEYOND THE IDEA PHASE
INSIGHT 9: EXECUTE YOUR MARKETING PLANS

Your press release should follow the standard format: typed and double spaced on white letterhead with a contact person's name, title, company, address and phone number in the upper right-hand corner. Below this information, put a brief, eye catching headline in bold type. A dateline—for example, "Los Angeles, California, December 2, 2002"—leads into the first sentence of the release. Limit your press releases to one or two pages at most.

If you've already created a marketing plan designed to help you spread the word about your business. Now's the time to establish your marketing infrastructure. You work against yourself when you're not prepared to respond to opportunities that result from your marketing efforts. Your stationery, business cards and marketing materials should be ready for distribution. If your customers can reach you via e-mail, set up auto responders to handle their queries. Have a phone system in place that allows customers to easily get in touch with you. Develop a Web site that offers information on your company and its products and services. Whatever response methods buyers can use to contact you; you should have materials that can be sent via those same mediums. Jump into action: Mail a press release to the local media announcing the opening of your business. Do a joint mailing with other complementary businesses to widen your reach. Beat the deadline for your Yellow Pages ad, and talk with your manufacturer about co-op advertising opportunities. Take advantage of all free directory listings. Contribute an article to a trade journal. Send out special offer postcards to prospects. Create a coupon offer. Make a speech at a networking event. Track the results of your devices by asking all respondents how they heard about you.

NETWORKING

The ability to network is a crucial skill any start-up entrepreneur must have. How else will you meet the clients and contacts necessary to grow your business? The trick with networking is to be proactive. This means taking control of the situation instead of just reacting to it. Networking requires going beyond your comfort zone and challenging yourself.

Try these tips:
1) **Set a goal to meet five (or more) new people at each event.** Whenever you attend a group, whether a party, mixer or industry luncheon, make a point of heading straight for people you don't know. Greet newcomers

(they'll love you for it!). If you don't make this goal a habit, you'll naturally gravitate towards the same old acquaintances.

2) **Try one or two new groups per month.** You can attend almost any organization's meetings a few times before you must join. This is another way to stretch yourself and make a new set of contacts.

3) **Carry business cards everywhere.** You never know when you might meet a key contact, and if you don't have your cards, you lose. Take your cards to the gym, parties, the grocery store, even when you're walking the dog.

4) **Don't make a beeline for your seat.** Take advantage of networking time before you have to sit down. Once the meeting starts, you won't be able to mingle.

5) **Don't sit by people you know.** Mealtime is a prime time for meeting people. You may be in that seat for hours, so don't limit your opportunities by sitting with friends. Remember, you're spending precious time and money to attend this event.

6) **Get active.** People remember and do business with leaders. Don't just warm a chair; join a committee or become a board member. If you don't have time for that, volunteer to help with hospitality at the door or with checking people in. This gives you a great reason to talk to others, gets you involved in the inner workings of the group, and provides you with more visibility.

7) **Be friendly and approachable.** Make people feel welcome. Find out what brought them there and see if there is any way you can help them. Introduce them to others, make business suggestions or give them a referral. What goes around comes around. If you make the effort to help others, you'll find people helping you.

8) **Set a goal for what you expect from each meeting.** Your goals can vary from meeting to meeting. Examples include learning about the speaker's topic, looking for new prospects, discovering industry trends or connecting with peers. If you work from home, you may find your purpose is simply to get out and talk to people face to face.

9) **Be willing to give to receive.** Networking is a two-way street. Don't expect new contacts to shower you with referrals and business unless

you're equally generous. Follow up on contacts; keep in touch with them; and share information that might benefit them.

INSIGHT 9.1: MARKETING YOUR BUSINESS

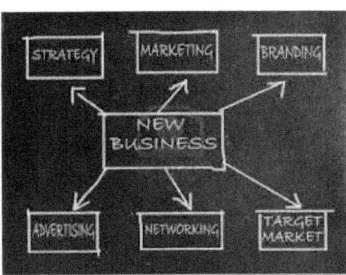

Figure 7: Business Insight

Marketing is an integrated process through which companies build strong customer relationships and create value for their customers and for themselves. It is the process by which a business decides what it will sell? To whom? When and how? And then does it. Marketing involves the strategic planning of a business (or other organizational provider) through to every customer engagement, including market research, product development, branding, advertising and promotion, methods of selling, customer service, and extending to the acquisition of development of new businesses.

SUCCESS FACTORS IN MARKETING

The key success factors are those elements that are necessary in order for the firm to achieve its marketing objectives. A couple of examples of this include:

a) Access to essential unique resources
b) Ability to achieve economies of scale
c) Access to distribution channels
d) Technological progress

It is necessary you remember that the key success factors may change over time, especially as the product progresses through its life cycle.

TOOLS FOR MARKETING

Social Media Marketing: This is one very effective way you can market your products and services more judiciously with little or no money from your pocket if you know how. It can be beneficial to your business if you use it the right way.

Real Estate Marketing: This demands you to be trendy and innovative in order to attract clients to your business and not throw away your money.

Marketing in Page: As an entrepreneur, any effective marketing strategy that will build relationship and get new clients to your business must interest you. In this marketing strategy you can market your business using Facebook or twitter. This is an effective platform to boost sales and earn more profits.

Strategies for Marketing Page: Another platform for marketing is usage of websites i.e. building a website that advertises you and what you are selling. It has been noted that most people prefer to use search engines in searching for goods and services so using websites that drives traffic to your site would be very important if you want the world to know what you do.

Marketing among Friends: This can be another means of advertisement because your friends can serve as great tool in telling others about you and reasons why they should patronise your product or services. But on the other hand, some people prefer to do business with people they know and they can trust rather than dealing with a complete stranger they don't know.

Marketing Strategy: This involves how the marketing plan will work in relations to all factors of business entity and activity, particularly including competitors, customers and demographics, technology and communications.

INSIGHT 9.2: BUSINESS SALES APPROACHES

There's no one best way to sell. Your personality and background will determine which type of sales technique is most effective for you. Even if you have a methodology that works well, it's a good idea to try a different approach now and then. Trying new methods keeps you out of a route, and you may be surprised by how well a new strategy works for you. In fact, many salespeople do best by using a combination of approaches, such as:

The Instant Buddy

People will be more willing to buy from someone they like. Salespeople who use this approach are warm and friendly, asking questions and showing interest in their prospects. They try to connect on an emotional level with a prospective customer. This approach can be very effective, but only in the right hands. Don't try to make friends with a prospect unless you really mean it – people can tell if you're faking it, and they'll be very unhappy with you. You'll also need to do some follow through to demonstrate that you really do like the prospect. For example, if you chat about the prospects eleven-month old baby during your appointment, you should follow up by sending a card and/or small gift on the child's first birthday.

The Guru

Salespeople who prefer a more logical and less emotional approach often set themselves the task of becoming experts in anything and everything related to their industry. They position themselves as problem-solvers, able to answer any question and tackle any issue that the prospect lays before them. The guru approach requires plenty of work learning the relevant information and keeping up with changes in your industry. But if you're willing to put in the time it takes, you can do very well both in selling to your prospects and generating plenty of referrals. Once customers realize what a great resource you are, they're quite likely to send friends and co-workers with questions straight to you.

The Consultant

This approach combines the 'guru' and 'buddy' approaches. The salesperson who elects to use the consultant approach presents herself as an expert who has the customer's best interests in mind. She knows all about her company's products and by asking a prospect a few questions, she can match him up with the best product for his needs. As an approach that combines the best qualities of the first two methods, it's extremely effective. But it also requires a great deal of time and effort on a salesperson's part. You must be both knowledgeable and able to make an emotional connection with your prospects. If you can manage both of these feats, your sales will take off like a rocket.

The Networker

Networking can be a big help for any salesperson. The dedicated networker takes it to the next level, setting up and maintaining a web of friends, co-workers, salespeople from other companies, customers and former customers, and anyone else he meets. A strong enough network will create an ongoing flow of warm leads that can provide most or even all of the salesperson's needs. With this approach, you'll spend a great deal of time cultivating people. It's a highly effective technique for salespeople who enjoy attending various events, parties, and so on and meeting new people. Just remember that you'll need to reciprocate by doing favours and sending leads back to the people who've helped you in their turn.

The Hard Seller

Best described as "scare the prospect into buying," the hard sell approach is what gives salespeople their bad reputation. Hard selling involves getting someone to buy a product even though he doesn't want or need it. Methods range from bullying ("Buy this now or you'll feel stupid tomorrow") to manipulation ("If you don't buy from me, I'll lose my job") to outright deception ("This product has a much better safety record than the competition").

No ethical salesperson should use a hard sell approach. Sadly, there are still salespeople who use this type of sales strategy, even though the result is customers who never buy again and, sooner or later, a bad reputation for the company as a whole. Stick with one or more of the first four approaches – they are all both effective and ethical.

HOW TO APPROACH PRODUCT BASE BUSINESS?

A strong first impression will greatly increase your chances of selling your products to a business owner or a potential customer. Knowing how to approach a business and zero in on its needs is a key trait of a successful salesman. Learning this approach is more challenging than implementing it. Once you have perfected your pitch, you need to learn to project confidence. If you believe in what you're selling, the business will believe in it. If you don't sound convincing, you will likely leave without making a sale.

Sell your Invention Idea Find Companies that Help Inventors. Request Free Invention Kit on this site www.inventionideas.org

Procedure 1

Select a sample of the best products from your inventory. Ensure that the products are intact, in working order and of the highest quality.

Procedure 2

Design a presentation suited to your products. Either arrange a sample in an appealing, logical order, or put together a portfolio that clearly displays photographs of what you have to offer. Your display should leave no doubt about the quality and usefulness of your products. Products should be grouped by type, price or style.

Procedure 3

Select companies that you feel could benefit from your products. Start with companies in your geographic location. If successful, you will make a number of contacts you can use to generate further leads.

Procedure 4

Write down a cold-call script. This is the general pitch you will make when you contact a company. Do not read this verbatim as it will sound artificial and forced. Use it as a general guide. Practice out loud several times before actually making the call.

Procedure 5

Write down a list of questions you think the company may ask during the initial call. Determine the best way to answer them and write it down as well. Being prepared will allow for a more effective approach.

Procedure 6

Contact your targeted companies and make your pitch. Be prepared to adapt to questions the receptionist may ask you. If you get a question you haven't received before, add it to your list. Make an appointment to pitch your product if the company is open to a presentation.

Procedure 7

Dress professionally the day of the presentation. Wear a clean, pressed suit, and make sure to shave, if needed, and style your hair appropriately. Make sure your presentation is organized and clean.

Procedure 8

Arrive at the company a few minutes early. If you arrive too early, you run the risk of looking overeager and needy. If you arrive late, it looks unprofessional.

Procedure 9

Present your product confidently. If you don't believe in what you're selling, the company won't either.

Procedure 10

Review your presentation once you are finished. Assess what worked and what could be improved. Use the experience to improve the next time you approach a company to sell your products.

ITEMIZING STARTING A PRODUCT-BASED BUSINESS (google.com, ITEMIZING STARTING A PRODUCT-BASED BUSINESS)

1. Check your idea.

Before plunging head on to your entrepreneurial venture, your first step should be to ascertain the viability of your business. After developing the product, check your potential competitors in the market, both direct and indirect. If you have created a unique Chinese sauce, for example, you need to check out your indirect competitors including makers of other Spanish sauces. How will your sauce be used and what food products go along with it? Why will people use your sauce? It's one thing to have a good idea, and another to create a demand for your idea.

2. Check the market for your product.

You may have a great product, but are you in the right market? You may have a great idea for winter gear, but if you live in sunny California, you may have little demand for your product. How will you reach your market? What are the buying behaviours of your consumers? How many of your products do they buy in a month? Or is your product seasonal? If so, how will you survive the full season? Your market (perhaps you could open an online store instead of a retail store) will define your distribution mechanism, pricing structure, and other business variables.

3. Know your legal structure.

Your legal structure will depend on the liability you are willing to take, the number of investors, the tax structure, etc. If you are 1-person business, you may start out as sole proprietorship. But if you have partners or investors, you can either start a partnership, LLC or corporation. Learn the pros and cons of each structure and pick one that is most suited to your circumstances.

4. Availability of financing.

Even with a great idea and a ready market, you are bound to fail if you do not have adequate capital. Know your manufacturing and operational, and other start-up expenses. Determine where you will get the money – from your savings, relatives and family, friends, bank, angel investors, or SBA. If you are planning to invite partners to the venture, clarify the roles and responsibilities of each and make sure that all agreements are made in writing.

5. Plan out your operations.

Look for suppliers and distributors. Identify where you can get your ingredients and raw materials. Think how the packaging will be done; many great new products languish in store shelves because of poor packaging. How well your product or service is presented will determine the initial consumer acceptance or rejection. Determine where and how you will sell the product. A specialty product, for example, must not be overly distributed as it could lose its perception as a specialty good. A mass-market product, on the other hand, must be distributed with consumer convenience as the prime consideration.

6. Develop your marketing program.

How will you move your product? How will people know that your product exists? You need to think how you will market and promote your product. Will you advertise in a publication that reaches your market? How much will that cost? Your marketing strategy should be based on how your product will reach and affect your target market. Your product must be designed and marketed to clearly demonstrate how it will satisfy an unsatisfied need.

7. Write a business plan.

After doing steps 1-6, you will have enough information to help your need to write a business plan. This is essential as it helps you think through your business and what you really need to do. If you are looking for investors, they will also want to see your business plan.

8. Know the zoning regulations, if you are planning to do your business at home.

Some counties may have limitations on what you can do inside your house for commercial purposes. Zoning considerations usually include the amount of traffic, disturbance levels, and safety considerations. Take this time to check out the licenses and permits that your business may require. If you will be selling food products, consult your government's food administration office.

9. Initiate the business registration process.

Depending on the complexity of your legal structure, you may need to consult a lawyer. After you have filed your business registration and fictitious name, open a separate bank account for your business. You may also need to get an Employer Identification Number if you live in United States.

10. Get insurance to protect your property from damage, theft or other unforeseen circumstances.

Risk and entrepreneurship always go hand-in-hand, and your goal is to minimize your risks. However, beware of "overprotection" or getting too much insurance for your business. The rule of thumb is to carry insurance only on what the business cannot afford to cover in the event of misfortune.

11. Protect your product.

If you created an original Chinese sauce or a new thermal system for mittens, protect it with patents. It may be expensive and time consuming, but it reduces the risk of someone else claiming your product as their own.

12. Get your business cards ready, as well as brochures, stationary and other business forms.

If you are planning to promote your product on the web, start creating your online presence. You're now ready to open your business! Set a starting date, and plan out this event. You may send press releases to local newspapers about your great new sauce for example. You can take this opportunity to spread the word about your business. Starting a business is not easy as 1-2-3. There will be a lot of challenges along the way. But if you believe in yourself and in your product, you will go a long way.

INSIGHT 9.3: RE-THINK YOUR SALES METHOD
(GARY LOCKWOOD) **SALES APPROACH PERSPECTIVE**

Demanding customers - fierce competition - breath-taking technological innovation...

These are the realities of today's global marketplace... realities that have changed forever the way we do business, especially the way we sell. Gone are the days when salespeople could rely on charming small-talk and aggressive closing techniques alone to generate business.

Many traditional selling approaches regard selling as something the seller does to the buyer. They sell them something. The result of this attitude to sales is that many salespeople adapt a manipulative, almost coercive style of selling. Some salespeople think of selling as pushing a customer into buying, and success as a victory. Often, people fear salespeople and distrust them. They think of salespeople as fast talking and slick. They are wary of being sold something they really don't need or want. Have you ever been sold something, and then regretted it later? How did you feel about the salesperson?

The more modern and enlightened view of selling is that the role of the sales person is to help the customer make good buying decisions. Someone seen as an ally and adviser. A business partner who can be relied upon to provide valuable help and advice as well as supply vital goods and services. The outcome of a sale is not that one-person gains at the expense of the other, but that a win-win outcome is forged by the two parties who both leave feeling good about the transaction and with a positive commitment to each other.

The role of the professional salesperson is largely a product of this century. Before the industrial revolution, the people who made things were also responsible for selling their goods. As the availability of consumer goods expanded, the need arose for people who specialized in guiding consumer decisions. The role of salesperson has changed dramatically over the years, largely as a result of the changing relationship between availability of products and services being sold and the demand of the consumer for those products and services. Since World War II, with the increasing growth of enabling technology, and the explosion of competition, we have seen availability outstrip demand. In those situations, we started to see sellers pushing their goods and services at consumers. We began to experience the manipulative salesperson. This is the perception that many people have today of salespeople. The smooth-talking con man so well depicted in movies such as "Used Cars", "Tin Man", and "Glen Garry Glen Ross".

How do we re-establish a more positive relationship between product/service availability and consumer demand? Three strategies:

1. Clearly identify each customer's unique needs and requirements.

2. Tailor your goods and services to meet those needs at a fair price.

3. Ensure a long-term relationship by attaining customer satisfaction.

Clearly identify each customer's unique needs and requirements. Manipulative salespeople focus on trying to manufacture a need in a customer where none exists. We may, however, be able to bring existing needs to the surface simply by clarifying the customers understanding of the symptoms they are experiencing. Many people make a very good living out of helping people identify which particular need may be causing a symptom, then advising them on how to alleviate it. This includes not only medical doctors but also good salespeople. The most skilled salesperson will guide a customer through a discovery process designed to uncover and articulate the customers' needs and wants. In addition, the effective salesperson will help the customer reach an understanding of the consequences of inaction plus the value in making a change. The more clearly your customer sees the depth of the ramifications of inaction, plus the range of positive benefits of taking action, the more likely they are to want to do something about it. This is called "tension for change". The customer who has decided that they have a need and that they really wish to do something about it, will then be in a position to seek solutions. Tailor your goods and services to meet those needs at a fair price for most businesses, offering generic products and services is a recipe for disaster. With the vast array of choices available, customers want a solution that is right for them in their own special situation. Frequently, this can be accomplished by listening carefully to the needs and wants of your customers, then packaging a combination of your products and services that specifically addresses those customer's needs.

To do this requires these skills:
- ✓ The ability to understand what the customer wants, and recognise the core issues and peripheral issues that are important to them;

- ✓ The ability to identify the relevant features of your products and services that are appropriate for this customer;

- ✓ Ability to communicate the specific benefits, gained by using your products and services, that are meaningful to this customer;

- ✓ Willingness to deliver the package of products and services with emphasis on the desired results expected by this customer.

Develop a long-term relationship by attaining customer satisfaction Truly effective salespeople succeed because they are genuinely curious and concerned about people in general - and customers in particular. Their desire to understand the customer takes priority over their desire to sell their products and services. The delightful irony, of course, is that the very reason they are successful at selling is because they have made their desire to sell a secondary issue. The primary issue is the relationship they have with their customer.

The surest way to cement a long-term business relationship with your customer is to remember that no sale is completed until the customers' expectations have being met or, preferably, exceeded. There are many salespeople who take customers for granted. The excitement of new sales often leads to ignoring existing customers. The result is constant pressure to create new business from scratch. Meanwhile, some of your best prospects are right there under your nose, in your own customer base.

The "traditional", fast talking slick sales person is no longer effective in today's global marketplace. Dynamic and highly competitive, our market consists of well-educated, savvy consumers looking to the modern salesperson for guidance in making well-informed buying decisions. Those unwilling or unable to adapt not only experience declining sales, but also risk severing long-term customer relationships. The challenge is enormous and the stakes are high. Remember, customers buy for their reasons, not ours. When we strive to form a partnership with our customers, providing them with valuable help and advice as well as supplying vital products and services, we virtually ensure sales success.

INSIGHT 10: IMPLEMENTATION OF DEVELOPED MARKETING AND CUSTOMER SERVICE PLANS

Without marketing, no one will know your business exists—and if customers don't know you're there, you won't make any sales. When your marketing efforts are working, however, and customers are streaming through the door, an effective customer service policy will keep them coming back for more. So now it's time to create the plans that will draw customers to your business again and again. A marketing plan consists of the strategies and devices you're going to use to communicate to your target audience. A customer service plan focuses on your customer's requirements and the ways of filling those requirements. The two work in concert. Descriptions of your market and its segments, the competition and prospective customers should be in your business plan. This is the start of your marketing plan. Based on this information, you can begin choosing the communication channels to use to get the word out about your business: radio, TV, billboards, direct mail, flyers, print ads, etc. Then prioritize your tactics and begin with the ones that your research has shown to be the most effective for your audience. For example, a TV repair service's marketing program may be supported mainly by paid advertisements in the phone book, since "Television Repair" is one of the most often looked-up headings by homeowners.

b) Market, market, market

Advertise in your local newspaper is an obsolete practice, but good old guerrilla marketing isn't. Put flyers up in local supermarkets, church bulletin boards, community centres, and in the mailboxes of homes in surrounding neighbourhoods. The customers will flock if you have a selling point that stands out. If your business is cantered on a product, you may want to consider initiating a start-up campaign. You'll be confident that people are interested in what you're selling, and it's a great way to start your business backed up by a client base.

c. Listen to feedback

One of the biggest mistakes new business owners make is ignoring what potential investors have to say. Some entrepreneurs are so wrapped up in the "my way or the highway" type of thinking that they're unaware anything could be improved (a great example of this is the show "Kitchen Nightmares." Be open to suggestions. Your customers might have ideas that didn't cross your mind when creating the business plan. Being active on social media, offering comment cards, and having an e-mail or phone line specifically for idea-generation is a good way to open the lines of communication. The most important thing to remember as you start your new business is to never stop learning. You won't know everything there is to know about your industry or business, whether you've being in business 6 months or six decades. Don't be afraid to ask for help along the way.

HOW TO START A PRODUCT BASED BUSINESS?

INSIGHT 10.1: WAYS TO APPROACH YOUR BUSINESSES IN SELLING HANDMADE GOODS IN WHOLESALE

"If you don't create wealth you end up with losses, bills to pay, indebtedness and there is a limit to the kind of people you will be able to touch because you are bound perpetually with expenditures, wastage and maybe a forfeiture of things you use to own" **by Matthew Ashimolowo**

Case Study: (google.com, HAIR START-UP BUSINESS) **In United States (But Its Concept Is Applicable Anywhere You Are)**

Here is an anonymous story of a man who started a business (in his own words)

I decided to go over how to approach local businesses first, rather than making a business plan first. This just happened to be the sequence I went about it. I felt like I had to know where I would be selling and what price points I could meet, it also determined the type of product I made, which in my case were hair bows. Of course, this was my unique experience, so just take away what you can and apply it to your situation.

For my personal experience it was walk into the store get a dialogue going and ask if they would be interested in seeing my work. I had already determined that I wanted to sell at a children's boutique so that is where I centred my attention. I saw that the boutique had only one type of hair accessory and knew that I could offer them something different that they could easily sell – and basically that is what I told them.

I introduced myself and asked if she were the owner/manager and then told her how much I loved her store, and how it was just the place I was looking to sell my handmade hair accessories. She then asked about my product. I said something along the lines of "I love the hair bows you have, and I think what I make would be a great addition to them. I make hair fascinators, rosette headbands......" It was about right there in the dialogue that she interrupted me and said "Yes, that is what we have had customers requesting! Especially the fascinators for pictures." I offered to bring some in for her to look at she said that would be great, and that was it!

I was so excited I went to three more boutiques that day and pretty much had the same response from each of them. I was set to make enough money to pay for our entire trip to California the way I saw it. But in the days following I came to my senses and a few conclusions:

- if I sell my hair accessories to all the boutiques in town there would be less demand for my product
- if I sell my hair accessories to all the boutiques in town, I was bound to lose credibility with all shop owners
- if I sell to only one boutique within a certain number of miles, I would have an incentive for the shop owners – they would have an exclusive product

So, I decided to only take my product back to one local boutique, the first one I had approached. I chose that boutique because of all the ones I had visited, I felt it had the best chance of moving the most product. They had a great sales mentality. The more they sell, the more I can sell to them. It was simple. Plus, I liked her and knew she was excited about doing business with me.

When I returned with my product, I informed her that I would sell to her exclusively, and because of that I needed to sell at a bulk rate of at least $300 dollars to start. Meaning that I couldn't just sell her $100 dollars' worth of hair accessories and have it been worth my time. After the initial first purchase we could see how well they sold and determine a monthly inventory that could work for both of us. She agreed to my terms and bought $360 dollars' worth that day. Wahoo!

That got me excited and I decided to reach out to a couple boutiques in surrounding areas that would not be competitors to my local boutique. I had found one large boutique about 2 hours' drive away, and one that was an hour. I figured I could make one trip to them and after that mail or make a monthly trip. I approached both of them by telephone. One owner asked me to bring them in for her to see, and the other asked if I could send her an e-mail with pictures first. I sent the e-mail with my terms of selling exclusively to her in that area, and she told me to come on in. Both seemed genuinely interested and I was confident that they would be new customers.

But then life happened! My house went on the market and I am now moving across the country this week. So, I have just stuck with my original shop owner and it has worked great. I am able to sell $300 of my product a month to her with only 12 hours of work each month. If I were staying in the area, I am certain I would have had a couple more boutiques to sell to, and I could have brought in a solid $900 extra income a month. When I look at the time, I have to spend on it that would probably be my max.

Bottom line is brick and mortar businesses have an overhead they need to cover. They have to man the shop itself and they don't have time to make all the product to sell as an online shop does. They rely on quality products they can buy at wholesale. So, if you have a great product that you know they can sell, let us then know! They will more than likely be excited about the chance to work with you.

Remember that if you are trying to sell a product you are a salesman, so you have to think like one. Talk to them in a language that lets them know you understand their business. For instance, "I know you have a lot of customers shopping for special occasion dresses, we could make customer hair pieces to make an easy add-on sale". Provide examples of trends and how your product will meet those trends. The shop owner is running a business, and the more you show you can think from their perspective the better. If they can make money selling your product and if you can help them see how – you have yourself a sale.

Here are a few tips to take away:

    a. Don't pop in on a busy Saturday afternoon when they are busy

    b. Dress nicely and smile

    c. Be enthusiastic, excited, and confident about your product

    d. Offer suggestions for how best to display your product

    e. Offer products that are easy add-on sales

    f. Present a unique product that is in demand and on trend

    g. Know their customer base and what would sell

    h. Offer product suggestions

Now for field research. I basically thought of a few different places that might buy handmade goods and then called them up or went in to talk to them. I just wanted to demonstrate how you can think outside of the box when looking for potential businesses to work with. Hopefully it will give you an idea how you can branch out with whatever your product is. In all of the instances I explained that I was doing research for an article on selling handmade goods, and wanted to know how best someone could approach them for doing business on a wholesale basis.

1. I called a large store that sells mainly gift items of all sorts and asked for the manager. Because of the size, I was certain it was running by employees rather than the owner, so I opted not to go in. She said that they are always on the lookout for local handmade goods, and actually had a section just for that – who knew! She stressed that it had to be top quality and that any returns fall back on the wholesaler. They preferred an appointment to be set up with a formal meeting.

2. I went into a high-end salon and spoke with the owner. I went when I knew it would be a slow time and he had a few minutes. I told him why I was there and he said he had never thought to bring in anything handmade. I explained how hair accessories would be a great add-on sale, and trust me this industry makes a good amount of their money on these kind of sales (I used to do hair – I made half my money from product sales). **He was excited about the idea and said that he would love to just have someone offer!**

3. I went into a local high-end china type store – they sell nice china, silver flatware, and gifts. When I explained why I was there (speaking with the manager) she said she really didn't think there was anything handmade they could sell. I offered a few suggestions such as hand-embroidered dish towels and aprons. She thought for a minute and said that might work, and she would definitely consider working with someone on a wholesale basis.

4. I went into a bridal boutique and took a few of my wedding-ish hair accessories with me. I told her why I was there and she said that they actually carry hair accessories and can't sell them. I explained that online there is an entire blog community devoted to weddings and they feature a lot of handmade goods and brides are probably drawn to that. They carried old fashioned hair pieces and maybe offering a few retro or elegant pieces, and flower girl type might do well. I couldn't tell if she was offended or not (I hope not!), but said she would buy from me on the spot. I wasn't selling, but hey, that could have been a sale!

5. I have a local coffee shop I frequent so I asked the owner if she ever thought about bringing in some handmade gifts for the holidays. She said no, but if someone came in with something she loved and on target to her customer base she would definitely consider it, especially if it were offered in a ready to give package. She preferred someone to call first to set up an appointment.

So, there you have it! They were all interested! I hope this encourages any of you that are looking for a second source of income. I can think of several different businesses I could have contacted with several different product ideas; vet office for handmade pet items – tutus for dance studios – shoe clips for shoe stores – camera straps for camera shops – the possibilities are endless! Just remember from part one – keep it simple.

INSIGHT 10.2: HOW TO SELL A PRODUCT

Selling a product isn't as complicated as it's made out to be. At its most basic, a sales program is defined principally by what you sell, who you sell to, and how you sell. Beyond that, it all boils down to staying focused on the details outlined next, suitable for both sales' representative and for owners of small businesses

Love what you're doing when you're selling a product. The popular image of a salesperson as someone willing to "sell at all costs" is not the reality across the board in sales. A good salesperson loves sales, is motivated by what they're selling, and transfers this enthusiasm and belief to the customer. Indeed, the customer is given options, including the one to walk away, in order to avoid such undue pressure.

Learn how to listen to customers and to read their body language. Avoid interrupting or disagreeing with a customer, and provide your customer with space to talk. Know how to interpret a customer's folded arms, eye contact, and manner of standing towards or away from you. Make the customer comfortable and you're off to a good start in selling your product.

Be knowledgeable about the product. There is nothing more infuriating to a potential customer than to come across a half-hearted salesperson who claims uncertainty about what the product can and can't do, what it's made from, and what happens when things in it stop working. It is absolutely vital to know your product range inside out and if you do not know something a customer asks for, you let them know you'll find out and get back to them as soon as possible.

Help the customer see the perks. As well as getting good product information to the right people, it is important to translate the product's features into benefits for the customer, thus making it easier for them to buy.

1. Have you used the product, tested it, tried it out, or worked with it-- whichever is relevant?
2. Do you feel comfortable about being able to talk to a customer as someone totally familiar with the product?
3. Ask yourself one simple question: Why should a customer buy my product? If the only answer you can come up with is "So I can get paid," you're selling the wrong product.

Ensure that the product has being adequately explained. Good product information, including retail packaging is very important. Lots of salespeople and sales managers don't like to admit that sales can be completed by product information. They like to think it is their personal charm, intelligence, and determination that closes sales. For the most part, that is bunk. Not only can sales be made by product information, most sales *are* made this way. And this is truer today than in the past because of the proliferation of "big-box stores" and other forms of product sales without the benefit of interpersonal relationships.

- The product information should be informative, true and complete. Ideally, it should give the prospective buyer all the information they need to buy on the spot.
- For most prospects shopping without assistance, clear and easy to understand information, as described above is important.

Make the benefits of the product loud and clear. Besides the actual utility, beauty, or even fame of the product, what are you offering above and beyond? Make it clear to the customer what key benefits the product brings to them. Such as guarantees, warranties, and after-sales service.

SESSION 4: 5 BEST PLACES TO ADVERTISE ONLINE
1. Blogs/Websites or Online Newspapers
Depending on what you are advertising, you can find lots of top blogs, websites of online newspapers in Nigeria where you can place your adverts on and get-well targeted sales and brand exposure. You can find these blogs, websites or online newspapers by searching for them via Google.com. When you find these top blogs, websites or online newspapers, check out the "Advert" page for the advert prices. Make sure you contact the owners. Also, make sure you request for their blogs, website or online newspapers traffic stats.

2. Facebook
Facebook is a good place to advertise online in Nigeria. At the moment of writing this, there are millions of Nigerians on Facebook. Your business is sure to get the needed sales and brand exposure that you really need. You can spend few thousands of Naira on advertising on Facebook and make millions in return if what your business is offering is what people really need and also if you only advertise to your business' target market.

3. Google
Google is also a good place to advertise online in Nigeria. At the moment of writing this, Google is the number one search engine people use to find information. There is a high probability that people will buy your product or service if you advert is displayed when they search for information related to your business. It is easy to advertise on Google using Google AdWords. Just like Facebook, you can also spend few thousands of Naira on Google AdWords

and make millions in return if what your business is offering is what people really need and also if you only advertise to your business' target market.

4. Twitter
Just like Facebook and Google, you can get lots of Nigerians on Twitter. The same principle applies for advertising on Twitter. In this case, you advert will be shown as promoted tweets. You are advert will be shown to your target market. The other good thing is that, your promoted tweets can be retweeted and many more people will be able to see your advert and make purchase of what you are advertising.

A FEW SITES TO ADVERTISE YOUR PRODUCT/SERVICES/PROPERTY

- www.google.com/adwords
- www.lamudi.com.ng,
- www.efritin.com
  www.nigeriapropertycentre.com
  www.privateproperty.com
  www.locanto.com.ng
- www.nairaland.com
- www.twitter.com
- www.instagram.com

- www.bunchbay.com
- www.mobofree.com
  www.jumia.com
- www.tolet.com.ng
  www.instablog.com
- www.vconnect.com
- www.youtube.com
- www.facebook.com
- other social media sites

SESSION5: CONNECTING WITH THE BUYER
Understand the motivations of the buyer. When presenting the product to the customer, bear in mind that most successful products and services are bought, not sold. They are bought by people who have needs, and believe that the product will satisfy that need. This is often the result of marketing rather than selling, however. Selling the product rather than just offering it for sale almost always involves an emotional component.

   a. Take some time to look at the marketing side of the product. What images and promises have being created by the marketing around the product that you're trying to sell? In what ways can you continue this theme where it seems most appropriate to maintain the promised satisfaction the marketing offers?

b. During your presentation, confirm that your prospective potential buyer will want or need your product. You will need to do this through a range of methods, including observing their reactions, listening to them carefully, and asking them clear questions about what they need.

c. If you're visiting your potential buyer's office, look at their wall and desk. What photos, posters, or images can you see? Are there images of family, pets, vacations that will provide you with a connection to this person's wants?

Know how to open with a customer. Instead of asking the close-ended question "May I help you?" ask the more positive, open-ended "Are you looking for something for yourself is it a gift for someone special?" And be alert to making comments on the product before getting into a deeper discussion with the customer, such as "These long-legged computer stands are really popular this summer."

Convert the customer's motivations into the product's characteristics. In marketing, this is known as "positioning", and it consists of equating the product with the customer's hopes and desires.

The following positioning factors are all important when selling a product:

1. Position the product in the best spectrum of the market possible. Mark H, McCormack calls this finding your "biggest bulge of buyers", and not pitching the product too high or too low in terms of affordability and luxury.
2. Position the facts about the product according to the person you're selling it to. You may have a handful of different facts, but it's up to your skill to know which of those facts best serve each individual sale.
3. Position the facts so that they reflect the desired perception. However, don't forge facts or lie outright. This is about perception, not deception.
4. Position the facts so that they transcend the product itself. This means that the desirable, positive values associated with the product sell the product and have very little to do with the product itself. Companies that excel at this include Coca-Cola, Apple, and many designer goods or labels.

Understand all the aspects that fit into the end sale of a product.
Advertising, merchandising, and marketing are support functions for selling. Selling is the goal of these support functions and a good salesperson needs to have a decent understanding of each of these aspects in a product's life.

1. Read basic texts on marketing. These will quickly bring you up to speed on many of the tactics and techniques underlying advertising, merchandising, and marketing. In addition, texts on starting a small business will often provide useful overview information of this type.
2. If your product is more for work than for play, learn a little about finance to quantify its benefits. If it's for a business, learn more about accounting to explain how it will make the investors as well as the employees happy.

Be honest. Long-term lovers of your product will only come about if you've being honest with them. This means being transparent in your delivery of product information and also admitting your own lack of knowledge or mistakes you've made where needed. Don't be afraid of honesty; it builds trust.

1. Think like (not about) your customers. Think about what you'd like to hear and learn about the product if you were in the customer's shoes.
2. Don't take the easy way out and brush your customer off when stock is low or your knowledge is sparse. Always make a genuine effort to follow up customer wants, and to physically take customers to a product, and demonstrate it, where possible. A customer given a hands-on demonstration will feel more involved in the sale and more likely to purchase than one who is told "It's in aisle five that way" and given a brisk hand wave.

Give your customer some importance. Pay attention to his questions, answer them and make them feel like the centre of attention.

- If you aren't able to handle all your customers effectively, hire sales executives to assist you in business.

SESSION7: IMPROVING SALES
spread your product information. It is important to make your product information available through as many channels as possible. Today, the range of potential placements has increased a great deal thanks to the advances in communications. Give your potential buyers many possible places to find out more about your information including in the following ways:

1. Promote your product through representatives, dealers, salesmen, radio, TV, word-of-mouth by customers, mail and e-mail (in various forms), distribution at trade shows, seminars, telephone, fax, computer networks, product packaging, airline magazines, retail storefronts, space ads, and the

Internet. And consider the worth of product placement in movies, sports games, and other big events that are televised.

2. **Use social media**. This is now a very important part of getting products out into the broader, global marketplace. Places Facebook and interest can be great launching pads for your product.
3. **Use local community events**. Donating your product to a local school gala for auctioning to raise school funds can be a great way to get your product known, as well as getting the goodwill from the community who recognizes your generosity.

Get creative. Sales can only be increased by certain things over which you have control but which are not necessarily self-evident. Sometimes price changes are required; other times, you'll need tweaks to the product, or a broadening or contracting of your product range. All of this will be evident from undertaking regular inventory checks and follow ups on sales performance. Some methods to increase sales include:

1. Selling more of your existing products to your existing customers - which probably means new sales methods will need to be implemented.
2. Adding new products.
3. Adding new customers.
4. Having an exclusive product for a set period of time that everyone wants.

INSIGHT 11.3: CONCLUDING SALES
i) CLOSING THE SALE:
There are many styles and methods of closing a sale. One of the most effective has the mnemonic, ABC: "Always be closing." As you confirm your prospective buyer's interest in the product, put forward trial closes like, "Does this sound like the product you want?" When answered in the affirmative, this may mean you have completed the sale on that product, and it is time to build the sale with related products.

Be prepared to give customers time to consider. Appearing overtly pushy is a turn off for many modern-day buyers who do their own survey internet research before coming to see you. They may want to go home and do a quick online search; let them do so with your enthusiastic and supportive pitch in their mind. If you've being truthful, helpful, considerate, and enthusiastic and the information you've given them matches with what they read online, it'll be your business they come back to for the product, or your product they'll prefer over a competitor's.

SESSION 1: (GOOGLE.COM, 7 WAYS TO PROMOTE YOUR BUSINESS ONLINE FOR FREE)

The Internet is teeming with marketing platforms that don't cost a dime—you just need to know where to look.

1. Use the three big local listing services

Registering your business with **Google Places** allows it to be found more easily on Google searches and it shows up on Google Maps. All you have to do is fill out the form and register, then get your business verified through their confirmation process, which can be done either with a phone call or snail mail. Yahoo! also has a big database of businesses called **Yahoo! Local**. It's free, and is certainly worth the few minutes it takes to set up. Microsoft's **Bing** has a similar service that's easy to sign up for.

2. Embrace social media

Social media isn't just a tool to gain exposure—it has now become a necessary time investment for every business to make. You can tie in ads and offers on your Facebook page and have a direct channel with your customers on Twitter. Networking on LinkedIn—both at the personal and company level—can be another way to help your start-up.

3. Start a blog

A blog not only helps your company get its name out through followers, but is a way to connect with your consumers more directly. But remember that one of the major keys of blogging is to keep your stream updated as frequently as you can. A dormant, abandoned blog is worth nothing.

4. Put up multimedia on YouTube and Flickr

YouTube provides a free way to distribute creative promotional videos, but in order to succeed you must put up content that people want to view and are relevant to your business—a simple ad will not work. A Flickr profile can also help by giving you one place to compile all the photos for your business, and allows you to link back to your website.

5. SEO your company website

Search engine optimization cannot be underestimated in the world of constant Googling. Pick up a book or head over to an online how-to-guide on SEO and make sure your site is primed for performance on search engines.

6. Press releases

Every time your business does something newsworthy, don't hesitate to shoot off a press release—maybe folks will pick up on it. They're a powerful media tool to use to help generate publicity, and having free distribution of them is a bonus. There are dozens of websites out there that you can use for your press releases, such as **PRLog** and **24/7 Press Release**.

7. Join a relevant online community and contribute

Every niche has communities online that you can get involved in. But just signing up for a forum and posting everyone in a while about your business isn't beneficial for anyone, and will likely just annoy people. Actively contribute and build a rapport with the community, while keeping your business out of it. Passively promote your business by putting a link in your signature or mentioning it only when the context is appropriate.

SESSION 8: TROUBLESHOOTING POOR SALES

Review. At regular intervals during and after the sale of your product, there should always be a review. Is the product selling well? If not, why not? Are stocks low or are you still tripping over product that has dust on it? Bear in mind the image that slow-moving or unsold products can create in the minds of a customer. Finding dust on items tells the customer the product has being there for some time and may be out-dated. Seeing the same display month in and month out suggests to the customer that the product is stale and not very popular. Always review the viability of the products with these questions:

1. Can the product be deleted from your line if it's not selling so well? Try not to add new products until you've removed the old ones or you may just have too many choices and less leverage with which to convince the potential buyer. If you're a business owner, you also risk tying up too much of your cash in stock that has the potential to go obsolete faster than you can move it.

2. Can you liquidate obsolete products?

3. Can you look back over your target market and sharpen the focus? You may have been missing the best fit within the market for your product.

4. Re-evaluate product mix, product design, product location and selling methods if your product is in severe sales decline.

5. You should be nice to the buyer.

In A Situation of Concluded Transaction

a. Send out invoices with accurate details indicating sales date and due date if any was agreed
b. Call within the week of sending in the invoice to verify if it has been received and acted upon
c. Call in a few days to the due date of payment for reminder to ensure early payment
d. Call back if you have not received the payment a day after the due date of payment. Ask for a specific date it would be paid by them while staying polite and friendly
e. If the payment is still not met, call to verify why and insist it is paid quickly to avoid any unnecessary legal actions that might soar the relationship already in existence
f. If nothing happens one week after send in a letter of warning stating the involvement of police and legal action if the money is not paid (cooperate body)
g. But if it is one man's business there is no need of sending a warning letter just make use of whatever legal options you have to recover your money
h. (Cooperate body) if payment still not made then you can take the matter up legally to ensure you recover your money or consider it as bad debt and move on.

INSIGHT 11: PERFORMANCE REVIEW AFTER MEETING YOUR FIRST CUSTOMERS

You have a profile of the end user of your product or service. Now's the time to get in the habit of "talking up" your business—telling everyone you know about it. Ask for referrals from colleagues, suppliers, former employers and other associates. You can improve the quality of your referrals by being specific in your request. For example, an insurance broker developed a successful referral network by asking existing clients if they knew anyone who was "in a two-income professional family with young children," rather than just asking if they knew anyone who needed insurance. Consider offering free consultations or an introductory price to first time buyers. Consider joining forces with a complementary business to get them to help you spread the word about your new venture. For example, a carpet cleaner might offer incentives to a housecleaning service if they'd recommend them to their regular customers. Once you've done work for a few satisfied customers, ask them for a testimonial letter to use in your promotional materials.

"An Organisation can only walk the talk when its managers deliberately shape its internal reality to align with its brand promise values must be internalised by the organisation shaping its instinctive attitude, behaviours and priorities." **By Brad Van Auken**

PERFORMANCE REVIEW AND COMMUNICATION

- ✓ Sending Release Letter to the press (media) about your business on start-up, including sending a letter to C.A.C (Corporate affairs Commission).
- ✓ Evaluating methods and Tools that attracted Customers to the company (Advertisement and Marketing)
- ✓ Reviewing monthly target met and how much is needed to be inputted to increase sales and Publicity.
- ✓ Using Key Performance Indicator to access the growth and strength of the company.

Performance Management: An organization will benefit from establishing an effective **Quality Management System** (QMS). The cornerstone of a quality organization is the concept of the customer and supplier working together for their mutual benefit. For this to become effective, the customer-supplier interfaces must extend into, and outside of the organization, beyond the immediate customers and suppliers. There are different areas that address performance management such as: Quality Planning, Quality Assurance, and Quality Control.

INSIGHT 12: EVALUATE, INNOVATE AND ADD CREATIVITY TO YOUR BUSINESS SYSTEM

In the words of **George Bernard Shaw** *"Imagination is the beginning of creation. You imagine what you desire, you will what you imagine and at last you create what you will"*

Using Quality management system concept to grow the company and goal implementation to create structure and transition of jobs to be done using a centralised system of management or decentralized system of management depending on the style and type of business you are into. In this stage business advancement is made possible through innovation and creativity. A business without creativity is like a boat with lots of holes all round and hoping to travel a mile on water, without actually sinking before arriving at its destination.

13 BUSINESS START-UP SURVIVAL RULES EITHER AS AN IDEA OR

1. **PICK A GOOD CO-FOUNDER:** Co-foundership is like entering into marriage, before you decide you need to make a person your co-founder you must first test that the person is someone you can work with and more importantly both of your share the same belief and passion. Then for the most important part your co-founder must possess a complimentary skill to your skills. Never pick anybody your co-founder

out of ego, firm or the money or status of the person because at the end it will come back to haunt you and may eventually lead to the collapse of the business. Be wise and choose carefully because if you rush in, you will definitely rush out of the partnership business.

2. **LAUNCH FAST:** Don't spend so much time planning, up to the point that you turn your plans to an academic research or thesis. You need to know your launch date when the business starts running otherwise you might end up not starting the business at all and eventually leads the idea into a death phase or endless loop of planning.

3. **LET YOUR IDEAS EVOLVE:** As you run with your idea, over time your idea begins to mature and grow and it gets up to the point where the idea starts attracting people, resources and organisations eventually becomes a working growing organisation. So, don't be scared of your idea from evolving into a business and eventually into something bigger than you because that is the reason why you started the business in the first place.

4. **UNDERSTAND YOUR USERS:** Never go into a business thinking everyone is your target audience or everyone will patronise your business because thinking such will eventually lead to bankruptcy if the target audience is not properly understood or harnessed. See it in this way that your money is in the pocket of your target market (potential customers) so all you have to do is figure out a strategy that will help you get the money from the pocket of your potential customers to your own pocket or bank account which turns out to become sales to your business.

5. **BETTER TO MAKE A FEW USERS LOVE YOU**: Don't get over your heads about how beautiful your business ideas are and neglect customer service satisfaction because at the end it will be all about customer satisfaction otherwise you will run out of business faster than you can still in business.

6. **OFFER SURPRISINGLY GOOD CUSTOMER SERVICE:** Without customer service there can be no repeat sales. As a friend of mine would always say *"customers are always right"*.

7. **SPEND LITTLE:** Manage the little resources at your disposal because if you don't manage the limited resources with you, it may never grow to become huge enough to grow the organisation to become a multi-national corporation.

8. **GET PROFITABLE:** Profitability is not based on the idea itself but in the execution of the idea with a synergy of people and resources. There is no stupid idea, there are only lazy thinkers who have failed to recognised the circumstances that make an idea profitable in short and long run.

9. **AVOID DISTRACTIONS:** Don't get into multiple business idea execution at the same time because you will sink resources into multiple businesses and at the end failure is inevitable for all business idea invested into. Rather take the business idea one after another, start with one develop it and grow it into a profitable organisation before starting and implementing another business idea to avoid wastage of investment and resources at the end of the day.

10. **DON'T GET DEMORALISED:** Don't let past business failure become a limiting factor to starting a profitable business. Instead of punishing yourself or beating yourself up for it, sit down and find out where you missed it and what made your past business fail. Learn from them and move on otherwise you will pass away with your past and may not achieve that dream you have always wanted to see actualized.
"Remember winners never quit but losers look for opportunity to quit".

11. **DON'T GIVE UP:** The secrets behind successful businesses is their resilient drive for success. So, if you want to reach for the stars you must first learn how to get there. Never stop pushing through because at the end you will smile.

KEEP GOING, DON'T EVEN THINK OF STOPPING NOT EVEN FOR A MOMENT OR SECOND BECAUSE THE WORLD IS WAITING FOR YOU.

INSIGHT 12.1: QUALITY MANAGEMENT SYSTEM
Quality Planning

1. The process of identifying which quality standards are relevant to the project and determining how to satisfy them.
2. **Input includes**: Quality policy, scope statement, product description, standards and regulations, and other process Output.
3. **Methods used**: benefit / cost analysis, benchmarking, flowcharting, and design of experiments
4. **Output includes**: Quality Management Plan, operational definitions, checklists, and Input to other processes.

Quality Assurance

1. The process of evaluating overall project performance on a regular basis to provide confidence that the project will satisfy the relevant quality standards.
2. **Input includes**: Quality Management Plan, results of quality control measurements, and operational definitions.
3. **Methods used**: quality planning tools and techniques and quality audits.
4. **Output includes**: quality improvement.

Quality Control

a) The process of monitoring specific project results to determine if they comply with relevant quality standards and identifying ways to eliminate causes of unsatisfactory performance.
b) **Input includes**: work results, Quality Management Plan, operational definitions, and checklists.
c) **Methods used include**: inspection, control charts, pareto diagrams, statistical sampling, flowcharting, and trend analysis.
d) **Output includes**: quality improvements, acceptance decisions, rework, completed checklists, and process adjustments.

A fully documented QMS will ensure that two important requirements are met:

1. The customers' requirements – confidence in the ability of the organization to deliver the desired product and service consistently meeting their needs and expectations.
2. The organization's requirements – both internally and externally, and at an optimum cost with efficient use of the available resources – materials, human, technology, and information.

A QMS must ensure that the products/services conform to customer needs and expectations, and the objectives of the organization. Issues to be considered when settings up a QMS include its:

1. Design
2. Build
3. Control
4. Deployment
5. Measurement
6. Review
7. Improvement

Taking each of these in turn:

1. **Design** and **build** include the structure of the quality management system, the process, and its implementation. Senior managers must lead its design to suit the needs of the organization, and this is ideally done using a framework to lead the thinking. Design of the QMS should come from determining the organization's core processes and well-defined goals and strategies, and be linked to the needs of one or more stakeholders. The process for designing and building the QMS must also be clear with the quality function playing a key role, but involvement and buy in to the system must also come from all other functions.
2. **Deployment** and implementation are best achieved using process packages, where each core process is broken down into sub-processes, and described by a combination of documentation, education, training, tools, systems, and metrics. Electronic deployment via Intranets is increasingly being used.
3. **Control** of the QMS will depend on the size and complexity of the organization. ISO is a site-based system, and local audits and reviews are essential even if these are supplemented by central reviews. Local control, where possible, is effective, and good practice is found where key stakeholders are documented within the process and where the process owner can control all the process. Ideally, process owners/operators are involved in writing procedures.
4. **Measurement** is carried out to determine the effectiveness and efficiency of each process towards attaining its objectives. It should include the contribution of the QMS to the organization's goals; this could be achieved by measuring the following:
    1. Policy definition completeness
    2. Coverage of business
    3. Reflection of policies
    4. Deployment
    5. Usage
    6. Whether staff find the QMS helpful in their work
    7. Speed of change of the QMS
    8. Relevance of QMS architecture to the job in hand

A form of scorecard deployed through the organization down to individual objective level can be employed, and the setting of targets at all levels is vital.

> ➤ **Review** of the effectiveness, efficiency, and capability of a QMS is vital, and the outcome of these reviews should be communicated to all

employees. Reviewing and monitoring should be conducted whether improvement activities have achieved their expected outcomes.

- **Improvement** should follow because of the review process, with the aim of seeking internal best practice. It is part of the overall improvement activities and an integral part of managing change within the organization.

Eight quality management principles, upon which to base an efficient, effective, and adaptable QMS should be considered. They are applicable throughout industry, commerce, and the service sectors:

1. Customer focus
2. Leadership
3. Involving people
4. Process approach
5. Systems approach
6. Continual improvement
7. Factual decision making
8. Mutually beneficial supplier relationships

Taking each one in turn, they are explained more fully as:

- An effective QMS must ensure that the organization has a strong **Customer Focus**. Customer needs and expectations must be determined and converted into product requirements.
- Top management must demonstrate **Leadership**. Providing unity of purpose through an appropriate quality policy, ensuring that measurable objectives are established, and demonstrating that they are fully committed to developing, sustaining, and improving the QMS.
- Managers must ensure that there is **Involvement of People** at all levels in the organization. This includes ensuring that there is awareness of the importance of meeting customer needs and wants, in doing this and people are competent, based on appropriate training and experience.
- An effective QMS must be a strategic tool designed to deliver business objectives, and must have, at its core, a **Process Approach**, with each process transforming one or more inputs to create an output of value to the customer. The key business processes may be supported by procedures and work instructions in those cases where it is judged necessary to rigidly define what rules are to be followed when undertaking a task. Most organizations will have core business processes

that define those activities that directly add value to the product or service for the external customer, and supporting processes that are required to maintain the effectiveness of the core processes.
- The understanding of the many interrelationships between these processes demands that a **Systems Approach** to management is adopted. The processes must be thoroughly understood and managed so that the most efficient use is made of available resources, to ensure that the needs of all the stakeholders –customers, employees, shareholders, and the community - are met.
- Customer satisfaction is a constantly moving entity depending on changes in technology and the market place, so an effective QMS must be in a state of Continual Improvement.
- For this to be achieved, attention needs to be given to both the voice of the customer - through complaint analysis, opinion surveys and regular contacts – and the voice of the processes – through measurement, monitoring and analysis of both process and product data. This will result in **Factual Decision Making**.
- Each organization is itself only a link in the chain of a larger raw material process, and for the long-term needs of the stakeholders there needs to be **Mutually Beneficial Supplier Relationships**.

Service Quality

1. **Time and Timeliness**–customer waiting time, completed on time
2. **Completeness**–customer gets all they asked for
3. **Courtesy**–treatment by employees
4. **Consistency**–same level of service for all customers
5. **Accessibility and Convenience**–ease of obtaining service
6. **Accuracy**–performed right every time
7. **Responsiveness**–reactions to unusual situations

Figure 8: Quality vs Quantity

1. THE 5-S QUALITY MANAGEMENT SYSTEM

Workplace Standardization and Organization

Description

5S is a process of work place organization and housekeeping which is carried out gradually and systematically.

The 5S method is a structured program to implement workplace organization and standardization. A well-organized workplace motivates people, both on the shop floors as well as others. 5s improves safety, work efficiency, improves productivity and establishes a sense of ownership.

The 5-S system is a series of activities designed to improve workplace organization and standardization. These five activities, all of which begin with the letter S, include:

5S is developed in Japan and stands for

1. **Seiri (Sort)**: Remove all unneeded items and keeping what is needed
2. **Seiton (Organizing)**: Set limits and create temporary location indicators. Place things in such a way that they can be easily reached whenever they are needed
3. **Seiso (Cleaning)**: keeping things clean and polished; no trash or dirt in the workplace
4. **Seiketsu (Standardize)**: Maintaining cleanliness after cleaning-perpetual cleaning.
5. **Shitsuke (Self-discipline)**: Commitment, a typical teaching and attitude towards any undertaking to inspire pride and adherence to standards established for the four components.

This basic philosophy is applied in unique ways for many different situations such as:

to improve or design workstations, to improve overall plant organizations, to improve plant safety, to create visual aids, to standardize systems across work areas so employees can help each other out easier, and to increase efficiency and quality.

Benefits

1. reduces inventory,
2. efficient on workplace usage,
3. reduce time for searching spare parts,
4. reduce oil/water/air spilled,
5. reduce un stabilization,
6. preventive of machine function,
7. cleaning and checking machine condition,
8. improving working condition,
9. reduce work accident,
10. increase discipline,
11. follow procedure,
12. and better relationship among employees
13. Improve quality
14. Achieve work standardization
15. Decrease changeover time
16. Reduce cycle time

Key to successful implementation of 5S

1. **Get everyone involved:** 5s is not to be the responsibility of a concerned few. It is a concern of every one to act. All level of management should take part in decision making required to ensure 5S implementation. Incorporate 5S activities as part of company small group activities.

2. **Get company authorization:** 5S activities should not be performed in a secret or disguised such as overtime work. Get management approval for all 5S activities. Make sign and poster as means to promote 5S for everyone. Conduct a general monthly meeting where company and managers can address 5S issues and themes.

3. **Final responsibility rests with the president:** the 5S will not be taken seriously until all managers and even the company president takes personal responsibility and interest on its implementation. Nothing could be worse for the success of 5S implementation than to have managers who "pass the 5S implementation buck" to their subordinates. Company managers must take a strong leadership role in 5S promotional meetings and other 5S events.

4. **Make yourself understood and be aware of:** don't leave people wandering "why are we are sticking red tags on things?" Hold 5s promotional meetings to clearly explain 5s and to entertain all questions from all participants. Present actual examples of successful 5s implementation or take participants on tour to successful 5s workplaces.

5. **Do it all the way:** when establishing proper arrangement, make sure you carry out red tags campaign and to use correct red tagging formats and procedures. When establishing orderliness, use signboards, make sure the signboards have proper formats, description, and location. Prepare your company's own 5s manual, complete with all the necessary details

6. **Don't stop halfway in establishing 5s:** don't do things halfway, once the 5s promotional organization and method s have been established, get started and stick with it. When developing red tagging and signboards throughout the company, make sure that everyone gets involved. Once you have laid the foundation by establishing proper arrangement and orderliness, start developing discipline habit to keep the foundation strong.

7. **5s is a Halfway towards other improvement:** don't stop with 5s; follow through with zero defects, cost reduction, and other productivity and quality improvement. Once the office has been cleaned up, start putting casters on drawer cases to make them easily movable. Eliminate defects as close to their source as possible and implement flow process.

SESSION1: TOYOTA COMPANY BUSINESS START-UP STORY
The country's first car, a steam-powered vehicle, was produced just after the turn of the century, followed in 1911 by the introduction of the DAT model, forerunner of Datsun/Nissan, Toyota's nearest rival today. The Toyoda family patriarch, Sakichi, the son of a poor carpenter, had invented the first Japanese-designed power loom in 1897 and perfected an advanced automatic loom in 1926, when he founded Toyoda Automatic Loom Works. He ultimately sold the patents for his design to an English firm for $250, 000, at a time when textiles were Japan's top industry and used the money to bankroll his eldest son Kiichiro's venture into auto making in the early 1930s.

Numerous stories have sprung up over the years concerning why the auto company was named Toyota rather than Toyoda. A Business Week article claims the family consulted a numerologist in 1937 before establishing its first auto factory: "Eight was their lucky number, he advised. Accordingly, they modified their company's name to Toyota, which required eight calligraphic strokes instead of ten. Sure enough, what is now Toyota Motor Corp. soon became not only the biggest and most successful of Japan's automakers, but also one of the most phenomenally profitable companies in the world." But a New York Times story notes the family changed the spelling in the 1930s because "it believed the sound [of the new name] resonated better in Japanese ears."

After Eiji joined the family business in 1936, he worked on the A1 prototype, the forerunner of the company's first production model, a six-cylinder sedan that borrowed heavily from Detroit automotive technology and resembled the radically styled Chrysler Airflow model of that period. During those early years, Toyoda gained lots of hands-on experience. "I tried in the past to see how much I could really tell by touch," he said in The Wheel Extended. "It was hard for me to recognise a difference of one hundredth of a millimetre. I must have had a lot of free time. Still, I think it is important to know how much of a difference one can sense." It was a philosophy he shared with his cousin Kiichiro, who often told his employees: "How can you expect to do your job without getting your hands dirty?"

In this spare time, Eiji Toyoda studied rockets and jet engines and, on the advice of his cousin, even researched helicopters. "We gathered materials in an attempt to make a helicopter and make prototype rotary wings," he said in The Wheel Extended. "By attaching the wings on one end of a beam, with a car engine on the other, we built a contraption that could float in the air.... We weren't doing it just for fun. However, the war intensified, and it became hard to experiment because of a shortage of materials." The war left Japan's industry in a shamble, and the automaker began rebuilding its production facilities from scratch. Recalled Toyoda: "Everything was completely new to us. Design and production, for example, all had to be started from zero. And the competitive situation allowed for not even a single mistake. We had our backs to the wall, and we knew it."

But while Kiichiro Toyoda was rebuilding the manufacturing operations, Japan's shattered economy left the company with a growing bank of unsold cars. By 1949, the firm was unable to meet its payroll, and employees began a devastating fifteen-month strike—the first and only walkout in the company's history—which pushed Toyota to the brink of bankruptcy. In 1950, the Japanese government ended the labour strife by forcing Toyota to reorganize and split its sales and manufacturing operations into separate companies, each headed by a non-family member. Kiichiro Toyoda and his executive staff resigned en masse; Kiichiro died less than two years later.

Eiji Toyoda, meanwhile had being named managing director of the manufacturing arm, Toyota Motor Company. In what some automakers must view as a supreme irony, he was sent to the United States in 1950 to study the auto industry and return to Toyota with a report on American manufacturing methods. After touring Ford Motor's U.S. facilities, Toyoda turned to the task of redesigning Toyota's plants to incorporate advanced techniques and machinery. Returning from another trip to the United States in 1961, only four years after the establishment of Toyota Motor Sales USA, a prophetic Toyoda told employees in a speech recorded in a company brochure: "The United States already considers us a challenger.... But we must not just learn from others and copy them. That would merely result in being overwhelmed by the competition. We must produce superior automobiles, and we can do it with creativity, resourcefulness and wisdom—plus hard work. Without this ... and the willingness to face adversity, we will crumple and fall under the new pressures."

In 1967, Toyoda was named president of Toyota Motor Company—the first family member to assume that post since Kiichiro resigned in 1950. The family power wasn't consolidated until 1981, when Sadazo Yamamoto was replaced as president of Toyota Motor Sales by Shoichiro Toyoda, son of Kiichiro and nicknamed the "Crown Prince" by the Japanese press. A year later, the two branches of the company were unified in the new Toyota Motor Corporation, with Eiji Toyoda as chairman and Shoichiro Toyoda as president and chief executive officer. A Business Week article at the time quoted a Japanese economist as saying the return of the Toyoda family to power was a "restoration of the bluest of blue blood." At this stage of the company's history, there may be a strong family presence (after a stretch of non-family leadership for most of the post-war period), but not "control" in the Western sense. The top three family members own just over one percent of Toyota Motor stock, according to Britain's Financial Times. In contrast, the Ford family in the United States controls 40 percent of the voting power in the Ford Motor Company.

The Toyota's led their company to a record year in 1984. Toyota sold an all-time high 1.7 million vehicles in Japan and the same number overseas. Profits peaked at $2.1 billion for the fiscal year ending March 31, 1985. While that performance would certainly earn Toyota a mention in automotive history books, Eiji Toyoda and his company may be better remembered for a distinctive management style that has being copied by hundreds of Japanese companies and is gaining growing acceptance in the United States. The Toyota approach, adopted at its ten Japanese factories and 24 plants in seventeen countries, has three main objectives: Keeping inventory to an absolute minimum through a system called Kanban, or "just in time," crossing that each step of the assembly process is performed correctly the first time, and cutting the amount of human labour that goes into each car. Despite the predominance of robots and automation at Toyota, the company firmly believes in the principle of lifetime employment; displaced workers are not laid off, but frequently transferred to other jobs. Toyoda believes the day when robots totally replace humans is a long way off. He told The Wheel Extended: "At the current stage, there is a greater difference between humans and robots than between cars and magic clouds. Robots can't even walk yet. They sit in one place and do exactly as programmed. But that's all. There is no way that robots can replace all the work of humans."

Due in part to that sort of philosophy, it's not surprising that company loyalty is so high. Toyota's 60, 000 employees in Japan, for instance, are encouraged to make cost-cutting suggestions, an idea that Eiji Toyoda borrowed from Ford after his first visit to the United States. Since the system began in 1951, tens of millions of suggestions have flooded the executive offices. "The Japanese," asserts Toyoda, "excel in improving things."

FINAL SESSION: NIGERIA TAX, POLICY AND RATES IN NIGERIA
Laws to Note When Setting Up a Small Business in Nigeria

CORPORATE TAX RATE IN NIGERIA

Nigeria Taxes	Last	Previous
Corporate Tax Rate	**30.00**	**30.00**
Personal Income Tax Rate	**24.00**	**24.00**
Sales Tax Rate	**5.00**	**5.00**

INCOME CHARGEABLE
A Business Name owner in Nigeria shall pay tax for each year of assessment on the aggregate amount from every source of income for the year. This includes the profits from trade or business, salaries, wages, fees, allowances or other gains or profits from employment including compensations, bonuses, premiums or benefits given or granted by an employer to an employee, profits and premiums arising from rights granted to another person for the use or occupation of property, dividend, interest, annuity.

THE TAX IDENTIFICATION NUMBER
A Business Name owner must register with and obtain a Tax Identification Number ('TIN') from the State Board Internal Revenue to enable the payment of

taxes such as Personal Income Tax, Withholding Tax and also for VAT purposes.

A TIN is an identification number for the business which is used by the Internal Revenue Service in the administration of Tax. A TIN must be furnished on Returns, Statement and other Tax related documents.

FILING OF RETURNS

All taxable persons are required to prepare and submit annual self-assessment tax returns within 90 days from the commencement of every year and include the amount of tax payable. For each year of assessment, you are required to file a return of income in the prescribed form and containing the following information, with the relevant Tax authority where the taxable person is deemed to be resident:
- the amount of income from every source of the year preceding the year of assessment,
- Such particulars as may be required for the purpose of the Act with respect to any such income, allowances, reliefs, deductions etc.
- A declaration by him or on his behalf that the return contains a true and correct statement of the income disclosed on the form, in accordance with the provisions of the Act.

PAYE

Persons on paid employment pay their personal income tax through the Pay as You Earn (PAYE) system. Under the system, employers deduct the prescribed tax from workers' salaries and pay directly to the FIRS through the designated banks on behalf of the employees on a monthly basis

THE RELEVANT TAX AUTHORITY

The State Boards of Internal Revenue collect the Personal Income Taxes of:
- Individuals in their various states of residence
- Body of individuals such as communities, families that run a business
- Business names
- Executors of estates of deceased persons and trustees of trusts.

The Federal Inland Revenue Service collects Personal Income Taxes of:
- Persons employed in the Nigerian Army, the Nigerian Navy, the Nigerian Air Force and the Nigerian Police other than in a civilian capacity;
- Officers of the Nigerian Foreign Service;
- Non-residents who derive income or profit from Nigeria

While there is no promise yet to simplify the applicability of these laws, Odunoluwa Longe, Co-founder/Lead Counsel the Longe Practice LP, an entrepreneur-focused legal practice and a Mentor on Nigeria's largest entrepreneurship community, Mara Mentor, helps simplify the understanding of the laws regulating small business. Read, imbibe and implement.

LAWS PERTAINING TO CREATION OF ENTITIES
•Companies and allied matters act
Popularly referred to as CAMA is the genesis of all business entities in Nigeria. It creates the Corporate Affairs Commission which is the regulator of almost all business entities in Nigeria and provides for the creation of various business entities and their general operating guidelines. Most common entities for SMES in Nigeria are:

•Business Name which can be used by a sole proprietor or several individuals; with the promoters having no limited liability.

II. Limited Liability Company "LTD" which may have at least two but not more than 50 shareholders. Shareholders liability is limited to their separate equity contribution.

III. Partnership can be formed by a maximum of twenty people who have unlimited liability for (1) themselves as individuals; (2) for every other partner in the business; and (3) the partnership as an entity. CAMA also provides for the Limited Partnership which is simply a partnership whereby some partners are able to limit their liability. At least one partner must be a general partner with no limited liability in a Limited Partnership

•Lagos State partnership (amendment) law, 2008
Although limited in applicability being a state law, it is instructive to mention this law as it also provides for the creation of another type of business entity known as the Limited Liability Partnership "LLP". Currently, only Lagos State has a law permitting the creation of LLPs. The LLP is a form of partnership whereby all the partners have limited liability. Unfortunately, there is uncertainty regarding the legal status and recognition of an LLP in other parts of Nigeria outside of its state of creation.

•Other entities under CAMA that are not commonly used by SMEs include: Public Liability Company "PLC", Company Limited by Guarantee "LTD/GTE", Incorporated Trustees, Unlimited Liability Company (UNLTD) etc.

•Laws pertaining to taxation
"…but in this world, nothing can be said to be certain, except death and taxes". This statement is as valid today as it was in 1789 when Benjamin Franklin made

it. The general belief is that there are myriad of tax regulations at all government levels in Nigeria such that it appears a business owner would be left with nothing after paying all the requisite taxes. Of course, this is not totally correct as taxes applicable actually depend on the business entity adopted by an SME and sometimes, the nature of business. For instance, Business Names and Partnerships are not eligible to pay company-imposed taxes and as such are exempt from almost all taxes at the federal level except Value Added Tax (VAT)

Taxes Payable to Each Government Level in Nigeria:
•**Federal Taxes:** If your business entity is a company (whether, limited or unlimited, private or public), you have to pay companies income tax which is provided for under the Companies Income Tax Act. Other taxes payable to the federal government include withholding tax and capital gains tax on companies and Value Added Tax. There are other taxes which may be payable to the federal government depending on the type of entity, industry etc., however the highlighted taxes are almost always compulsory for all companies.

•**State Taxes:** Personal Income Tax, Withholding Tax and Capital Gains Tax on individuals are taxes payable in all states and generally applicable to all individuals. Some states may impose other taxes, For instance, Lagos State charges the Sales Tax.

• **Local Government Taxes:** This is one messy taxation level that unfortunately is usually abused by most local governments in Nigeria. There are a number of taxes that may be enforced at this level such as shop and kiosk rates, tenement rates, market taxes and levies and more ridiculous ones such as radio and television licence fees, vehicle radio licence fees etc.

The above is by no means an exhaustive list of taxes payable but are generally applicable especially the mentioned federal and state taxes. I would advise the proprietor(s) of any SME to consult a lawyer for guidance on the most tax-efficient entity before proceeding to incorporate. It would help to develop a relationship with a local government official in the local government where your business is situated so as to stay informed on the necessary taxes payable at that level.

• **Laws Pertaining to Daily Operations**
The operating laws applicable for each SME would depend on the type of business carried out by the SME and/or the industry within which such SME operates. For instance, an SME involved in production or sale of foods and drugs would be regulated by the National Agency for Food and Drug Administration and Control (NAFDAC) guidelines, an SME involved in telecommunications would be guided by the National Communications

Commission (NCC) guidelines, and one that creates intangible properties would want to take cognisance of the various Intellectual Property ("IP") laws. I would expatiate briefly on the IP laws as I get a lot of enquiries regarding these below:

- **Patents and Designs Act governs patent registration in Nigeria.** An invention is patentable if it is (1) New; (2) resulted from an inventive activity and is capable of use in an industry; and (3) constitutes an improvement on a patented invention. Nigeria patent law is on a first to register basis which makes the registrant a Statutory Inventor, however, if there is an objection which is proven to the satisfaction on the patent registry, an objector may be registered as the true inventor of an invention

- **Trademarks Act governs the registration of trademarks in Nigeria.**

To be registerable, a trademark must have at least one of the following:
The name of the company, individual or firm represented in a special or particular manner;
The signature of the applicant for registration, or some predecessor in his business;
An invented word or words;

A word or words having no direct reference to the character or quality of the goods to which the trademark applies and not being according to its ordinary signification a geographical name or surname;

Any other distinctive mark. Trademarks are registered in various classes, and a violator can be prosecuted. There is also the option of getting a lawyer to write a "Cease and Desist Letter" to a violator before exploring litigation. Note that Nigerian laws at this time do not provide for the registration of service-marks although there is a bill before the National Assembly to amend this among other amendments

Copyright Act is applicable for the protection of (1) literary works; (2) musical works; (3) artistic works; (4) cinematograph films; (5) sound recordings; and (6) broadcasts. It is not unusual to find some people who register their business plans, codes, formulas, etc. as literary works pending the creation of the final patentable product as a protective measure while discussing with investors. While a single article is not able to do justice to all the laws applicable to SMEs in Nigeria, I hope some clarity has being provided as to the available business entity options, how to determine applicable taxes and the available IP protection laws. Generally, my advice for all SMEs is do not be penny wise, pound foolish; at the commencement of your business, speak to a lawyer who can advise on the various laws applicable to your own specific situation. It is always cheaper on the long run.

FEDERAL INLAND REVENUE SERVICE IN NIGERIA (FIRS)–
INFORMATION ON VALUE ADDED TAX (V.A.T)
What is Value Added Tax?

Value Added Tax (V.A.T) is a consumption tax paid when goods are purchased or services are enjoyed. For simplicity sake V.A.T is a tax levied on consumption. It is payable only when taxable goods or services are consumed. Consequently, if there is no consumption the tax is not collectible

VAT was introduced by the enactment of the VAT act in 1993 to replace the then sales tax. It is collected by the federal inland revenue service (F.I.R.S) on behalf of the federal government of Nigeria (FGN).

Registration under VAT Act

Registration for VAT purpose is free and compulsory for all business entities including manufacturers, wholesalers, retailers, distributors, banks and financial institutions, importers and exporters, oil and gas companies and suppliers of goods and services in Nigeria. Also, government organisations and non-Governmental organisations (NGOs) are required to register for VAT

Benefits of Registration

The benefits a taxable person stands to gain from voluntary registration include:

- Claim of credit for any input VAT paid on purchase of goods
- Government patronage
- Claim of refund on excess tax paid

Taxpayer Identification Number (TIN)

All registered persons under the VAT Act administration are issued with TIN on registration with the FIRS after presentation of relevant documents. The documents required for TIN to be issued are:

Individuals

- Duly completed taxpayer registration input form
- Valid means of identification: international passport/National identity card/Driver's License
- Valid e-mail address and telephone number

Companies, business or Enterprises

1) Duly completed taxpayer registration Input Form

2) Certificate of incorporation/registration Memorandum and Article of Association (Where applicable)
3) Documents containing the following information:

   a. Registered address of company/Enterprise
   b. Principal place of business
   c. Date of commencement of business and accounting year end
   d. Name of bankers, auditors and Tax consultants

4. Valid e-mail address and telephone (GSM) number

FIRS expectations from Taxable persons under the VAT Act

In line with their vision to deliver quality service to all taxpayers in partnership with all stakeholders and make taxation the pivot of national development, FIRS expect the following from taxable persons:

1. **Registration:** It is the obligation of all taxable persons/collecting agents to comply with the VAT Act by registering with the FIRS and obtaining their taxpayer identification Number (TIN).
2. **Charging of VAT on taxable goods and services:** All taxable persons are required to add 5% VAT on all taxable transactions (goods or services). This should be clearly stated on the invoices issued to customers.
3. **Keeping of Records:** the administration of the VAT Act relies heavily on proper record keeping by taxable persons. All taxable persons are to ensure that records of all their business transactions are properly kept.
4. **Filing of VAT Returns:** The VAT Act requires all taxable persons to file VAT returns, using form 002, to Tax office on or before 21st day of the month following the month of transaction.
5. **Remittance of VAT:** Remittance of VAT by all taxable persons (Including collecting agents) is to be made concurrently with filling of the VAT returns i.e. 21 days after the month of transaction. All VAT remittances are to be made only through approved collecting banks or other payment channels e.g. e-Taxpay, Remita, internet banking etc
6. **Cooperation with FIRS officials:** FIRS carries out monitoring visits to taxable persons to educate them and monitor compliance with the VAT Act. Taxable persons are required to cooperate only with identified staff of the FIRS
7. **Notification of change:** All taxable persons are required to notify FIRS of any changes regarding their operations e.g. change of address, business line or regarding any compliance challenges faced by them.

Rights of Taxable person

1. It is the right of a taxable person:
2. To be given a taxpayer identification Number (TIN) free of charge immediately on request or to be provided with reason for failure to issue TIN
3. To object disputed VAT assessment as specified in the VAT Act
4. To appeal against a notice of refusal to amend a VAT assessment as specified in the VAT Act
5. To claim INPUT tax (on goods purchased or imported directly for resale and goods that constitute stock-in-trade) by deducting it from OUTPUT tax
6. To demand for proper identification from any person claiming to be an official of FIRS
7. To be granted refund on excess VAT paid with the option of using it to offset future VAT liability
8. To be issued receipt for all VAT remittances/Payment to the tax office
9. To be educated/enlightened by FIRS in area of concern.

VAT Compliance pitfalls to avoid

1. Failure to register and obtain a TIN
2. Failure to keep proper business records
3. Failure to charge VAT on taxable goods or services
4. Charging VAT at an incorrect rate
5. Failure to prepare and file tax returns on or before due date
6. Failure to remit all VAT collected on or before due date
7. Engaging the services of touts or any tax official to transact tax business on your behalf. Taxpayers are advised to engage the services of recognised members of approved professional bodies i.e. CITN, ICAN OR ANAN
8. Engaging in any form of tax evasion practices
9. Transacting business with any person/entity without a valid TIN
10. Failure to notify FIRS on change of business address

ELECTRONIC-TAX PAYMENT

1. **e-Tax Pay:** Log on to the internet banking platform of your bank
2. Click on **NIBSS e-bills Pay.**
3. Click on the e-taxpay tab or type federal inland revenue service in the search bar.
4. Input your Tax Identification Number (TIN) then verify and confirm your TIN details before selecting the type of tax you are paying
5. Enter the amount, confirm all details and click: continue to pay
6. e-acknowledgement is automatically sent to your e-mail

7. Your FIRS official receipt is sent to your e-mail 24 hours after receipt of payment
8. Click on the indicated link to download and print your receipt.

Remita

1. Go to www.firs.gov.ng
2. Click on e-services
3. Click on Remita
4. Select tax type
5. Enter your TIN payment amount, tax year, taxpayer's full name, e-mail address and phone number
6. Enter the CAPTCHA image
7. Click on processed to payment
8. e-Acknowledgement is automatically sent to your e-mail
9. Your official FIRS receipt is sent to your e-mail 24hours after receipt of payment
10. Click on the indicated link to download and print your receipt

E – REGISTRATION

To do business online with the FIRS, Register and be Authenticated at www.firs.gov.ng and follow these easy steps

1. Log in and proceed to the e-services tab
2. Click on the log in or register tab and input your tax Identification Number (TIN) or RC number
3. Choose a username and password upon successful registration.
4. Click on register
5. A security PIN will be sent to your e-mail for authentication to complete the process.

E – FILING

The federal inland revenue service (FIRS) has automated its tax administration processes through the integrated Tax Administration System (ITAS)

To file online

1. Go to www.firs.gov.ng
2. Click on e-services
3. Click on e-filing
4. Click on download e-filing access form
5. Complete the form

6. Ensure that it is duly signed by the taxpayer and/or authorized officer of the taxpayer
7. Select your tax office, scan and e-mail the completed form to your tax office
8. Check your e-mail for your user ID and password
9. Log into ITAS e-filing portal with your ID and password
10. Upload your return
11. Click submit
12. Document Number will be provided automatically
13. Click on payment

CONCLUSION OF START-UP INSIGHTS

8. RESULTS: Ripping the fruit of your Labour, by following the process from **Step 1** to **Step 12**

THE NIGERIAN LABOUR LAW 9 TIPS FROM EMPLOYERS TO EMPLOYEES (AS AT 2019)

(Lawpadi, 2019) The Nigerian Labour Act is the primary legislation which deals with the relationship between an employer and its employees. It contains quite a few provisions which govern this relationship dynamic, and all the regulatory processes applicable for employers.

Firstly, and most importantly, it appears that the Labour Act is not applicable to all classes of employees in Nigeria. The Act uses the word 'workers' in describing employees, and defines workers as not including persons exercising administrative, executive, technical or professional functions as public officers or otherwise. This means if the nature of your role is administrative, executive, technical or professional, then you are not covered by the Act. The Labour Act **only covers employees engaged under a contract of manual labour or clerical work in private and public sector.**

TIP 1: Forced Labour is illegal. The first (and in our opinion, most important) thing every Nigerian should know is that it is illegal to force anyone to work for you. It is every Nigerian's right to be free from forced labour, and this right is guaranteed under the 1999 constitution. Apart from existing in the constitution, it is also restated in the Labour Act. Therefore, if you or someone you know is being forced to work against your will, you can report to the police as it is a crime. However, the Labour Act gives the government the ability to be able to requisition people to work during an *emergency or a calamity*, and this will not be classed as 'forced labour'

TIP 2: All employees must have a written contract. The Labour Act states that an employer must give an employee a written contract within 3 months of the commencement of the employment. The contract must have the certain key terms – name of employer/employee, nature of employment, duration, wages etc. The key thing here is to ensure that the employee is protected by all the relevant terms being reduced to writing so the employee knows what is expected of him/her. Also important is that if there is any change in the terms of the employment, it should be made known in writing to the employee within 1 month.

TIP 3: Payment of wages. Any contract where the whole or part of the worker's wages is made payable in any other manner apart from legal tender shall be illegal, null and void. Therefore, it is illegal for your employer to attempt to pay you with things other than money. A few other key things to note around wages is:

- It is illegal for any contract to be for the payment of wages at intervals exceeding one month unless with the written consent of the State Authority. This means if your employer makes you sign an employment contract where the employee is to be paid every quarter or every 6 weeks etc., such a contract is illegal.

- No employer can impose any restrictions as to the place and way the employee can spend his/her wages. So, your employer can't insist that you only buy lunch from the office canteen.

- Employers are not allowed to provide an advance of wages more than 1month wages

TIP 4: Salary Deductions. Employers are not allowed to deduct an employee's wages for any reason, unless reasonable deduction for injury/loss caused to the employer by the employee, but only with prior written consent of an authorized labour officer. Also, if you are lucky enough to have your employer mistakenly overpay you, then you should know that the money which was overpaid can only be deducted within 3 months from the date of the overpayment. Any attempt by your employer to deduct the overpayment from your future salary after the expiration of this 3-month period is illegal

TIP 5: Illegal to prevent employees from joining trade unions and other labour associations. No employment contract can prevent workers from joining trade unions, and any contract which makes it a condition of employment that the worker should relinquish membership of a trade union or prejudices workers by reason of trade union membership is illegal.

TIP 6: Rest Hours, Sick Leave, and Holidays for Employees.

- If a worker is at work for more than 6 hours a day, he/she must be given at least 1 hour of rest-interval in that day. Further, in every period of 7 days, a worker is entitled to at least 1 day of rest which must not be less than 24 consecutive hours. So, for instance if you work Sunday all through Saturday, you must have the whole of the following Sunday as a mandatory day off.

- Every worker is also entitled to 12 days' sick leave for temporary illness certified by a registered medical practitioner.

- Every employee after 12 months of continuous service is entitled to a holiday with full pay of at least six working days (this is exclusive of all the public holidays)

TIP 7: Maternity and Paternity leave. All female employees are entitled to at least 12 weeks' maternity leave with full pay. Unfortunately, the Nigerian Labour Act does not recognise paternity leave and makes no such provisions. However, in Lagos State civil servants are entitled to 10 days' paternity leave within the first 2 months of the birth of the baby.

TIP 8: Transfer of employment. An employee must consent to the transfer of his/her employment from one employer to another for it to be valid, and the transfer must be endorsed by an authorized Labour officer. So, if for instance your company is taken over by another company, your employment will not automatically move to this new company (employer) without first consulting you and getting your agreement to transfer your employment.

TIP 9: Termination of employment. With respect to the termination of an employment contract, the Labour Act provides for minimum notice periods:

1. Where the employee has been employed for a period of 3 months or less, either party may terminate the contract with a minimum of 1-day notice

2. Where the employee has been employed for a period of 3 months but less than 2 years, either party may terminate the contract with a minimum of 1-week notice

3. where the employee has been employed for a period of 2 years but less than 5 years, either party may terminate the contract with a minimum of 2-weeks' notice

4. Where the employee has been employed for a period of 5 years or more, either party may terminate the contract with a minimum of 1-month notice

5. When giving notice of termination of employment contract where the notice is 1 week or more, the notice must be in writing

QUOTES: FOOD FOR THOUGHT

"People who cannot control their cash flow end up working for those who can" **by Robert Kiyosaki**

"Making more money will not solve your problems if cash flow management is the problem and the people who understand the power of financial numbers have power over those who do not" **by Robert Kiyosaki**

"The Ability to convert cash invested into labour or assets into continuous cash flow straight into your bank account is your start-up journey to wealth" **by Eneanya Austin.**

"When a man hopes to do the possible and thinks impossible, emptiness, failure, frustration awaits him ahead. But when a man thinks the impossible, to achieve the impossible requires going the extra mile because only then, is impossible possible if you can think possibility even though challenges wait along the way" **by Eneanya Austin.**

"No matter the complexity in any system there is always a molecularly/unit system approach to such complexity. Every complex system is created on connected structure in which that system is driven" **by Eneanya Austin.**

"Learn from the mistakes of others and create a better solution to avoid the mistakes because by so doing you would have saved yourself a thousand life time of making the same mistake they made" **by Eneanya Austin.**

"Citadel of Learning grows on the Platform of Assimilation and meditation then powered by a will to execute and implement thoughts/knowledge acquired, by so doing you will become a walking/working Authority in that field" **by Eneanya Austin.**

"The only Place Where Success comes before work is in the dictionary" **by Vidal Sassoon.**

CHAPTER 8
TIPS ON MANAGING YOUR COMPANY

"A successful Management system synchronises 5 elements: Planning, Supervising, Organising, Leading, and motivation. You cannot Create Wealth if you do not put a good management system in place" by **Matthew Ashimolowo**

Managing a company requires knowledge, dedication, organizational skills and ingenuity. To effectively manage a company, get informed about hiring and managing employees, budgeting, marketing, and tax and employment laws. Here are a few strategies for the successful management of a company.

Outline your vision for the company. Think about the ultimate goal of your product or service. The overall vision for the company may be to address a need, provide a service or create something new. Generating revenue is a given goal for companies, so the vision statement should be broader than a statement about profits.

Analyse the company budget. Assess your financial status. The development of new products and services requires staff and resources. Determine how much money you can devote to these expenses. Factor in overhead costs for rent, utilities, marketing and other business-related expenses. Create a contingency fund to set aside in the event of emergency needs. Hire a finance person, if necessary, to handle these tasks.

Make decisions about marketing efforts. Marketing activities in larger companies are generally handled by a department or a team of people. In a small business, you may be responsible for overseeing marketing efforts. Determine how you will market your products or services. Delegate marketing tasks to employees and monitor their progress.

Hire and manage employees.

1. Advertise for qualified workers. Choose from a variety of methods for hiring new employees, such as posting Internet advertisement, hiring a recruitment firm, placing an advertisement in the newspaper or spreading the word in niche-specific networks. To attract qualified candidates, be specific about your hiring needs and requirements.

2. Interview prospective employees. Put applicants at ease by being personable and communicative. Project a professional image during the interview by being attentive and dressed in business attire. Limit the conversation primarily to business-related matters.

3. Familiarize yourself with employment laws. Study the requirements in your jurisdiction and industry for laws related to employee hours, breaks, tax requirements and benefits.
4. Decide on your management style. Empower employees by explaining tasks and allowing them to manage their duties, checking in with you for clarification as needed. Alternatively, schedule regular check-in sessions with employees to evaluate progress on specific projects or tasks.
5. Address employee needs and conflicts. Create an environment of open communication for employees to approach you regarding professional conflicts. Address conflicts by listening, asking questions, showing objectivity and taking a solution-oriented approach to resolving problems.

Assess company progress. Decide on a regular time frame for evaluating your company's progress towards its goals. You might engage in this assessment on a weekly, monthly or quarterly basis. Take this time to evaluate your marketing efforts, product sales, financial health, employee issues and all other business-related matters.

Take courses in business management. In the process of managing a company, you may recognise skill areas in need of strengthening. Conflict resolution, marketing knowledge, technical skills and employee management are a few of the areas that may need further development. Contact colleges, universities or business institutes for course offerings. Being mentored by experienced business leaders is also an option.

INTRODUCTION: ROLES AND RESPONSIBILITY OF CHIEF EXECUTIVE OFFICER (google.com)
Leader

1. Advises the board
2. Advocates/promotes organization and stakeholder change related to organization mission.
3. Supports motivation of employees in organization products/program and operations

Visionary/Information Bearer

1. Ensures staff and Board have sufficient and up-to-date information
2. Looks to the future for change opportunities
3. Interfaces between Board and employees
4. Interfaces between organization and community

Decision Maker

Formulates policies and planning recommendations to the board

Decides or guides courses of action in operations by staff

Manager

1. Overseas operations of organization
2. Implements plans
3. Manages human resources of organization
4. Manages financial and physical resources

Board Developer

1. Assists in the selection and evaluation of board members
2. Makes recommendations, supports board during orientation and self-evaluation
3. Supports Board's evaluation of Chief Executive

Responsibilities of Chief Executive Officer by job description

1. Board Administration and Support

Supports operations and administration of board by advising and informing board members, interfacing between Board and Staff and supporting Board's evaluation of chief executive

2. Program, Product and Service Delivery

Oversees design, marketing, promotion, delivery and quality of programs, products and services

3. Financial, Tax, Risk and Facilities Management

Recommends yearly budget for board approval and prudently manages organization's resources within those budget guidelines according to current laws and regulations

4. Human Resource Management

Effectively manages the human resources of the organization according to authorized personnel policies and procedures that fully conform to current laws and regulations.

5. Community and Public Relations

Assures the organization and its mission, programs, products and services are consistently presented in strong, positive image to relevant stakeholders

6. Fund raising (non-profit specific)

Oversees fund raising planning and implementation including identifying resource requirements, researching funding sources, establishing strategies to approach funders, submitting proposals and administrating fund-raising records and documentation.

SESSION 1: 7 LEADERSHIP PRINCIPLES TO LEARN FROM AN EAGLE
1. Eagles fly alone and at high altitudes, they don't fly with sparrows, ravens and other small birds.

INTERPRETATION: Stay away from narrow minded people, those that bring you down. Eagles fly with eagles. Keep good company.

2. Eagles have accurate vision. They have the ability to focus on something as far as 5km away. No matter the obstacles, the eagle will not move his focus from the prey until he grabs it.

INTERPRETATION: Have a vision and remain focused no matter what the obstacles and you will succeed.

3. Eagles do not eat dead things, they feed only on fresh prey.

INTERPRETATION: Do not rely on your past success, keep looking for new frontiers to conquer. Leave your past where it belongs, in the past.

4. Eagles love the storm. When clouds gather, the eagle gets excited, the eagle uses the storms wind to lift itself higher. Once it finds the wind of the storm, the eagle uses the raging storm to lift itself above the clouds. This gives the eagle an opportunity to glide and rest its wings. In the meantime, all the other birds hide in the branches and leaves of the tree.

INTERPRETATION: Face your challenges head on knowing that these will make you emerge stronger and better than you were. We can use the storms of life to rise to greater heights. Achievers are not afraid to raise to greater heights, Achievers are not afraid of challenges, rather they relish them and use them profitably.

5. When a female eagle meets a male eagle and they want to mate, she flies down to earth, picks a twig and flies back into the air with the male eagle in hot pursuit. Once she has reached a height high enough for her, she drops the twig and let it fall to the ground while she watches. The male eagle chases after the twig and catches it before it reaches the ground, then brings it back to the female eagle. The female eagle grabs the twig and flies to a much higher altitude and drop the twig again for the male eagle to chase. This goes on for hours with the height increasing each time until the female eagle is assured that the male eagle has mastered the art of picking the twig which shows commitment. Then and only then will she let him mate with her.

INTERPRETATION: Whether in private life or business, one should test the commitment of the people intended for partnership.

6. Eagles prepare for training; they remove the feathers and soft grass in the nest so that the young ones get uncomfortable in preparation for flying and eventually flies when it becomes unbearable to stay in the nest

INTERPRETATION: Leave your comfort zone if you must breakeven and achieve new frontiers there is no growth in comfort zone.

7. When the eagle grows old, his feathers becomes weak and cannot take him as fast and as high as it should. This makes him weak and could make him die. So he retires to a place far away in the mountains. While there, he plucks out the weak feathers on his body and breaks its beak and claws against the rocks until he is completely bare; a very bloody and painful process. Then he stays in this hiding place until he has grown new feathers, new beaks and claws and then he comes out flying higher than before.

INTERPRETATION: We need to shed off old habit no matter how difficult on things that drags us back and adds no value to our lives should be allowed to go.

SESSION 2: OUTLINE GROWTH STRATEGIES

Entrepreneurship does not necessarily require extraordinary ability but finding what you can do well and establishing it

In the words of **Mark Twain**, *"Twenty years from now, you will be more disappointed by the things you didn't do than by the ones you did do, so throw off the bow lines, Sail away from the safe harbour. Catch the trade in your sails. Explore, Dream, Discover."*

If your business isn't growing as fast as you'd like, you may have reached a degree of saturation within your existing target market(s). In order to grow faster, you may be well advised to look to new markets for growth. The following are five examples of marketing strategies you can implement to create sales for your business within new markets:

Expanding your product line or service offerings.

You can identify and access new markets that currently exist within your business's target market(s) by adding new products and/or services. By creating these new products or services, your business can reach members of target markets who were otherwise inaccessible to your business using its existing product/service mix.

Using strategic marketing alliances.

These alliances allow your business to sell its products and services through other existing businesses. Your business will be able to access the target markets these alliance partners currently serve, without having to do any additional marketing.

Opening a new location.

Once your business is successfully operating in and serving an identifiable target market area, it may be time to consider expanding with one or more branch locations. The key to creating and successfully operating a new location is to be certain that a strong demand already exists within this target market for your business's products and services. It takes considerable time and money to create demand where it doesn't currently exist. Additionally, you must ensure that these potential customers within this new location are in fact new potential customers, not existing customers of your business.

Marketing on the Internet.

If your business's products and services can be delivered to potential customers throughout the country and the world, you can gain access to the largest target market anywhere: the collection of potential customers you can reach via the Web. Although it's difficult to rely on potential Internet customers to "find" your business's Web site, using search engines for example, you can promote sales by aligning your business with existing successful Internet businesses. You can arrange for your business's URL to be displayed on a "click through basis by other Internet businesses. In this manner, you can generate customer leads from people who click through to your business' site.

SESSION 3: OUTSOURCING MANUFACTURING FOR PRODUCT BASED BUSINESSES (google.com)

Outsource Manufacturing: Outsourcing production can have some advantages for a new start-up product provided there are existing suppliers qualified to manufacture the items to your specifications. Control over the new product can be documented in contractual agreements.

When Is Outsourcing Reasonable?

Some of the advantages of outsourcing are:

1. **Financial benefits**—Improvement of balance sheet by reducing or eliminating assets and increased cash flow
2. **Strategic optimization**—Focus on core mission and allocation of operations to more profitable activities
3. **Better Supply Chain Management**—Ability to select suppliers who are leaders in their specific categories
4. **Market discipline**—Opportunity to focus company payroll and resources on growing your market share
5. **Technology**—Gain access to state-of-the-art technologies
6. **Flexibility**—Resources can be redirected to the company's core operations and new product development.

Cost advantages from outsourcing can come from following factors:

1. **Cheaper labour and lower asset cost**—the most common regions for outsourcing manufacturing are Asia, Latin America, and Eastern Europe Additionally, the cost to set up business (land acquisition, construction, etc.) is lower.
2. **Economies of scale due to pooling**—this effect is most pronounced in manufacturing when fixed costs are high and pooling across organizations result in lower per unit cost for all.
3. **Expertise due to learning curve**—the idea, also known as experience curve, was examined and popularized by BCG in 1960s. The theory says that an organization reduces its cost by 25% every time it doubles its production. Though the exact figures may not hold for all industries alike, the concept is still valid. As a company increases production, it learns how to better use its equipment, how to standardize and optimize processes and how to better use equipment. Employees gain expertise and become more efficient resulting in higher productive and increased cost savings.
4. **Lower fixed cost**—in outsourcing, the company only pays for the variable cost of production and does not incur upfront fixed cost for setting up the operations. As a result, the barriers to entry are lowered. Companies that earlier found the business unviable could now enter and also be competitive.

Factors to keep in mind when outsourcing:
1. Look for compatibility and management philosophies that align with your own
2. Focus on the best solution, not just lowest price
3. Develop detailed RFPs (Requests for Proposal), contracts that incorporate up-to-date legal caveats
4. Share risks and rewards
5. Involve key players
6. Document the transition phase
7. Communicate clearly from the beginning

Identifying the right manufacturer: It is important to select a manufacturer with experience and certifications in producing products similar to the one you are seeking to outsource. Do not select a factory who you will be putting in business for the first time. Location of the manufacturer is very important.

10 factors to be considered when qualifying a manufacturer:
1. **Legal** – Does the CMO hold the necessary manufacturing authorizations?
2. **Competence** – Can the CMO manufacture/test/pack the product(s) in question?
3. **Quality** – Does the CMO meet or exceed the quality standards of the sponsoring company?
4. **Capacity** – Does the CMO have the capability to meet sales demands?
5. **Cost** – Can the CMO supply the product cheaper than in-house production or competition?
6. **Commitment** – Does the CMO value your business?
7. **Continuity** – Is the CMO a secure and experienced business capable of long-term contract?
8. **Delivery** – Does the CMO deliver orders on time and in full?
9. **Communication** – Does the CMO have an infrastructure and culture capable of providing accurate, comprehensive and timely information?
10. **Cash resources** – Does the CMO invest sufficiently in maintaining up-to-date technologies?

Note: CMO means Contract Manufacturer organization (i.e. the manufacturer you are contracting)

How to Create a Request for a Proposal (RFP)?

A well-written RFP will clarify your objectives and the scope of the services you are seeking. It will also provide a structured format that delineates the way the contract manufacturer will present its capabilities, costs and expectations. Be sure to include these three requests, which are considered the most important requirements of any RFP:

- **References:** You want third party validation on the solution you're choosing.
- **Information on a manufacturer's organization:** Make sure you know how long they've being in the business, the company's stability, the tenure of the executive team, number of lifetime customers, customer retention rate, and so forth. You need to be sure that your business partner is prepared for a long-term commitment.
- **Information on research and development:** What percentage of the staff is committed to R and D? What's the company's monetary commitment to R and D? What's its release cycle?

RFPs typically have the following sections, though these are malleable and dependent on the nature of your project:

Introduction: Explain to potential bidders in broad terms why you are putting out an RFP and what you hope to accomplish by hiring one of them. You may also summarize key points from other sections, such as when their responses are due and when the project will start.

Background information: This section includes pertinent information about your organization and the history of the current project, leading up to the need for the RFP.

Requirements: This is the most important section and usually requires the most time. Included should be a detailed explanation of what you need the manufacturer to do, and a list of the information you expect to receive from the candidates.

Structure of the response: Present the structure of how you would like to receive the response. If the project is complex or highly technical, you can break down the requirements into bullet points to which the manufacturers are expected to respond.

A typical format for the response might include:

1. Executive summary (high level overview with key points)
2. Manufacturer company background information

3. Proposed services or deliverables (how the manufacturer will meet the RFP requirements)
4. Pricing
5. References

Product Design Basic Requirement:

From product concept to manufacturing and assembly, your product will be a success if you follow these twelve INSIGHTs:

1) Product concept:

What is your product and how is your product going to be used? This step includes brainstorming, sketching, and any other creative methods used to come up with a sellable product.

2) Research:

Know the current market and its demands. Are there similar products already being manufactured/sold? If there is a similar product, how is yours going to be better?

3) Product design development:

Using the information, you have gathered from your research you will be able to develop your product designs.

4) Research and development of the final design:

Creating accurate drawings with dimensions and material selection carefully considered will finalize your product design.

5) CAD (Computer Aided Design):

Using 3D modelling software, you will get a computerized 3D model of your final product design. These designs will highlight problem areas where the theoretical stresses and strains on the product will be shown. If there are any problems, you must address the design faults and revisit INSIGHT 4.

6) CAM (Computer Aided Manufacturing):

A prototype of your design will be created using computer aided engineering systems. The physical representation of your design will be used for testing and developing.

7) Prototype testing:

This is a critical phase, and you must be completely scrupulous in order to find out if your product will function properly. If it is not completely ready for manufacturing, you must return to the drawing board.

8) Manufacturing:

Once your product prototype is completely satisfactory, you can then move to the manufacturing process. Manufacturing costs depend on the complexity of your product. The number of components, material selection, and batch numbers must be considered to ensure healthy profits.

9) Assembly:

This is where your product finally takes form. It should be assembled using lasting materials and sound design. Quality assembly practices ensure a good product.

10) Feedback and testing:

The manufacturer will test your final product. Again, it is vital to be critical and honest in regards to the final product in order to decide whether any more product development is necessary at this point.

11) Product development:

If your testing and feedback highlight areas that need improvement, you will need to revisit your product development. However, a good manufacturing companies will have flagged obvious issues before you get to this stage.

12) Final product:

Now it's time to sell your product. The more you sell, the larger the manufacturing batches you can order, which will lower the cost of manufacture and increase your profits!

UNDERSTANDING START-UP COSTS, SAMPLES AND PRODUCT CHANGES

Gross margin is the money left after you have covered all the costs associated with the sale of a product or service (such as wages, materials, etc.). It is a measurement of your production efficiencies and it determines your breakeven point. It is a key calculation as you assess the risk and profitability within your company. Start-up costs are the expenses incurred during the process of creating a new business.

However, there are a few standard costs that are common to all business types:

1. Research expenses

2. Insurance, license and permit fees
3. Equipment and supplies
4. Advertising and promotion
5. Borrowing costs
6. Employee expenses
7. Technological expenses

To remain competitive in a changing business environment companies must be aware of all aspects of their business and look for ways to refine operations in order to reduce lead times, expedite speed to market, and reduce the cost of operations. All of these processes make the company more flexible so that it can respond to changes in customer demands and improve its market share.

Monitoring and Managing Production Quality Assurance

Quality assurance (QA) involves preventing mistakes or defects in manufactured products, guaranteeing that quality requirements will be fulfilled and avoiding problems when delivering solutions or services to customers.

Quality assurance is an integral part of monitoring and managing production and cannot be overlooked. Whether the item being produced is simple or complex, it is bound to have several steps in its production process. From manufacturer selection, to materials selection, to production and everything in between, quality assurance is vital every step of the way.

Monitoring and managing are essential parts of the process to ensure quality. Every stage of the production plan should possess a set of procedures to monitor and control the processes. First and foremost, the selected manufacturer must be evaluated in terms of its quality of technology, procedures, and labour. During the production and manufacturing stage, each product must have a pre-determined set of steps that will be followed to ensure their safety and quality. These monitoring procedures are used to foresee, detect, and repair any issues in quality.

For instance, one could make a manufacturing decision based on cost, but when dealing with outsourcing production, many other considerations such as quality, time, and technology should all be taken into account when making a decision.

Once a manufacturer has being selected for a certain product, every step of the production process needs to be monitored, ensuring that all specifications are followed. After the audits, a report should be compiled and shared that details progress including photos, videos, timing updates and anything else necessary to assure the quality of every product being manufactured.

Communication and Project Management

The goal of Project Communications Management is to ensure timely and appropriate generation, collection, storage, and distribution of project information. Successful project management depends heavily on quality communication. In order to accomplish a project successfully, everyone involved must take part in open and candid communication.

The project manager can often handle the communication through informal channels such as one-on-one meetings or calls to all of the team members and stakeholders.

The project manager must spend dedicated time keeping everyone on the project aware of statuses, issues, and changes all while maintaining the timeline. Also, stakeholder meetings hold much more weight and require large amounts of preparation. Throughout complex programs, the program manager spends the majority of their time maintaining communication and attending to risk management.

A project manager should incorporate a communication plan at the planning stage of the project. When making a communication plan, a project manager will have to ask the following questions:

1. What kind of communication is required? (Management meetings, team meetings, management reporting, project records, etc.)
2. Who needs to be communicated with? (Who should stakeholders, team leaders, team members, etc.)
3. What is the chain of command? (Everyone should know exactly to whom they should report progress/issues)
4. How frequent is communication required? (Scheduled meetings, open doors, progress reports, etc.)
5. What needs to be communicated? (Reports, meeting minutes, details or summaries, etc.)

To be successful in outsource manufacturing, document control and quality need to function in concert with your partner. From initial product specification to final sign-off, your product team must be in close contact with your outsourcing manufacturing partners to ensure that your cost, quality and schedule goals are met. Each step will work towards building a concurrent process between all project members.

With the production outsourced, the company can now focus its resources, on the areas that increase revenue and profit. If outsourcing reduces manufacturing costs, the company can increase its revenue through a better focus on sales and marketing therefore increasing its profit margin as well.

SESSION 4: NAFDAC GUIDELINES FOR ESTABLISHMENT OF FOOD MANUFACTURING PLANTS IN NIGERIA

1.0 GENERAL

1.1 These guidelines are for the general public and in particular industries that want to engage in food manufacturing.

1.2. These guidelines prescribe the minimum good manufacturing practice requirements for the facilities, controls to be used in the manufacture, processing and packing of products to ensure that they meet quality standards.

1.3. The guidelines should also apply to persons that may engage in some aspects of a manufacturing process e.g. packaging.

1.4. It is necessary to emphasize that no food product should be manufactured, imported, exported, advertised, sold or distributed in Nigeria unless it has been registered in accordance with the provisions of Act Cap F33 LFN 2004. Consequently, a food product shall not be manufactured in Nigeria unless the factory is inspected and certificate of recognition is issued by NAFDAC.

2.0 ORGANIZATION AND PERSONNEL

2.1 There should be an adequate organizational structure that clearly defines
a) Qualification of key personnel.
b) Responsibility

2.2 There should be an adequate number of qualified personnel to perform assigned duties.

2.3 Each key personnel engaged in food manufacturing should have
a) Adequate education
b) Experience

2.4 The quality control and production units shall be distinct organizational units that function and report to management independently of each other and of all other functional units

2.5 Personnel should wear protective apparel/gears, such as head, face, hand, and arm coverings to
protect products from contamination.

NATIONAL AGENCY FOR FOOD AND DRUG ADMINISTRATION AND CONTROL (NAFDAC)

2.6 Personnel should practice good sanitary and hygienic habits.

2.7 All personnel should have access to medical treatment and checks for communicable diseases and the records should be kept.

2.8 There should be adequate training for employees in the particular operations that they perform

2.9 Consultants advising on any form of manufacturing process should have sufficient education, training, and experience to advice on the subject for which they are retained.

3.0 PLANT AND FACILITIES

3.1 Building(s) used in the manufacture, processing and packing of food products should be Adequately located, constructed and of suitable size to facilitate cleaning, maintenance and Proper operations as appropriate to the type and stage of manufacture.

3.2 The building should have adequate space for the orderly placement of equipment and materials to prevent mix-ups between different materials.

3.3 The building should be designed to maintain orderly flow of personnel and materials

3.4 There should be defined areas of adequate size to accommodate the different operations in a logical order of production flow corresponding to the sequence of the operations.

Operational areas should include;
a. Cloakroom/ Toilet facilities (which should not open directly into the production area)
b. Raw Materials Store
c. Packaging Materials Store
d. Production Room
e. Finished Products Store

Quality Control Laboratory

3.5 Floors, walls and ceilings of smooth, hard surfaces that can be easily cleaned and disinfected routinely should be provided.

3.6 Ceiling boards should be made of non-asbestos and non-flaking material.

3.7 Windows and entrance doors should be screened with insect-proof netting and the doors should be self-closing to prevent contamination and be constructed in such a way as not to trap dust.

3.8 Adequate lighting should be provided in all areas to facilitate easy identification of materials, cleaning, maintenance and proper operations.

3.9 Adequate ventilation, cooling and exhaust systems should be provided where appropriate to minimize condensation in all the sections and in high risk food manufacturing appropriate air level purification should be put in place at the required section.

3.9.1 Pallets or shelves (not wooden) should be provided for storage of materials in the raw materials store.

Cold Storage:

3.9.2 A cold room should be provided for materials (raw material, packaging material or finished product) that require special storage conditions and should have the following features:

a. It should be an enclosure fitted with air cooling/freezing facilities.
b. A thermometer should be installed such that it can be read off without opening the cold Room.
c. A temperature monitoring chart should be kept to ensure that the cold chain is constantly maintained.
e. A stand by generator should be installed as alternative power source.
f. Illumination should be provided in the cold room.

3.9.3 **PRODUCTION SECTION**

A. In production section where water forms part of the production process, the walls and floor should be made of easily cleaned and disinfected non shedding durable material and should have smooth surface.

I. A functional air conditioner or cooling system shall be installed in this room to enhance Ventilation. However, for production rooms where heat and possibly dust from powdered Raw materials, exhaust fans and (or) dust extractors shall be used to enhance ventilation and Remove dust in this room.

ii. Illumination shall be via electric lighting and the room shall be sufficiently lit.

iii. Production equipment installed in this room should allow for smooth flow of production process and movement of personnel.

b. **Finished Product Store:**
This room shall be used for the storage of the finished products. Depending on the nature of the finished product, this room could be a dry store, cool room or cold room. Other features required in this room shall include;

I. The room shall be adequate in size for its intended use.

ii. Illumination shall be via electric lighting and the room shall be sufficiently lit.

iii. Depending on the nature of the product ventilation shall be via air conditioners or exhaust fans or limit of purified air system.

iv. The floor should be made of easily cleaned and disinfected non shedding durable material and should have smooth surface.

v. Storage of finished products shall be on pallets or shelves (not wooden) of sufficient Strength to carry the weight of the products. The arrangement should allow for easy cleaning and movement of personnel.

vi. Self-closing doors and windows should be screened with insect-proof netting.

vii. There should be provision for quarantine and approved products.

3.9.4 Factories sited in commercial areas are unacceptable.
3.9.5 The factory can either be a purpose – built structure or a suitably adapted building.
3.9.5 The factory shall be constructed of cement or concrete and not made of wooden or prefab materials.
3.9.6 The size must be adequate for its intended use to facilitate cleaning and proper operation.
3.9.7 The facility shall be fenced round with block walls of at least five feet high to prevent external interference and should be plastered.
3.9.8 The factory shall not be sited less than 100 meters from a refuse dump, abattoir, graveyard, oil depot (petroleum and vegetable), and canal or cement factory.

4.0 EQUIPMENT:
The design, material, construction, location and maintenance of equipment should be such as to make it adequate and suitable for its intended use. Its layout and design must aim to minimize the risk of mix-ups and permit effective cleaning and maintenance in order to avoid cross contamination, build-up of dust, dirt, food particle or any other contaminant that can affect the quality of the product. The parts of the equipment that make contact with products should be made of non-toxic/non-reactive materials such as food grade stainless steel etc.

5.0 WATER TREATMENT PROCESS:
Water which is used in the production of food products (production Water), washing of production equipment (Operation water) should be treated water and the facilities required should include the following;

5.1 The source of water shall be either via *public mains or spring or borehole of not less than 150ft depth.*

5.2 The distance of the borehole from the nearest soak-away pit or septic tank should not be less than 50 meters.

5.3 The borehole shall be fitted with a submersible pump of adequate power to pump the raw water out of the borehole.

5.4 **A raw water tank and treatment tank** shall be provided which should be made of treated PVC, stainless steel or galvanized steel. In case of galvanized steel, it shall be coated internally with food grade rubber paint.

5.5 **Industrial modules** containing sand bed and activated charcoal shall be provided.

5.6 **A treated water tank** shall be provided should be made of treated PVC, stainless steel.

5.7 **A set of serial micro filters mesh** of 5micron, 2 or 1 micron and then 0.5-micron pore sizes shall be provided.

5.8 **An industrial size UV sterilizer** shall be provided at required points in the water treatment process.

5.9 The Treatment process shall comprise of;

5.9.1 *Disinfection:* This process is carried out either through chlorination at 2 – 4 parts per Million (ppm), zonation via an ozonator apparatus, pH adjustment, ion-exchange, distillation or reverse osmosis.

5.9.2 *Filtration:* This process is achieved by passing the water through sand bed filters and then through activated carbon filters to remove the chlorine, colour, odour and taste from the water.

5.9.3 *Sterilization:* This is achieved by passing the water through and industrial size ultra violet sterilizer to kill off any other microbes that may have escaped the disinfection stage.

Other Requirements for Water Treatment Process:
Depending on the quality of the raw water, chemical coagulation, flocculation and settling using chemical coagulants like aluminium sulphate or neutralizing the carbonic acidity in the water by the use of suitable base like the hydroxide of sodium or calcium.

Hard water shall be treated by addition of water softeners such as zeolite or using Ion-exchange resins.

Aeration shall be carried out where raw water report shows a high iron content by exposing the water to air through aeration showers.

Chlorine concentration shall be calculated between 2 – 4 ppm and a contact time of Not less than 6 hours.

The sand bed filter should be recharged every 1 to 5 years while the activated carbon filter is done every 1 to 2 years depending on production output/volume.

Micro filters should be made of appropriate materials that do not shed particles into the water such as nylon, glass, stainless steel etc. and must be installed in descending order in terms of pore size towards the UV steriliser.

The UV sterilizer shall be fitted with an indicator or alarm system to signal when the UV bulb is burnt out.

The UV sterilizer shall be installed at the final point before the water used for production.

All piping should be on the surface for early detection of leaks and should be made of either PVC or stainless steel.

RAW/PACKAGING MATERIALS AND SOURCES:
Raw and packaging materials should be sourced from approved vendors. They should be of good quality in order to produce quality products. All incoming materials should be stored under appropriate storage conditions. Where applicable, the materials should be immediately tested by quality control (QC) to ensure conformity to specification.

VALIDATION OF EQUIPMENT AND PROCESS:
All equipment and processes must be validated. Validation is the establishment of documented evidence which provide a high degree of assurance that a specific process and equipment will consistently produce a product meeting its pre-determined specifications and quality attributes.
Types of validation include;
- ✓ Process validation
- ✓ Facility qualification
- ✓ Computer systems validation
- ✓ Equipment qualification
- ✓ System qualification
- ✓ Cleaning validation
- ✓ Methods validation
- ✓ Packaging validation

CALIBRATION OF EQUIPMENT:
Calibration should be carried out on laboratory and production equipment on a daily basis before the equipment can be used for production and adequate documentation should be kept. Calibration is the act of checking or adjusting (by comparison with a standard) the accuracy of a measuring instrument. Calibration can be broken down into;

8.1 Physical (temperature, relative humidity, pressure, time) Analytical Instrumentation (including pH, conductivity etc.

Optical (Turbidity, Osmometry, spectrophotometry)

Electrical (Voltage, Current, Resistance Frequency)

Dimensional (Length, Volume, Mass etc.) Most calibration activities can be classified as either *process calibration* or *laboratory calibration*

QUALITY ASSUARANCE:
QUALITY CONTROL
Cottage Food Producing factories are required to send samples from every batch of their finished products to a public analyst for comprehensive analysis and

document same in a file while rectifying any anomaly in the parameter reading by carrying out the needed process change(s) for the overall product quality conformity. However, for medium to large scale food industries, an in-house laboratory adequately equipped to carry out the most critical parameters on their raw materials, in-process and finished products shall be provided. A public analyst shall also carry out comprehensive analysis on every batch of finished products. The requirements in the laboratory include;

There shall be competent quality assurance personnel to man the laboratory.

The laboratory shall be adequately equipped to carry out the critical chemical and microbiological parameters on the raw materials, in-process and finished products.

There should be clear separation of responsibility between the quality assurance and production.

Adequate documentation of all analysis carried out should be properly filled.

Daily calibration and bi-annual validation of all laboratory equipment should be carried out and proper documents should be kept.

Shelf life studies of food products should be carried out to ensure that the stated shelf life on the product is adequate.

HAZARD ANALYSIS SYSTEM
It shall design and implement a hazard analysis system. Traditional internal audit by plants has shifted to own process assessment for associated hazards and the risk level at each stage of the production with a concurrent control measure(s) to eliminate or reduce such Hazards/risk factors to the barest minimum and thus assure the quality of the product in a Proactive and preventive practice.

One form of Hazard Analysis System could be derived from Industrial Guides/Codes, Research Findings, publications, Systematic Assessment of Food Environment, Assured Safer Food Catering. Etc.

Ultimately, the plant should adopt and practice the principles of Hazard Analysis Critical Control Point System which is the system of choice in food safety either on voluntary basis or Mandatory as in HACCP System certification. A thorough implementation of this reduces the cost of quality, prepares the staff for external audit and assures food safety.

ENVIROMENTAL SANITATION AND PERSONEL HYGIENE:
Appropriate sanitation measures should be taken to avoid contamination risks of all kinds:

The entire factory should be cleaned frequently and thoroughly in accordance with the standard operational procedure (S.O.P) for cleaning.

Equipment should be thoroughly cleaned in strict compliance to the S.O.P

Water system toilets and washing facilities should be appropriately located, designed, equipped and the sanitation shall be maintained satisfactory in strict compliance to the S.O.P

Eating, drinking and smoking should not be permitted in the production, laboratory and storage areas.

All operators should wear appropriate protective garments/gowning.

Production staff should undergo food handler's test/medical examination at least once a year.

Persons known to be suffering from communicable diseases or with wounds should be excluded from duty until they are certified medically fit again. Wastes should be adequately disposed of in strict compliance to the S.O.P.

Effective pest control program should be in place and executed satisfactorily in accordance to master validation plan.

DOCUMENTATION
The aim of documentation is to define the specification for all materials and methods of manufacture and control, to ensure that all personnel concerned with manufacture know what to do and when to do it. Documentation falls into three main categories;

Commitment Documentation: These are documents that describe the commitment of a factory to adhere to cGMP and HACCP plan e.g. quality manual, master validation plan, quality manual, sample collection, stability studies, HACCP record etc.

Directive Documentation: These are the documents that direct the technical staff on how to remain in compliance e.g. Batch Formulation Records.

Procedural Documentation: This describes the standard operating procedures, process validation, cleaning validation, etc.

CONSUMER COMPLAINT AND RECALL:
All consumer complaints must be thoroughly investigated and documented. They should be handled by technical personnel. The outcome of investigation should be communicated to management in order to prevent future occurrence. If a recall is decided upon, it should be done quickly using the production batch history through the product distribution records. All records of recalled products must be kept. In event of recall, NAFDAC must be fully notified of all actions at receipt of consumer complaint, during investigation and actual recall activity.

DISTRIBUTION SYSTEM:
Record of product distribution network must be properly kept for easy recall of defective Products. Distributors' names, addresses, fax, phone, e-mail etc. should be obtained.

TRANSPORTATION AND HANDLING:
Products should be handled and transported under conditions which prevent deterioration, contamination, spoilage and breakage to ensure that the product quality is maintained up to the time of delivery to the consumer.

15.0 LABEL
Product should be labelled adequately in English language and should also be in the three Nigerian languages (Hausa, Yoruba and Igbo}. The label should also contain the nutrition panel stating nutrient composition and within the label should be stated the net weight/volume of content, factory address, lot/batch number, usage instruction and NAFDAC registration number.

PRODUCT REGISTRATION
The food product should be registered with NAFDAC upon factory recognition and the following documents will be submitted for the processing of the product registration during review meeting at NAFDAC state office.

- A letter requesting for production inspection addressed to the Director (EID) should be submitted through the state office.

- The letter will be accompanied with the Standard Operating Procedures (SOP) for quality management system, Cleaning/Sanitation/Hygiene for plant/equipment, environment and personnel, Letter of appointment, acceptance , C.V and credentials of Production or plant manager and quality control Manager, Certificate of Food Handlers test for production staff, List of equipment, company organogram, certified copy of agreement/certificate of fumigation or record of plant in-house fumigation activities, , certify copy of product name trade mark acceptance/registration, certified copy of Company registration certificate or business name, payment receipt of registration fees, Filled Product Registration form, Borehole drilling geological report, vetted label/primary packaging material and payment receipt of product registration fees.

SESSION 5: FRANCHISING OR LICENSING FOR AN ALREADY EXISTING BUSINESS (google.com)
Once your business has matured to the point where it's both easily duplicable a doesn't rely on your presence in order to operate successfully, you may want to consider creating franchise opportunities that you can sell to individuals and/or investor groups that wish to own and operate a business similar to yours. A franchise of your business is, in effect, a copy of your business that can be sold as a stand-alone entity. You must be certain that your business can be operated in locations apart from the target markets it's served; otherwise it won't be sellable. Alternatively, you can license your business, whereby the right to operate a business like yours is sold to other entrepreneurs, within a set of certain guidelines and operating procedures.

What is franchising?
The term "franchising" can describe some very different business arrangements. It is important to understand exactly what you're being offered.

Business format franchise

This is the most common form of franchising. A true business format franchise occurs when the owner of a business (the franchisor) grants a licence to another person or business (the franchisee) to use their business idea - often in a specific geographical area. The franchisee sells the franchisor's product or services, trades under the franchisor's trade mark or trade name and benefits from the franchisor's help and support. In return, the franchisee usually pays an initial fee to the franchisor and then a percentage of the sales revenue. The franchisee owns the outlet they run. But the franchisor keeps control over how products are marketed and sold and how their business idea is used. Well-known businesses that offer franchises of this kind include Prontaprint, Dyno-Rod, McDonald's and Coffee Republic.

Starting a franchise company is not an easy or inexpensive process. There are a number of requirements you will have to meet and a few other things that, though not legally required, are also essential. These requirements include:

- **Legal.** You will be required to prepare a standard disclosure document for your franchise operation. This document, called the Uniform Franchise Offering Circular (UFOC) is required of all companies, by the Federal Trade Commission, if they want to offer franchises for sale anywhere in the United States. In addition, there are a number of individual states that have registration requirements you must meet if you are going to offer franchises in those states. You will need an effective and experienced franchise attorney to help you meet these legal requirements correctly. As with any adviser, make sure to check the experience and references of attorneys when making this selection.

- **Accounting.** You are going to need to prepare audited financial statements for the franchise company. This is actually one of the disclosure requirements under the legal section above so you won't be able to complete legal until you have your statements audited. You'll have to decide if you want to set up another company to franchise your concept or if you want to use the existing business entity you are operating as your franchise company. You'll need an experienced accountant to produce these audited statements and to advise you on the structure of your business enterprise. Again, make sure you are getting someone experienced in operating in the franchise arena and check references prior to deciding on this person.

- **Systems.** The heart and soul of any successful franchise company is systems. You will need to develop and completely document the systems that a franchisee will use to run their business successfully. You will need to develop a training program that will teach a new franchisee whatever they need to know to become a successful operator. You will need to formalize the marketing plans that a new franchisee will use to drive customers into their new unit. You will also need to design a sales system that you can use to recruit new franchisees into your franchise company. There's a mountain of work getting all your systems set up and ready to go. You can hire outside consultants to assist with all this work but if you do, make sure you check references very carefully since there is a wide variance in terms of what these folks do and what they charge for it.

- **Mindset.** One of the most important things you need to do in order to be a successful franchisor is to have the right focus and attitude. In your existing business, you're the boss, you have employees and they probably do what you tell them to do without much resistance. Franchisees are quite different from employees and you need to make sure you don't treat them as if they were employees. Successful franchisors use a lot of persuasion to get the franchisees to do what they want rather than issuing orders. It's not as fast or efficient but you'll find that you meet a lot of resistance from franchisees if you don't do it this way. I don't know about specific advisers related to this topic but there are numerous industry meetings and opportunities for you to interact with other franchisors and you should take advantage of all these as a learning experience.

Note that Most honest advisers in the franchise business will tell you that you'll need at least $500,000 to $1,000,000 in initial capital to even think about starting a franchise company. You will probably work harder than you ever have for at least 2-3 years before you even start to make any money on your franchise operations, and it could easily be 3-5 years.

The rewards and satisfaction of building a successful franchise company are incredible but so is the price that you'll pay to reach this goal. Make sure that you want to pay the price before you start this process and then go forward with realistic expectations and you should do fine.

HOW DOES FRANCHISING WORK?

Franchising is based on mutual trust between the franchisor and franchisee. The franchisor provides the business expertise (training, technology, advertisement/promotion, ongoing advice etc.) that otherwise would not be available to the franchisee. The franchisee brings the entrepreneurial spirit, capital and drive necessary to make the franchise a success by selling a franchisor products or services. The rules and regulations established by the franchisor must be followed by the franchisee. The franchisee fulfils payment obligations such as initial franchise fee and (in most cases) annual franchise royalty fee.

Some examples of franchises in Nigeria are Tantalizers, UPS, Kentucky Fried Chicken (KFC), and Mobil fuelling station, Total fuelling station, Mr. Biggs, Coca-Cola and Chicken Republic.

BENEFITS OF BUYING A FRANCHISE

People consider buying a franchise for many good reasons. The franchise concept provides a buyer (franchisee) with many important advantages over starting a new business from scratch. These advantages help a franchisee maximize the chances for success and be able to run the business effectively, enjoyably, and profitably.

1. When you acquire a franchise, you are normally entitled to franchisor-proven systems. As a franchisee, you have an operating manual to rely on that will help guide you to success in your new business.

2. With the franchise concept, your chances of failure are lower than if you start your business from scratch because the franchisor will use its experience, expertise, and proven resources to guide and support you in your business.
3. As a franchisee, you have exclusive rights in your territory. The franchisor cannot sell to any other franchisee in the same territory.
4. Obtaining a loan to finance your business may be easier. Banks sometimes consider lending money to buy a franchise with a good reputation.
5. As a franchisee of a reputable franchise, you will receive the benefits that accrue from selling an established brand of products or services. Also, you will enjoy low-cost advertising and promotions.
6. Under the franchise concept, the franchisor usually provides business support such as training, technology, advertisement/promotion and ongoing advice to the franchisee.

Is there a downside to being a franchisee?

Franchising is certainly not for everyone. Here are some of the potential disadvantages:

1. **Lack of control** - The essence of a franchise -- buying and operating a proven concept -- can make it seem like you're more of a manager than a boss. This may be difficult for some people, especially those that are more entrepreneurial. This type of person may find it hard to conform to someone else's system.
2. **Cost** - It can take a good deal of cash to open and operate a franchise. Upfront costs can be significant, and you may find that ongoing royalty fees will have a major impact on your cash flow.
3. **You're not alone** - Just as a franchisor's reputation can benefit your individual business, the franchisor's problems are also your problems. So if the parent company comes upon hard times, your individual franchise may also suffer because of how closely you're tied in.
4. **You're committed** - Your franchise agreement is a binding contract, and can be quite restrictive. You're locked in to certain business practices, fees, and even the look of your business. If you don't agree, you may have no recourse except to adhere to these guidelines.

What franchising laws do I need to be aware of?

You should consider having your attorney, accountant or other adviser review the disclosure documents and proposed contracts before entering into any agreement. This advice, coupled with your own research, can help save you money and keep you from making a bad investment.

What should I look for in the disclosure documents?

The disclosure document provided to you by the franchisor can serve as a window into the company's operations. It is important to review it completely (preferably with the assistance of an attorney, accountant or business adviser) to learn all you can about the franchisor.

Some things to look for:

1. Does the franchisor have a track record of success? - Learn all about the franchisor's personal and business names, its organization; its background; and its financial history. You'll also need to determine whether this success can be duplicated in your area.

2. **What will it cost me?** - The circular should have complete list of fees that you will be required to pay both to start your franchise and operate it. It will also tell you other obligations, such as inventory or equipment that must be purchased from the franchisor.

3. **Will my territory be exclusive?** - You will want to determine whether or not the franchisor can open other stores in your area, or even sell its product by mail order to customers in your region. You also might have to meet certain sales criteria to maintain your exclusivity.

4. **What products can I sell and how can I sell them?** - You may only be allowed to sell certain products that are on the franchisor's approved list. And you may be limited in the ways you can sell them. For instance, you might be allowed to handle walk-in traffic to your store, but you may be prevented from selling outside your location.

5. **What services will the franchisor provide to me**? - Look for what services will be provided to you prior to opening, and after you're open for business. You'll also want to read about what training is necessary, where it will take place, and what it will cost you. Also, check to see what trademarks and patents you will receive.

6. **Is there any bad news I should know about?** - The documents must disclose any actions involving violation of franchise law, fraud, embezzlement, or unfair business practices. They also must disclose whether the franchisor, any predecessors, or any partners or officers have

declared bankruptcy in the past 15 years. And be sure to read financial statements closely.

7. **How much can I expect to make from this business?** - The circular contains hypothetical profit projections, along with the formula for how these figures were created. Be aware that economic conditions vary from region to region, so these figures do not assure success of a particular outlet. Instead, use these figures combined with estimates of costs and expenses in your area.

What should I look for when selecting a franchise?

Here are some of the things you should look at when evaluating a franchise:

1. **Profitability** - Make sure that both the franchisor and individual franchisees are healthy.
2. **A track record of success** - Is this concept viable? Has it succeeded elsewhere? Does the franchisor have a good credit rating?
3. **A strong USP** - You'll want a business that stands apart from the competition, since you don't want to be perceived as selling the same old thing.
4. **Effective financial management and other controls** - A strong monitoring system will help you identify your problems and deal with them more effectively.
5. **A good image** - It's important that the public has a positive image of the franchisor, since you're basing your business on its reputation. Also, look for a concept that can expand nationally so your business can grow locally.
6. **Integrity and commitment** - You actually want the franchisor to spend a lot of time checking you out, because you want to make sure it has strong requirements for all its franchisees, since your success in intertwined with its.
7. A successful industry - Look for opportunities in industries that are growing.

TAKE YOUR PICK FROM THE BEST FRANCHISES IN UNITED KINGDOM

www.franchiseinfo.co.uk

Franchise info is a complete source of franchising information, offering a comprehensive directory of franchises for sale, as well as franchise and business focused advice and support

1. Make detailed searches from thousands of UK franchises
2. Create a favourites hotlist with the new save your search function
3. Gain free advice and information from a host of franchising experts
4. Sign up for Fran Mail, a free franchising e-newsletter
5. Exclusive online registration for the franchise exhibitions

Is there other research I can do to learn more about a particular franchise?

It's important to learn as much as you can before purchasing any kind of business so you can make an informed decision. There are a wide variety of sources you can approach to learn about a franchise opportunity. Here are some things you can do:

1. **Interview the franchisor** - Make sure that you feel comfortable with the franchisor, and that all your questions can be answered to your satisfaction.

2. **Interview existing franchisees** - Speak with current franchisees to see how they feel about the business. Are they happy with their investment? Are they making as much money as the expected?

3. **Read the business and trade press** - Spend some time in the library or on the Internet looking through the media. Often, you'll learn a lot more about the company than they volunteer in disclosure documents.

4. **Check references** - Don't just speak to franchisees. Call bank and other business references supplied by the franchisor.

5. **Go to independent agencies** - Find out whether any complaints have been lodged against the company.

6. **Get a credit report** - Get a report on the franchisor from Dun and Bradstreet, TRW/Experian, or one of the other credit reporting agencies. You'll learn a lot about how the company conducts business.

THE OFFICIAL JOURNAL OF THE BRITISH FRANCHISE ASSOCIATION (BFA): www.businessfranchise.com

What fees should I expect to pay for my franchise?

There are basically two types of fees you should expect to pay for your franchise -- upfront fees and ongoing fees.

The first is the initial upfront fee, which is what you pay the franchisor for the rights to open your franchise. Essentially, you are purchasing the rights to use the franchisor's trademarks, business methods, and distribution rights. This licensing charge can be significant, especially for a well-known, established franchise -- it's not unusual for it to be in the hundreds of thousands of Naira. Often, it is also based on the value of the territory or trading area, so the larger your market, the more you could end up paying.

Be aware that this upfront fee may be in addition to any other start-up costs you will have to incur. The initial franchise fee may or may not include things like training costs; start-up promotional fees; inventory; build-outs (some franchisors require your space to have specific architectural elements); equipment/fixtures (you may be required to purchase or lease specific equipment and fixtures from the franchisor); and any other costs that are necessary to open your business.

You will also have to pay ongoing fees to maintain the rights to your franchise. Most franchisors charge a royalty fee, typically a percent of your gross sales, not your profits. This royalty fee can range from 1 percent to as much as 15 percent, although 5 percent is typical. Remember, you are paying this royalty on gross sales (your total receipts, less sales tax, returns and refunds), so it can potentially take a significant bite out of your profits.

Some franchisors charge a regular fee (payable weekly, monthly or quarterly) in lieu of royalty payments. This type of fee may also be part of the mark-up you are charged for goods or services you are required to purchase.

It is also common for franchises to pay a portion of the franchisor's local, regional and national advertising and promotional costs. These fees are usually put into a co-operative advertising fund that ultimately benefits all franchises through increased exposure to your trade name.

Should I look into established franchises or rising stars?

This is one of the key decisions you will need to make if you decide to go the franchise route. There's a trade-off you will need to evaluate in terms of risk and ultimate payoff.

A franchise with an established track record has many benefits -- significant name recognition; proven marketing methods; entrenched business plans and training systems; strong management; and a history that is easy for you to investigate. On the downside, you might find that the franchisor has already saturated your market (so good locations may not be available, or other outlets may encroach on your area); fees may be higher; and you may find that the larger the company, the harder it is for you to be heard should any disagreements arise.

An emerging franchise gives you the chance to get in on the ground floor of what could be a highly profitable growth opportunity. Newer franchises also tend to have lower upfront and royalty fees, and they may be more willing to negotiate and accommodate individual franchises. On the other hand, smaller franchise opportunities may lack name recognition; they may not have enough experience to make their system work; you may find yourself being a test-case for their procedures; and the chance of franchisor failure could be much greater.

MERITS AND DEMRITS OF FRANCHISE

Then, we arrange merit, demerit to join franchise chain.

1. **Merit**

    1. Generally, chain name and mark, image known widely are available Without business experience, we can start business by instruction of the headquarters.

    2. As we perform business based on the results and experience that the franchise headquarters accumulated in the past, probability to succeed in individual in comparison with case to open is high.

    3. Management instruction (tax practice, accounts, law) and help (new product development, securing of stocking, sales promotion, education) by the franchise headquarters are received and can devote ourselves to business.

    4. We can do business as an independent company.

    5. The headquarters lays in stock in large quantities and it is cheap, stable, and can purchase high quality product and materials which we produced again.

    6. We can ask the headquarters for location investigation into opening of business article.

    7. We can participate in sales campaign which we made use of scale only in franchise chain including advertisement in.

    8. Your business is based on a proven idea. You can check how successful other franchises are before committing yourself.

    9. You can use a recognised brand name and trademarks. You benefit from any advertising or promotion by the owner of the franchise - the "franchisor".

10. The franchisor gives you support - usually including training, help setting up the business, a manual telling you how to run the business and ongoing advice.

11. You usually have exclusive rights in your territory. The franchisor won't sell any other franchises in the same region.
12. Financing the business may be easier. Banks are sometimes more likely to lend money to buy a franchise with a good reputation.
13. Risk is reduced and is shared by the franchisor.
14. If you have an existing customer base you will not have to invest time looking to set one up.
15. Relationships with suppliers have already being established.

Other Advantages of buying a franchise

Note: not all franchise systems will include these factors listed below.

1. Association with a well-established brand, reputation and product or service.
2. Assistance with site selection, lease negotiation, site development, builders and shop fitters.
3. Assistance with outlet design and equipment purchasing.
4. Initial management training and continuing management assistance.
5. Access to group/national market research, along with advertising and merchandising assistance.
6. Access to established standard procedures, operating manuals and stock control systems.
7. Assistance in securing finance and sometimes financial assistance in establishing the business.
8. Access to financing packages which may be more attractive and easier to access than for non-franchised businesses. and
9. Access to established financial systems and checks which can provide early warning signals to highlight trouble spots.

Disadvantages

1. Costs may be higher than you expect as well as the initial costs of buying the franchise, you pay continuing royalties and you may have to agree to buy products from the franchisor.
2. The franchise agreement usually includes restrictions on how you run the business. You might not be able to make changes to suit your local market.
3. The franchisor might go out of business, or change the way they do things.
4. Other franchisees could give the brand a bad reputation.
5. You may find it difficult to sell your franchise - you can only sell it to someone approved by the franchisor.
6. Reduced risk means you might not generate large profits

Other Disadvantages of buying a franchise:

1. less autonomy in some business decisions (franchisees generally have to operate the business according to the franchisor's operations manual).
2. restricted territory in which you may operate and/or promote your business.
3. ongoing payment of fees to the franchisor.
4. less control if you decide to sell your franchise business as there will be a set of procedures for you to follow, including getting the franchisor's approval of the buyer.
5. if you sell the business you will usually have to pay a fee to the franchisor as outlined in the franchise agreement.
6. restraint of trade provisions on the sale or termination of the franchise that may be more onerous than required if a non-franchised business is sold.
7. at the end of the franchise term, the franchisor is not obliged to renew the franchise, in which case the business and its goodwill revert to the franchisor.

OTHER INFORMATION ON FRANCHISING

1. A franchise business is most preferred kind of start-up business with about 91% of all franchises reporting profitability across the globe, as per British Franchise Association (BFA). Franchising Business model is one of the attractive and most successful business formats of the day. Many prospective entrepreneurs chose buying a franchise over starting with a business of their

own due to the various perks of buying a franchise. However, it is important to know that franchises have their own advantages and disadvantages.

2. Ongoing support is one of the key merits of a franchise business, as there is a franchisor that is always looking over the business protecting interest of both self and the franchise. Along with this come various advantages, such as

a. A reputed brand name
b. A guide who helps in entire set up and start-up of the business
c. A fraction of a market that is ready for your product or services
d. A proven business process and operations ready to be implemented
e. An ongoing research and development taken care of by franchisor
f. Timely up gradation, innovation and introduction of newbie
g. Receive extensive training
h. Approval on loans is simpler as bankers find franchise as a lower risk business
i. Marketing is usually undertaken by the franchisor for entire region, with costs shared among all the franchises. Hence there is a reduced burden of planning for marketing and the cost as well is shared.
j. There is access to bulk purchasing

4. Brand Proven Formula Aided Set Up Easy Financing Shared Marketing Cost Lower Risk Ongoing Support Dependence Strict Adherence Ongoing Costs All or Nothing Territory Restriction Fixed Term Agreement

5. Even though franchise business is gaining high reputation and is leading model of business which is proven to even bear economic downturns, it also comes with many disadvantages mostly related to decision making crucial for business because of which it is important to explore the downside of franchise business before making the investment and be prepared.

6. Franchise Business is quite dependent on the parent company

a) The operational procedures are adhered to diligently and strictly; non-adherence may result in losing the business
b) Less autonomy on overall business
c) Restricted territory of operation
d) Ongoing payments, fees and other charges
e) Fixed term agreement, renewal of which depends on franchisors discretion
f) Less control on sale of franchise, and a fee is paid for same as well
g) You cannot pick and choose the elements from the design; it is all or nothing that a franchisor offers "Owning a franchise allows you to get into business and operate it with the necessary training.

7. Every style of business, perhaps, has its own advantages and disadvantages. As a prospective entrepreneur it depends on you to decide what kind of start-up suits you as an individual and a businessman.

8. Indian Institute of Hardware and Technology (IIHT) has its own pros and cons, however it ensures that all decisions are taken in the best interest of the business itself and the franchises. This is essential as the interest of entire business and all franchise depends on how each franchise individually performs. IIHT Franchise has its presence in countries such as China, Malaysia, Turkey and Nigeria to name a few, and has being flexible to change its processes and operations to customize the business to suit the demands of the local market in the respective country like any international franchise business. IIHT has a reputation for timely up gradation and introducing courses in latest.

SESSION 6: CHOOSING THE RIGHT FRANCHISE: TED IWERE TEN KEY FACTORS TO CONSIDER (IWERE)
How does one shop for a franchise? What factors should one consider before buying a particular franchise? Should one always go for the most popular brand? Should one go for the trendiest brand? These questions are pertinent because the success of a franchise business largely depends on finding the right franchise. The questions are also important because the fast food industry is not the only industry where franchising opportunity exists. In Canada, for example, according to Doing Business in Canada guide, there are approximately 1,100 franchise brands and 78,000 franchise units in operation throughout the county and they cross more than 40 different sectors of the economy, including retail, hospitality, automotive and health care. In the United States, there are approximately 3,500 franchise brands. In the United Kingdom, a NatWest/British Franchise Association survey conducted in 2009, found that there were 838 franchisors actively operating in the country with an estimated 34,600 franchisees. There are at least ten factors that a prospective franchisee must consider and evaluate before buying a franchise. The list is by no means exhaustive and is in no particular order.

1. Evaluate Your Skills: You know your goals, your habits, your limitations, your educational and technological background and the skill sets that you bring to the table. What is your experience as a business owner or manager? Will you need special training to run a particular franchise? What skill sets do you already have and which franchise can best maximize those skill sets? It would make little sense to invest in an automotive franchise if you know next to nothing about cars, are not excited about the auto industry, and cannot afford the time or money investment needed to acquire the necessary training.

2. Evaluate the Industry: Is the industry growing or declining? What are the future projections for the industry? Is the industry likely to become obsolete soon due, for example, to technological changes? Imagine the range of products and services that were once considered indispensable but have become obsolete or are about to become obsolete because of changes in technology. As products such as films (and film cameras), compact discs, records, VCRs, and landlines go, so do services associate with them. Conversely, one can think of products and services that are not presently in high demand but which may become very popular in the future as a result of technological and demographic changes. For example, with a growing middle class and a growing number of parents willing to spend money on the education, entertainment and overall development of their children, kids' franchises (e.g. educational franchises, child care franchises, fitness franchises) could become winners in Nigeria in the near future.

3. Evaluate the Economy: When the economy is robust and more and more middle class are created, this typically translates into more options for prospective franchisee because more people have the money to spend on services that may have once being considered luxuries. For example, in a thriving economy, services such as pet care and services, coffee shops, ice-cream shops, and fitness/nutrition services can be good options for a prospective franchisee. Conversely, when the economy is weak or unpredictable, prospective franchisees may be better of choosing recession-proof brands. Recession-proof brands offer services that people always need regardless of the state of the economy such as child care, elder-care, and health care.

4. Evaluate the Demand: Is there a demand for the product and service that a given franchise is offering? A franchise must and should make sense in the domestic market where a prospective franchisee hopes to operate. A prospective franchisee should pay attention to products and services that people cannot afford to live without (e.g. child care and healthcare) as well as luxuries that have become more affordable to a growing middle class (e.g. fitness). Regarding the sectors or industries with greatest opportunities for franchising, this will vary from country to country. What is working in the United States may not necessarily work in Nigeria. According to Entrepreneur.com, in the US, the **Top 10 Franchises for 2013 are**: Hampton Hotels **(1)**, Subway **(2)**, Jiffy Lube Int'l Inc. **(3)**, 7-Eleven Inc. **(4)**, Supercuts **(5)**, Anytime Fitness **(6)**, Sevpro **(7)**, Denny's Inc. **(8)**, McDonald's **(9)** and Pizza Hut Inc. **(10)**. Although hugely successful in the US, some of the popular US franchises may not be popular in Nigeria. Automotive franchises (e.g. Jiffy Lube) may not work in a country like Nigeria where road-side mechanics are readily available. However, automotive franchise may work in a city like Abuja with a growing and affluent middleclass willing to splurge on expensive cars.

5. Evaluate Local Culture, Tastes, and Habits. Consider South-South Franchising Opportunities: In thinking about franchising in Africa, it is important to remember that the culture and taste of consumers in developed countries may be different from those of consumers in Africa. The best performing franchising sectors in Brazil in 2007, in terms of revenue growth, were not necessarily the best performing sectors in the US but were personal accessories and footwear (24.4%), other retail business and services (24.2%), and information technology (IT) services (20.4%). The question to ask is what will work given local tastes and habits. In this regard, prospective franchisees would be well advised to consider promising opportunities in other developing countries. Given similarities in weather, culture, or economy, it is possible that what works in one developing country may also work in another developing country. This could explain the success of some South African franchises in Nigeria.

6. Evaluate the Competition. Danger of Being the First or Last in Line: Competition is good for business and for consumers. However, excessive competition may completely wipe out the profit expected from a franchising deal. Is the demand for the product and service undercut by competition from other businesses that offer similar products and services? Given the rise in online business, competition can be local, regional, national and even international. Competition can also come from other franchisees in a franchisor's network or even from company-owned outlets. A prospective franchisee must evaluate fully the level of competition to expect in a given industry and with a given franchise. While caution suggests that it is better to go for a known and proven brand, new brands get into the market every day and many are doing remarkably well. Entrepreneur's ranking of the top new franchises (those in the market for less than five years) indicates that many new brands are doing very well.

According to Enterpreneur.com, the Top 10 New Franchises for 2013 in the US are: Kona Ice (1), Menchie's (2), Orange Leaf Frozen Yogurt (3), ShelfGenie Franchise Systems LLC (4), Bricks 4 Kidz (5), Smashburger Franchising LLC (6), GameTruck Licensing LLC (7), Paul Davis Emergency Services (8), Signal 88 Security (9), and Mac Tools (10). Note however that while it is foolhardy to get into a business where competition is stiff, it is also risky to be the first franchisee in a system. Being the first in the system may mean limited name and brand recognition for the company and its product or service. To be the first is also to deal with many unknowns (about the quality of franchisor's product and service offered, about a franchisor's reputation regarding fairness, and about consumer perception of a given product or service).

7. Evaluate the Brand. What do you know about the quality and reputation of the brand that you are considering? Does the brand have a good track record? It is important to consider the quality and reputation of the brand in the franchisor's home country as well as in other markets that the franchisor is operating in. When considering a brand what factors must one consider? At least four. To come up with the list of Forbes Top 20 US Franchise Brands in 2011, Forbes Magazine compared four variables: estimated minimum initial investment (including initial fees plus equipment costs); total locations; survival rates (measured as the percentage of closings during the previous three-year period to the total number of existing locations); and the number of training hours offered to new franchisees measured against the start-up costs. *The top 10 on Forbes list* were: Domino's Pizza (1), 7-Eleven (2), Kumon North America (3), McDonalds USA (4), Papa Murphy's International (5), Merry Maids (6), Great Clips (7), Sport Clips (8), Edible Arrangements International (9), and Jimmy John's (10).

8. Evaluate Affordability and Credit Availability. What can you afford? One's franchising goals depend largely on what one can afford. There are several questions to consider. How much does a particular franchise cost? Do I have access to financing? Does the government provide any kind of financing opportunity? Are bank loans accessible and available? These questions are important because lack of funds is one of the top reasons' franchisees go out of business. Access to capital can affects franchising decision in at least three ways. First, affordability and credit availability will determine the sector/industry you can get into. For example, hotel franchises are inherently much more expensive than fast food franchise or a dating service franchise. The start-up costs for Hampton Hotel franchise ranges from US$3.7M – US$13.52M. Compare this to the start-up cost for a McDonald's franchise ($1.07M – 1.89M), a 7-Eleven franchise ($30.8K – 1.5M), Anytime Fitness franchise ($56.3K – 353.9K) or Bricks 4 Kidz franchise ($33,800 – $51,050). Second, even within an industry, financial considerations will also affect the particular brand one acquires. Within the same industry, more established brands are likely to be much more expensive than newer brands. Compare the start-up cost for a McDonald franchise ($1.07M – 1.89M) to those of Smashburger Franchising LLC ($560.5K – 909.5K). Third, cost will also affect whether one decides to go for a single-unit franchise, an area-development franchise or a master franchise. Note however, the potential profitability of a franchise is not determined by the price of the franchise; a low-cost franchise may be a bigger earner than an overpriced or expensive franchise.

9. Evaluate the Franchisor: While a brand may be a good quality brand, the franchisor may be going through turbulent times, may be involved in multiple law suits brought by past and present franchisee, may be in bankruptcy, or may simply be caught up in a number of issues that can affect and ultimately destroy a franchise arrangement. A prospective franchise must therefore carefully research the franchisor. In some countries it is very easy to evaluate the franchisor because of mandatory disclosure laws. In the U.S. for example, a franchisor must complete an extensive disclosure document called the Franchise Disclosure Document (previously known as the Uniform Franchise Offering Circulate (UFOC)). Nigeria does not have any mandatory disclosure requirement. Consequently, it is up to the franchisee to carry out necessary due diligence. Examples of issues that merit examination are: the business experience of the franchisor, the franchisor's current directors and executive officers, allegations of fraud embezzlement, fraudulent conversion, misappropriation of property, or restraint of trade, that may have been brought by a present or former franchisee or franchisees and which involves or involved the franchise relationship, and whether the franchisor has filed for bankruptcy or has being adjudged bankrupt.

10. Evaluate Your Team. Do you Have a Winning Team? Can you put Together a Winning Team? Do you have a team of professional advisers (lawyers, accountants, etc.) that can help you with the legal, business, and financial aspects of a franchising deal? Do you have a cohesive team that can help you make your franchise a success once the deal is concluded and the agreements are signed? When one is thinking of a cohesive team one has to consider employees, suppliers, investors, business partners and even one's family. Regarding employees, what is the labour market situation in the industry and in the geographic area that you plan to operate? How are changes in the population affecting the available labour market? Can you adapt to changing employee base? Would you have ongoing access to excellent legal and accounting services?

At the end of the day, there is more to choosing and operating a successful franchise than a few dos and don'ts. Wisdom, perseverance, and above all prayers, are important. With these three one cans go against all odds and still succeed. Walt Disney, the founder of the hugely successful theme park that almost every child in the world dreams of visiting, once said: "We did it (Disneyland), in the knowledge that most of the people I talked to thought it would be a financial disaster – closed and forgotten within the first year." Albert Einstein once said, "A person who never made a mistake never tried anything new." This is so true for franchising. Franchising is not for the faint hearted. Mistakes can and do sometimes occur along the way. A person who is very fearful of failure is not likely to be able to invest the capital and time necessary to make a franchise unit succeed. Prayer remains the key. Abraham Lincoln 1809-1865, Sixteenth President of the USA, once said, "I have been driven many times to my knees by the overwhelming conviction that I had nowhere else to go. My own wisdom, and that of all about me, seemed insufficient for the day." Finally, Benjamin Franklin 1706-1790, one of the Founding Fathers of the United States and a scientist, publisher, author, inventor, and a diplomat, had this to say about prayers: "Work as if you were to live a hundred years. Pray as if you were to die tomorrow."

10 COMMON MISTAKES OF PROSPECTIVE FRANCHISEES

1. Not reading, understanding or asking questions about the disclosure document. These documents are typically long, sometimes 80 pages, but it is very important that you read and understand each item, 1 through 23, of the Uniform Franchise Offering Circular (UFOC). As you read the document, keep notes on those areas that are confusing and unclear. While you may want your attorney's opinion, give the franchisor the benefit of the doubt and first ask its representatives to explain their understanding. Then check the remainder of your concerns with your attorney. Check the document's date. If it is current, you may want to request a previous document for comparison.

One of the most common problems between new franchisees and the franchisor is a misunderstanding as regards responsibilities. Among other things, this can cause problems in meeting the schedule for Grand Opening dates. Read the disclosure document and the franchise agreement carefully as of what your responsibilities are. Also pay attention to the stated obligations of the franchisor, especially item eleven of the UFOC. Do not assume the franchisor is responsible for details of a particular support service. If it is not spelled out, get it in writing. List all of your concerns, and clarify which duties, obligations and responsibilities belong to whom.

2. Not understanding or having an inaccurate or incomplete interpretation of the franchise agreement and other legal documents to be signed. You and your attorney should carefully review the franchise agreement, the lease or real estate agreements, and any other contracts. First, make a list of questions to go over with your attorney, then present your concerns to the franchisor. Get the franchisor's clarifications in writing. There may be very little that you can change in these standardized agreements, but things can be added. There is no reason the franchisor cannot give you additional documentation to clarify something in the agreement that is confusing to you or your attorney.

3. Not seeking sound legal advice. Locate and retain an attorney, preferably one experienced in franchising.

4. Not verifying oral representations of the franchisor. You can avoid this mistake if you take the proper precautions. You may want to tape-record all your meetings with the franchisor. If you ask permission to do so, it is generally admissible in court if the need arises later. It also lets the company representatives know that you are tracking their words. You can do this politely, but if you prefer, take compendious notes of all your meetings. Later, review and summarize the details of your discussion, noting any items requiring clarification. Send a registered letter to the franchisor and a copy to the representatives memorializing your notes with a request for their response to any items you want clarified. Do not leave anything unresolved.

Due diligence also includes verification. If there have being any oral representations, of which you are uncertain, try to verify these with previous and current franchisees as well as through additional meetings with the franchisor. As stated in item 2 above, get anything orally promised in writing if it differs from other literature and the disclosure document.

5. Not contacting enough current franchisees. The section of the disclosure information on "Past, Current and Future Franchisees" is a valuable starting point for locating franchisees. It is imperative to discuss any concerns you may have with existing franchisees. If the franchisor gives you a tour that includes two or three franchisees, get back to them later and ask any questions that could have being confrontational or embarrassing if asked in front of the franchisor. Another important factor here is to find out whether the franchisor has introduced you to specific franchisees compensated for their help to solicit new franchisees. Ask them directly, then follow up with letter stating their answers to your questions. It is surprising how an inaccurate response might change once it is in writing.

Other than the franchisees introduced to you by the franchisor, to get a true picture, you can survey others listed in the disclosure document not versed in soliciting prospective franchisees. Find out from them if the franchisor has a reputation for honesty and fair dealing. It is of paramount importance to contact existing franchisees of the franchisor to verify their experience of the accuracy of previous disclosure documents. Also, ask their opinions of the accuracy and completeness of the current one. Further, you can solicit their help in verifying any other information not provided in the disclosure document.

When interviewing other franchisees, try to cover a large cross section of franchisees. Seek answers from those that:

a) Are in different locations,

b) Have one franchise,

c) Have multiple franchises,

d) Have being in business a long time,

e) Are still new,

f) Are successful, and

g) Are not doing so well.

For the latter, try to determine the reasons. Specifically, ask the franchisees if they feel that the franchisor exercises too much control, or not enough. Is the franchisor always willing to help? Has the franchisor held up its end of the obligations regarding ongoing support assistance and training?

Information from franchisees about their first year in business and their experience with the franchisor can be extremely enlightening. Under the FTC requirement, while the offering circular must disclose a list of existing franchisees, this record does not have to be complete. If you find the list provided to you is incomplete, ask the franchisor for a complete registry.

6. Not confirming the reasons for failed franchises. Locate some franchise outlets that are closed, sold, or have changed ownership to company-owned, and find out the reasons for their change of status. Contact the original owners and get their stories. If no two is alike, you may want to pay them less heed. If, on the other hand, there is a common story, the underlying problem may be something you want to avoid. Nevertheless, for fairness, get the franchisor's version.

7. Not having enough working capital. Make sure you have enough capital to cover every cost associated with the business including all pre-opening costs, enough set aside for your family budget, and enough operating cash for the business to make it through the breakeven point.

8. Not recognizing the need for financing, not knowing how to make a proper loan request and not developing a true and accurate financial statement. If business accounting is not your forte, solicit the help of a good accountant.

9. Not meeting the franchisor's key management personnel at their headquarters and the field representative assigned to your territory. Quite often, the sales representative will do such a good job in building your confidence that you may not bothered with trying to meet the other important personnel or traveling to the headquarters before signing the franchise agreement. Do not make this mistake. Meet the other franchisor personnel and verify the information provided by the sales representative. After the franchisor defines your territory, also meet the field representative or district supervisor that will be working with you. It is important that your personalities are sufficiently harmonious to be able to work effectively together. Although you may not be able to determine this at first, you can find out the field representative's length of time on the job, training, and other experience levels.

If you foresee problems, it is better to address them and try to work them out before you sign the agreement.

10. Not analysing your market in advance. While the franchisor may help with site selection, it is still your responsibility to decide for yourself whether a particular location is desirable and promising. It is important to confirm the market for your product or service in this area. If competition exists, there are several things to consider. Do the competitors have any weaknesses that you will be able to avoid in your business to capture more market? Are the competitors so strong that their market saturation may be hard for you to penetrate? If a local competitor dominates the market, entering it may turn into a competitive struggle that will increase your working capital requirement. Also, evaluate your franchisor's marketing strategy; find out the amount of advertising and promotional dollars intended to help. Although helpful, it is not a good idea to rely totally on your franchisor for your market research. It is to your advantage to do your own market analysis and develop your own marketing plan. If your findings support a strong market for a "virgin" area, you may want your agreement to include a right of first refusal to buy additional franchised outlets in the subject territory before the franchisor considers other prospective franchisees. If you consider this, you will be under a timetable to expand according to the franchisor's goal. If you cannot meet the stated expansion goal, you will forfeit the area. If you are looking into a franchised area controlled by a sub-franchisor, research the sub-franchisor with the same determination and persistence you used evaluating the franchisor--maybe even more.

CHAPTER 9
WAYS TO GROW A SMALL BUSINESS INTO BIG BUSSINESSS

SESSION 1: OVERVIEW (google.com)

ome of the biggest conglomerates today started small. Microsoft started in Bill Gates' garage; and so, did Apple, which was started in the garage of SWozniacki. Mark Zuckerberg started Facebook in his dorm room, and so did Michael Dell when he started Dell. Mattel was also started in the garage of designer and co-founder Harold Mattson, while Google initially operated in the garage of Susan Wojcicki, currently a vice-president at the company. However, these businesses grew and became the largest companies in their industries and in the world. These once-small businesses succeeded with the right product offerings, marketing savvy and solid management skills.

One of the primary reasons that smaller businesses fail to grow and create attractive sustainable profits is that business owners and managers fall into the trap of working 'in' their businesses and fail to take the time or effort to work 'on' their businesses. It is incredibly easy to get caught in this trap. You start, buy or launch a business and initially, to keep costs down, you do almost all the work yourself. You develop products, make sales, service customers, issue invoices and keep the financial records yourself. The motivation of working for yourself and being your own boss enables you to work hard and focus on delivery to clients. As you deliver to clients so you win more work, requiring you to work harder. As the owner of the business you get busier and busier, working late into the night and also on weekends, just to get everything done. This level of activity is not sustainable. Soon you get tired, your family starts to complain and your positive upbeat attitude becomes sour and negative. You miss a few deadlines, fail to return phone calls and your clients, who were initially very impressed with your service, wonder what's happened. Some people realize that this cannot continue so, after some moments of self-reflection, they decide to scale back and operate at a level that is more sustainable. Others just continue to operate at a frantic pace but because of declining service levels some clients leave and the business stops growing. Whichever route the owner takes; the business reaches a level where it stops growing. The business owner has been caught in the trap of only working 'in' their business. To break out of this cycle, the business owner needs to make a transition from working 'in' the business to working 'on' the business. Working 'on' the business means taking time out from the day-to-day operations of the entity to focus on, and implement, critical bigger picture issues such as strategy, structures, systems and skills development. It is about building a platform for growth within the business that is not dependant on any single person for success. If you want to leave a legacy and make real money as an entrepreneur, then this is probably the most important lesson you can learn. Working on one's business takes discipline and effort. It does not come naturally to most people to work on their business; the natural default is to work in the business. There are many reasons why business owners avoid working on their businesses. Some use the excuse that they don't have time; others say that they don't want the operation to get too bureaucratic or corporate while others are oblivious to the difference between working in and working on a business. I believe that one of the primary reasons why so many entrepreneurs avoid working on their business is that they don't really understand how to. A business owner may decide that from next month he is going to devote a morning a week to working on his business but when that morning comes, he is uncertain of what to do with the time so he defaults to dealing with a client or preparing invoices. Working on one's business is a cyclical process that involves thinking and decision making about strategy, designing and implementing new structures and strategies, and facilitating the development of new skills.

Strategizing is about taking a step back and making some decisions about where you choose to operate and how you plan to win in those areas. In running a business, it is so easy to get swept up in what customers' demand that you never really take a step back to question whether your business is heading in the right direction. Many entrepreneurs invest a great deal of time and energy in devising a strategy for their business when they first launch, but they never revisit their strategy once the business is operating. You are in a much stronger position to make important strategic decisions after you have being operating for a while because you then have experience in the industry and greater insight into the markets, competitors and business model alternatives.

In the strategizing phase of the cycle you should spend time addressing the following issues:

VALUE: What value are we creating, how are we creating value and for whom are we creating this value? How will we create value in the future?

MARKETS: Are we operating in the right markets? Which markets will we focus on growing in the future?

COMPETITIVE ADVANTAGE: Are we winning in our markets? What can we do to have an even greater competitive advantage in our markets now and in the future?

ACTIVITIES: What are the core activities of our business? What do we choose to do and what do we choose not to do?

GOALS: What are our goals for the next 3 – 5 years? What do we need to do to deliver on those goals?

Structuring

To effectively deliver on a strategy a business needs structure. Structure is the right people in the right positions to do what is required to make the strategy happen. Even in the smallest, simplest businesses it is important to have some element of structure and as a business becomes larger so structure becomes more and more important. If you are in a small business with just one partner, structuring involves identifying your individual responsibilities and what you are going to outsource to external service providers. In a larger business it is about giving each person in a business a clear understanding of what they are required to do and how they will be held accountable for carrying out those tasks. As a business grows the business owner can easily lose sight of what everyone in the organisation is doing and this can result in duplication of work, lack of accountability and work overload. Working on the business therefore requires the leadership to review the structures and lines of responsibility to establish an effective and efficient organisation that can deliver on the strategy.

In the structuring phase of the cycle, you should spend time addressing the following issues:

SKILLS: What skills do we require in the organisation to deliver on the strategy? Do we currently have the right skills to deliver on the strategy? Where can we find the missing skills?

ROLES: How do we put people in roles that leverage their skills and enable us to deliver on our strategy? Describe each person's roles and the responsibility that goes with that role?

ACCOUNTABILITY: How will people be held accountable for delivering on the requirements of their roles? What will we measure? Who will do the measuring? How often will we measure performance?

Skills development

Systems invariably depend on people and for people to operate effectively within a system they often need to be trained. It is therefore essential to see skills development and training as a critical element of working on your business. If you don't train and develop people, then all your efforts in structuring and systematising your business are likely to be in vain. You do not necessarily need to do all the training yourself but you should oversee the training and take an active interest in the skills requirements and development of all the people in your business. The process of working on your business by strategizing, structuring, systematising and developing skills is a continuous cycle. Therefore, once you have been through the cycle after having developed or refined your strategy, created a structure, established systems and developed and trained people with the requisite skills then you need to start again with development and refinement of strategy. The more times that you go through the cycle the more your business is likely to grow.

In the skills development phase of the cycle you should spend time addressing the following issues:

PERFORMANCE REQUIREMENTS: At what level do I need the various people in my organisation to perform in order for the business to be successful?

PERFORMANCE GAPS: At what level are the people in my organisation currently performing? What are the gaps in their performance between what is required and what is currently happening?

TRAINING PRIORITIES: In what order should I address the skills gaps for maximum success and survival of my business?

TRAINING METHODS: How should I address each of the skills gaps? Which gaps are best addressed through formal training and which are best addressed through on the job coaching and mentoring? Who will I get to do all the required training?

SYSTEMATISING

To build a business with a real platform for growth, it is critical to identify the key activities relating to that business and to build systems that allow those key activities to be often replicated effectively. When most businesses start out, entrepreneurs perform most of the critical activities in the business themselves. The only way that entrepreneurs can facilitate real growth in that business is to translate what they do into a set of processes that others can execute. The critical systems within a business may vary slightly depending on the nature of the industry in which the business is operating but most businesses require systems and processes that relate to marketing and selling, product or service delivery, financial management and reporting, buying, and product development.

In the systematising phase of the cycle you should spend time addressing the following issues:

KEY PROCESSES: What are the key processes that create value for our customers and/or allow our business to run effectively and efficiently?

PROCEDURES: Do we have established documented procedures to deliver on our key processes easily and often? For which of our key processes do we still need to establish and document procedures?

AUTOMATION AND OUTSOURCING: What could we automate to reduce the dependence on people? Are there procedures within our processes that could be more effectively executed by external organisations?

THE TRANSITION

Making the transition from spending all your time working in your businesses to consistently dedicating time to working on your business is not easy. It takes discipline and dedication to get this right but such discipline and dedication should yield handsome returns in the long-term. Smaller business owners should aim to spend 20% of their time (the equivalent of one day a week) working on the business. Larger business owners or managers within larger enterprises can aim to spend as much as 80% of their time working on the business.

Therefore, the amount of time you aim to dedicate to working on the business should depend on the size of your business and how much you want it to grow. The higher your growth aspirations, the more time you should spend working on your business. If you are currently caught in the trap of working almost entirely in your business, make the transition over time. Start off by setting aside two hours a week to work on your business. In your first two hours review your strategy, in your second two hours examine your structure, in your third two hours evaluate your systems and in your fourth two hours consider your skills development. This will establish the platform for working on your business in month one of the transitions. Then in month two dedicate three to four hours a week to working on your business and take the time to address some of the issues that were identified in the review sessions in month one. Work with other senior people in the organisation on these issues. As you move into month three, try to dedicate a full half a day a week to working on your business and continue to increase the time you spend on these issues over time until you are working on strategy, structure, systems and skills development for a full day a week.

The effect of moving from a place of working entirely in your business to a place where you regularly dedicate time to working on your business will be amazing. You will realize a year down the line that you have a happier, more empowered, more focused workforce. You will discover that customers that you personally had nothing to do with are raving about your company's service. You will discover that you have more time for yourself and are able to approach work in a more balanced fashion and that the business is growing in a sustainable and profitable way. A well-known business philosopher, Jim Rohn, says: "If you go to work on your goals, your goals will go to work on you. If you go to work on your plan, your plan will go to work on you. Whatever good things we build end up building us." It is for this reason that we need to remove ourselves from our businesses to work on our businesses if we truly want our businesses to work for us so that we can make millions and leave a legacy.

Make an Impact! Make a Fortune! Leave a Legacy!

Some believe that entrepreneurship relates only to people who are starting and growing a new business. Yet time and time again I am strucked by how the principles of entrepreneurship have application within many different settings.

Entrepreneurship is primarily about the creation of value and the concept of value creation has relevance within many different spheres of society. We need people who are willing to take risks and be innovative in order to create new value in government, business, education and the non-profit sector. Thus, the principles that are consistently applied by successful entrepreneurs can be used in many different circumstances to enhance the world in which we live and to enable individuals to make a significant contribution.

For the bulk of Jack Welch's career, he was employed by one of the world's largest corporations, General Electric, yet it would be difficult to argue that he was not entrepreneurial. Tom Boardman used the entrepreneurial principles he learnt in establishing Boardman's furniture store early on in his career to turn around Nedbank, one of South Africa's largest financial services institutions. Nick Binedell showed entrepreneurial flair as an academic professor in establishing and growing the Gordon Institute of Business Science. Therefore, no matter where you find yourself, if you are able to apply and implement the following fundamental entrepreneurial principles, you are much more likely to be successful and to leave a legacy.

Establish and define a compelling purpose for what you are doing

The world's greatest entrepreneurs establish a purpose for themselves and their business that focuses on more than just making money. The Google Guys see their purpose as organising the world's information and Walt Disney felt his purpose was to make people happy.

People are compelled by purpose; they are energized by being part of something that they feel is bigger than they are. They want to work for something that they feel is meaningful. Therefore, if you wish to really succeed in your career, whether you are in a large corporation or in a small start-up, whether you are in government or an NGO you need to work hard to clearly understand, define and focus on your purpose.

Establish a point of differentiation that gives you a sustainable competitive advantage

Entrepreneurship is about being innovative and creating an advantage by being distinctly different from competitors. Doing more of the same will seldom, if ever, make an entrepreneur truly successful. Anyone who wishes to create long-term success needs to build distinctive points of differentiation. In a career, you need to establish a set of skills and competencies that set you apart and make you irreplaceable. It is by becoming irreplaceable that you are able to command higher compensation and yield more decision-making power within a corporation, government institution or any other organisation.

Focus on the creation of value for your chosen market

Entrepreneurs launching a new business need to focus intensely on giving their chosen market something that they need and want, if they wish to have any chance of surviving. It is this intense focus on the needs and wants of the customer that enables them to create value. Anyone who wants to succeed in a career needs to understand what he or she can do to create value for the organisation for which they are working. Take the time to understand what is valuable to your organisation and then focus intensely on delivering whatever that is effectively and consistently.

Work on your situation, not just in your situation

A related article in this magazine highlights how critical it is for entrepreneurs to work 'on' their business and to avoid the trap of just working 'in' their business. Working on your business involves stepping back and taking time to review strategy, establish structures, build systems and develop skills. In your career it is easy to get so wrapped up in what you are doing on a day-to-day basis that you never take the time to consider where you want to go and how you are going to get there. Working on your situation involves regularly giving yourself the time and space to redefine your goals and establish a plan for achieving those goals. It has been shown time and time again that those people who take time to reflect on where they have been and readjust where they want to go are more likely to be successful and have an impact than those who get caught in the trap of just working, working, working without ever reviewing where they are going or what they are doing. Being successful as an entrepreneur is a simple formula. You need to sell things for more than they cost so that you make a profit. Any money you spend in the process of generating revenue causes you to make less profit. Entrepreneurs therefore learn to spend as little as possible in order to avoid going into the red. Within a larger corporation people often lose sight of this simple equation causing them to spend irresponsibly without having anything to show for it. If you develop the habit of spending without thinking, you will be eroding value over time. You may be able to get away with this for a short period of time but it will eventually catch up with you. If you continuously think and act like an entrepreneur, questioning every item of spending, over time you will develop good, wealth generating habits in both your personal and your business life. Warren Buffet said: "Chains of habit are too light to be felt until they are too heavy to be broken." If, in your career and your life, you get too used to doing things in ways that do not create value and waste time, money and other resources, your career will be trapped on a downward spiral that will be very difficult to break out of. If, however, you try to think and act like an entrepreneur, focusing on purpose, differentiation, value creation, effective use of time and frugality, then you are likely to establish habits that will set you apart, causing you to be successful and leave a legacy.

SESSION2: BUSINESS COST
PROFIT EARNINGS AFTER START-UP COST

For an Entrepreneurial business there are two kind of ongoing cost incurred I) fixed cost ii) variable cost.

Fixed Cost is the cost you pay whether anyone buys anything or not. Which basically consist of rent, rates, service charge for your premises and staff cost for staff who earns monthly salary rather than by the hours they work, generally fixed cost are called fixed because they tend to be fixed for a few years and may change over some space of years but at the moment can be regarded as fixed. *Utilities* (while these vary depending on how much you use them for most business types, they tend to be stable regardless of how many sales the business makes) *Insurance payment*.

Variable Cost this is the cost you incur only when someone buys something. Variable cost goes up and down with sales which usually consist of whatever you are selling, if your business is a shop these will be the cost of whatever goods you are selling and the extra staff you take on to cope with sales. If your business is a manufacturer it will be the cost of your raw materials and non-fixed staff costs.

SESSION 2B: DEVELOPMENTAL PHASES OF BUSINESS MANAGEMENT
STAGE I: EXISTENCE

In this stage the main problems of the business are obtaining customers and delivering the product or service contracted for. Among the key questions are the following:

Can we get enough customers, deliver our products, and provide services well enough to become a viable business?

Can we expand from that one key customer or pilot production process to a much broader sales base?

Do we have enough money to cover the considerable cash demands of this start-up phase?

The organization is a simple one—the owner does everything and directly supervises subordinates, who should be of at least average competence. Systems and formal planning are minimal to non-existent. The company's strategy is simply to remain alive. The owner *is* the business, performs all the important tasks, and is the major supplier of energy, direction, and, with relatives and friends, capital.

Companies in the Existence Stage range from newly started restaurants and retail stores to high-technology manufacturers that have yet to stabilize either production or product quality. Many such companies never gain sufficient customer acceptance or product capability to become viable. In these cases, the owners close the business when the start-up capital runs out and, if they're lucky, sell the business for its asset value. In some cases, the owners cannot accept the demands the business places on their time, finances, and energy, and they quit. Those companies that remain in business become Stage II enterprises.

STAGE II: SURVIVAL

In reaching this stage, the business has demonstrated that it is a workable business entity. It has enough customers and satisfies them sufficiently with its products or services to keep them. The key problem thus shifts from mere existence to the relationship between revenues and expenses. The main issues are as follows:

a) In the short run, can we generate enough cash to breakeven and to cover the repair or replacement of our capital assets as they wear out?

b) Can we, at a minimum, generate enough cash flow to stay in business and to finance growth to a size that is sufficiently large, given our industry and market niche, to earn an economic return on our assets and labour?

The organization is still simple. The company may have a limited number of employees supervised by a sales manager or a general foreman. Neither of them makes major decisions independently, but instead carry out the rather well-defined orders of the owner. Systems development is minimal. Formal planning is, at best, cash forecasting. The major goal is still survival, and the owner is still synonymous with the business.

In the Survival Stage, the enterprise may grow in size and profitability and move on to Stage III. Or it may, as many companies do, remain at the Survival Stage for some time, earning marginal returns on invested time and capital and eventually go out of business when the owner gives up or retires. The "mom and pop" stores are in this category, as are manufacturing businesses that cannot get their product or process sold as planned. Some of these marginal businesses have developed enough economic viability to ultimately be sold, usually at a slight loss. Or they may fail completely and drop from sight.

STAGE III: SUCCESS

The decision facing owners at this stage is whether to exploit the company's accomplishments and expand or keep the company stable and profitable, providing a base for alternative owner activities. Thus, a key issue is whether to use the company as a platform for growth—a sub-stage III-G company—or as a means of support for the owners as they completely or partially disengage from the company—making it a sub-stage III-D company. Behind the disengagement might be a wish to start-up new enterprises, run for political office, or simply to pursue hobbies and other outside interests while maintaining the business more or less in the status quo.

SUB-STAGE III-D.

In the Success-Disengagement sub-stage, the company has attained true economic health, has sufficient size and product-market penetration to ensure economic success, and earns average or above-average profits. The company can stay at this stage indefinitely, provided environmental change does not destroy its market niche or ineffective management reduce its competitive abilities.

Organizationally, the company has grown large enough to, in many cases, require functional managers to take over certain duties performed by the owner. The managers should be competent but need not be of the highest calibre, since their upward potential is limited by the corporate goals. Cash is plentiful and the main concern is to avoid a cash drain in prosperous periods to the detriment of the company's ability to withstand the inevitable rough times.

In addition, the first professional staff members come on board, usually a controller in the office and perhaps a production scheduler in the plant. Basic financial, marketing, and production systems are in place. Planning in the form of operational budgets supports functional delegation. The owner and, to a lesser extent, the company's managers, should be monitoring a strategy to, essentially, maintain the status quo.

As the business matures, and the owner increasingly move apart, to some extent because of the owner's activities elsewhere and to some extent because of the presence of other managers. Many companies continue for long periods in the Success-Disengagement sub-stage. The product-market niche of some does not permit growth; this is the case for many service businesses in small or medium-sized, slowly growing communities and for franchise holders with limited territories.

Other owners actually choose this route; if the company can continue to adapt to environmental changes, it can continue as is, be sold or merged at a profit, or subsequently be stimulated into growth. For franchise holders, this last option would necessitate the purchase of other franchises. You can read up on chapter 8 for more details on franchise business.

If the company cannot adapt to changing circumstances, as was the case with many automobile dealers in the late 1970s and early 1980s, it will either fold or drop back to a marginally surviving company (endpoint four on Exhibit 4).

SUB-STAGE III-G.

In the Success-Growth sub-stage, the owner consolidates the company and marshals' resources for growth. The owner takes the cash and the established borrowing power of the company and risks it all in financing growth.

Among the important tasks are to make sure the basic business stays profitable so that it will not outrun its source of cash and to develop managers to meet the needs of the growing business. This second task requires hiring managers with an eye to the company's future rather than its current condition.

Systems should also be installed with attention to forthcoming needs. Operational planning is, as in sub-stage III-D, in the form of budgets, but strategic planning is extensive and deeply involves the owner. The owner is thus far more active in all phases of the company's affairs than in the disengagement aspect of this phase.

If it is successful, the III-G company proceeds into Stage IV. Indeed, III-G is often the first attempt at growing before commitment to a growth strategy. If the III-G company is unsuccessful, the causes may be detected in time for the company to shift to III-D. If not, retrenchment to the Survival Stage may be possible prior to bankruptcy or a distress sale.

STAGE IV: TAKE OFF

In this stage the key problems are how to grow rapidly and how to finance that growth. The most important questions, then, are in the following areas:

DELEGATION.

Can the owner delegate responsibility to others to improve the managerial effectiveness of a fast growing and increasingly complex enterprise? Further, will the action be true delegation with controls on performance and a willingness to see mistakes made, or will it be abdication, as is so often the case?

CASH.

Will there be enough to satisfy the great demands growth brings (often requiring a willingness on the owner's part to tolerate a high debt equity ratio) and a cash flow that is not eroded by inadequate expense controls or ill-advised investments brought about by owner impatience?

The organization is decentralized and, at least in part, or in divisions—usually in either sales or production. The key managers must be very competent to handle a growing and complex business environment. The systems, strained by growth, are becoming more refined and extensive.

Both *operational* and *strategic* planning are being done and involve specific managers. The owner and the business have become reasonably separate, yet the company is still dominated by both the owner's presence and stock control.

This is a pivotal period in a company's life. If the owner rises to the challenges of a growing company, both financially and managerially, it can become a big business. If not, it can usually be sold—at a profit—provided the owner recognizes his or her limitations soon enough. Too often, those who bring the business to the Success Stage are unsuccessful in Stage IV, either because they try to grow too fast and run out of cash (the owner falls victim to the omnipotence syndrome), or are unable to delegate effectively enough to make the company work (the omniscience syndrome).

It is, of course, possible for the company to traverse this high-growth stage without the original management. Often the entrepreneur who founded the company and brought it to the Success Stage is replaced either voluntarily or involuntarily by the company's investors or creditors.

If the company fails to make the big time, it may be able to retrench and continue as a successful and substantial company at a state of equilibrium. Or it may drop back to Stage III or, if the problems are intractable, it may drop all the way back to the Survival Stage or even fail. (High interest rates and uneven economic conditions have made the latter two possibilities all too real in the early 1980s.)

STAGE V: RESOURCE MATURITY

The greatest concerns of a company entering this stage are, first, to consolidate and control the financial gains brought on by rapid growth and, second, to retain the advantages of small size, including flexibility of response and the entrepreneurial spirit. The corporation must expand the management force fast enough to eliminate the inefficiencies that growth can produce and professionalize the company by use of such tools as budgets, strategic planning, management by objectives, and standard cost systems—and do this without stifling its entrepreneurial qualities.

A company in Stage V has the staff and financial resources to engage in detailed operational and strategic planning. The management is decentralized, adequately staffed, and experienced. And systems are extensive and well developed. The owner and the business are quite separate, both financially and operationally.

The company has now arrived. It has the advantages of size, financial resources, and managerial talent. If it can preserve its entrepreneurial spirit, it will be a formidable force in the market. If not, it may enter a sixth stage of sorts: ossification.

Ossification is characterized by a lack of innovative decision making and the avoidance of risks. It seems most common in large corporations whose sizable market share, buying power, and financial resources keep them viable until there is a major change in the environment. Unfortunately for these businesses, it is usually their rapidly growing competitors that notice the environmental change first.

KEY MANAGEMENT FACTORS

Several factors, which change in importance as the business grows and develops, are prominent in determining ultimate success or failure.

We identified eight such factors in our research, of which four relate to the enterprise and four to the owner. The four that relate to the company are as follows:

1. Financial resources, including cash and borrowing power.

2. Personnel resources, relating to numbers, depth, and quality of people, particularly at the management and staff levels.

3. Systems resources, in terms of the degree of sophistication of both information and planning and control systems.

4. Business resources, including customer relations, market share, supplier relations, manufacturing and distribution processes, technology and reputation, all of which give the company a position in its industry and market.

The four factors that relate to the owner are as follows:

1. Owner's goals for himself or herself and for the business.

2. Owner's operational abilities in doing important jobs such as marketing, inventing, producing, and managing distribution.

3. Owner's managerial ability and willingness to delegate responsibility and to manage the activities of others.

4. Owner's strategic abilities for looking beyond the present and matching the strengths and weaknesses of the company with his or her goals.

As a business moves from one stage to another, the importance of the factors changes. We might view the factors as alternating among three levels of importance: *first*, key variables that are absolutely essential for success and must receive high priority; *second*, factors that are clearly necessary for the enterprise's success and must receive some attention; and *third*, factors of little immediate concern to top management. If we categorize each of the eight factors listed previously, based on its importance at each stage of the company's development, we get a clear picture of changing management demands.

SESSION3: MANAGEMENT SKILLS FOR BUSINESS SUCCESS
1) **Leadership skills**
   a. Lead by example
   b. Set achievable, realistic and measurable goals
   c. Plan, direct and coordinate goal-oriented activities
   d. Treat others as himself and motivate them to achieve results

2) **Decision making skills**
   a. A leader must have decision making ability
   b. A leader is creative and believe in himself
   c. Have positive attitude to issues as they arrive
   d. A leader is patient in reaching a rational decision

3) **Time Management Skills**

   a) Prioritize daily activities and allocate time and deadline on each activity
   b) Time is the greatest asset of the entrepreneur
   c) Set time to seek new opportunities, solve problems and create activities
   d) Schedule time to review daily goals, outcomes or achievement
   e) Planning, organizing and scheduling are the keys to successful time management

4) **People Management Skills**

   a) Knowing your workers and how to treat them
   b) No business can succeed without the full support of employees
   c) Manage people as asset

d) Motivate workers for productive activities

e) Offer fair rewards

5) **Money Management**
   a. Managing business finance is the hall-mark of business
   b. Good financial planning (budget planning and control) and ability to stick to them will determine business success
   c. Determine your expenses and income
   d. Be prudent in financial matters
   e. Allocate salary for your time and personal expenses
   f. Separate personal financial matters from business matters
   g. Document all financial transaction
   h. Prepare the cash flow statement weekly, monthly and quarterly
   i. Never dip hand into working capital
   j. Never use short-term loans (overdrafts) for long-term investment
   k. Engage the services of a book-keeper or accountant if you lack financial management skills

6) **Business knowledge**
   a. Know your business inside out
   b. Know your products and services and where they are needed most
   c. Know the step-by-step process about your business
   d. Find out the needs of your customers, their levels of demand and how to satisfy them
   e. Know your suppliers, customers and employees
   f. Understand what the business is made of and stay with what you do best
   g. Record existing experience for future use
   h. Develop human competencies through training and nurture them
   i. Manage the knowledge about the business as assets

7) **Information Technology Skills**
   a. Establish a corporate website

b. Use the internet to network and communicate with customers and other people. Nearly, all the networking sites are free
c. Facebook, twitter and LinkedIn are web-based tools that you should explore for this purpose,
d. Marketing and sales-sell your products and services to the whole world on amazon.com and similar websites
e. Online marketing and sales are ways your business can grow from a micro-enterprise into a multi-national concern
f. Advertising – advertising is a very important aspect of marketing
g. With the internet, an entrepreneur can deliver advertising messages to millions, if not billions of people, all over the world at next to nothing cost
h. Online meeting – with internet, it is possible to have a meeting with someone in Australia without leaving the comfort of your office
i. There are "chat rooms" you can subscribe to for the same purpose. For a more professional atmosphere, then subscribe to WebEx. Most are free.

To run a successful business, you need a diverse range of business management skills. When you start your business, which will likely include:

a) sales and marketing;
b) accounts;
c) human resources; and
d) Information technology (IT).

How confident do you feel in your ability to manage all of these?

It's a good idea to plan ahead of time how you're going to manage each area which may include delegating various functions to a business partner, that is if you have one if you don't then it is advisable to undertake additional training or contract a specialist or a consultant such as a I.T oriented specialist, business managers and marketers. Remember that although you need to understand, manage and take responsibility for every aspect of your business, you don't have to do everything yourself. You get somebody that you can trust based on well laid out contract to join you reason because in the nearest future the person can lay claims of having a share in the company if the company becomes successful and rich.

Some of the key areas you'll need to think about are outlined below.

What's next...?
- Do you need any licences or permits to start your business?
- Do you have the financial capacity to start your business?
- How feasible is your business idea?

Marketing, sales and promotion

Marketing is more than just selling and promoting your business. It's about identifying your customers and working out how to get them to purchase your product or service. Check previous chapters this area has being handled thoroughly but in the area of promotion it is necessary so as to create a basis of having potential clients and customers.

Human Resources

Human resources are about managing and looking after your staff. If you're buying an existing business or taking on a franchise you may find that you've got employees to manage before you even start your business. Reason for this is that employees are the back bone of your business they are the ones that will build your vision in your business for without them you would have difficult expanding your business to a global scale. Incentives, bonuses and monthly awards for staff will be a great way for celebrating their effort in your company with a good pay.

Understanding Business Financials

LIST OF TO DO ACTION

- ✓ Find out what's the supply cost
- ✓ Research about the income of people already doing the business
- ✓ Calculate how many sales you need to do to make your profit target work
- ✓ Work out how much you need to kick start your business

The primary objective of any business is to make a profit. Good financial management is essential to ensure your goal is achieved. The first step involves understanding your financial statements which is crucial to running your business successful.

Communication and Negotiation skills

Business is all about people regardless of your industry or the product or service you're offering. On a daily basis you will encounter a range of people including customers, suppliers, employees and business associates. Developing your communication and negotiation skills will be invaluable in a range of situations from negotiating a supplier contract to dealing with a difficult customer.

Knowledge of Business legal issues

Starting a business can be full of legal potholes for the unwary, whether its industry regulation, tax requirements, industrial relations, business structures, negotiating a commercial tenancy lease or contracts with suppliers. There are many legal issues to be aware of, so before you start a business, it's a good idea to engage a lawyer to advise you in these areas.

Logistics Expert

Logistics is about managing the procurement, supply and maintenance of products and operational goods. One of the major concerns for a business owner is stock control and there are many different approaches and programs to stock management. Before you start your business, you should think about how you'll ensure you have the right amount of stock at the right place and at the right time. Efficiently managing stock is important and will ensure your capital isn't tied up, and protects production if problems arise in the supply chain.

SESSION 4: (FORBES.COM, 2016) 12 FACTS YOU NEED TO KNOW FROM FORBES' 2016 BILLIONAIRES LIST

FORBES has spent the past 30 years scouring the globe to find all of the world's richest people and value their fortunes. This year's result: 1,810 billionaires from 67 countries worth a combined $6.5 trillion. Here are twelve things you should know about these 10-figure fortunes:

1. In the past 30 years, only 5 people have held the title of richest person on planet : Warren Buffett, Carlos Slim, Yoshiaki Tsutsumi and Taikichiro Mori. Bill Gates has being the world's richest person for seventeen out of the past 22 years.

2. The 500 richest individuals in the world are responsible for 64% of all 1,810 billionaires' wealth.

3. A record 66 members of the 2016 FORBES Billionaires List are under the age of 40 . That's more than triple the number four years ago and a seven-fold increase since 2010. A record 36 of these young billionaires have self-made fortunes.

4. Just 19 years old, Alexandra Andresen is the world's youngest billionaire and the second teenage billionaire to ever appear on the Billionaires List. Heir

to a family fortune built on tobacco, FORBES values her stake in investment company Ferd at $1.2 billion. Her sister, Katharina Andresen, is the second youngest billionaire at the age of 20.

5. New to the list this year, Zhou Qunfei of Hong Kong is the world's richest self-made female entrepreneur with a $5.9 billion fortune. She owns nearly 88% of Lens Technology, the world's largest makers of glass covers for mobile phones and tablets and a supplier to and Samsung. The company went public in May 2015.

6. Twenty-seven billionaire megadonors have publicly given a collective $46 million to presidential candidates who have dropped out of the race . Donald Trump meanwhile has spent just $18 million of an estimated roughly $300 million cash pile.

7. Mark Zuckerberg added $11.2 billion to his net worth in the past 12 months (more than any other billionaire) as Facebook shares rose 35%.

8. Despite a turbulent year for the world's wealthy, 198 newcomers added their names to the FORBES Billionaires List in 2016 . The richest new additions were Udo and Harald Tschira, who inherited shares in software giant SAP from their father Klaus Tschira, who died.

9. This past year, 221 billionaires got knocked off the FORBES Billionaires list ; not since 2009—when the credit crisis exiled 355 from the three-comma club—have so many gone down in one year.

10. Just two of the 20 richest people in the world held on to their rankings this year . Bill Gates is the richest man on the planet for the 17th time in the last 22 years. His buddy Warren Buffett remains the third-richest person in the world, despite losing $11.9 billion as shares of his Berkshire Hathaway tumbled 14%.

11. There are only 10 female billionaires who made or inherited their fortunes from technology . The richest is Steve Job's widow, Laurena Powell Jobs, who holds the largest individual stake in Disney and is worth $16.2 billion

12. New York City is still the world capital for the ultra-rich. Seventy-nine billionaires call the Big Apple home, holding a combined $364.6 billion in wealth. Mike Bloomberg is the city's richest, taking the spot from David Koch.

SESSION 6: BIOGRAPHY OF A FEW FAMOUS SUCCESS STORIES OF WEALTHY INDUSTRIALIST IN NIGERIA (wikipedia.com, 2016)

S/N	NAME	Company Name	(Industry)
1	**Alhaji Aliko Dangote**	Dangote Group	(Manufacturing, oil and gas,)
2	**Alhaji Sayyu Dantata**	MRS Group	(Oil and gas, construction)
3	**Chief Ade Ojo**	Elizade Motors Nig LTD	(Auto retailing)
4	**Chief Cletus Ibeto**	Ibeto Group	(Trading, manufacturing, oil and gas)
5	**Chief Molade Okoya Thomas**	Chairman CFAO Nig and other six French companies	(Automobiles)
6	**Cosmos Maduka**	Coscharis Group	(Automobile, manufacturing)
7	**Dele Fajemirokun**	Chaiman Aiico Insurance, Xerox Nigeria, Chicken Republic, Kings Guards	(Insurance, Security, Technology, Food retailing)
8	**Femi Otedola**	Forte Oil and Gas	(Oil and gas)
9	**Fola Adeola**	GTBank	(Banking)
10	**Hakeem Bello Osagie**	Etisalat Nigeria	(Telecom)
11	**Jim Ovia**	Zenith Bank, Visafone	(Banking, Telecom)
12	**Jimoh Ibrahim**	Nicon Insurance, Global Fleet	(Insurance, transportation, oil and gas)
13	**Leo Stan Ekeh**	Zinox	(Computer, technology)
14	**Mike Adenuga**	Conoil, Globacom	(Oil and gas, Banking, Telecom)

15	**Oba Otudeko**	Honeywell Group Nigeria, Pivotal Engineering, Airtel	(Manufacturing, oil and gas, telecom)
16	**Orji Uzor Kalu**	Slok Group	(Aviation, Shipping, publishing, manufacturing)
17	**Pascal Dozie**	MTN Nigeria, Diamond Bank	(Banking, Telecom)
18	**Prince Samuel Adedoyin**	Doyin Group	(manufacturing, pharmaceuticals)
19	**Tony Ezenna**	Orange Group	(Pharmaceutical, oil and gas)
20	**Umaru Abdul Mutallab**	former Chairman First Bank Plc	Mutallab Group
21	**Vincent Amaechi Obianodo**	Young Shall Grow Motors, RockView Hotels	(Transportation, hotels)

Aliko Dangote

Aliko Dangote GCON (born 10 April 1957) is a Nigerian billionaire, who owns the Dangote Group, which has interests in commodities. The company operates in Nigeria and other African countries, including Benin, Ethiopia, Senegal, Cameroon, Ghana, South Africa, Togo, Tanzania, and Zambia. As of February 2017, he had an estimated net worth of US$12.5 billion.

Dangote is ranked by *Forbes* magazine as the 67th richest person in the world and the richest in Africa; he peaked on the list as the 23rd richest person in the world in 2014. He surpassed Saudi-Ethiopian billionaire Mohammed Hussein Al Amoudi in 2013 by over $2.6 billion to become the world's richest person of African descent.

The Dangote Group was established as a small trading firm in 1977, the same year Dangote relocated to Lagos to expand the company. Today, it is a multi-trillion naira conglomerate with many of its operations in Benin, Ghana, Nigeria, and Togo. Dangote has expanded to cover food processing, cement manufacturing, and freight. The Dangote Group also dominates the sugar market in Nigeria and is a major supplier to the country's soft drink companies, breweries, and confectioners. The Dangote Group has moved from being a trading company to being the largest industrial group in Nigeria including Dangote Sugar Refinery, Dangote Cement, and Dangote Flour.

In July 2012, Dangote approached the Nigerian Ports Authorities to lease an abandoned piece of land at the Apapa Port, which was approved. He later built facilities for his flour company there. In the 1990s, he approached the Central Bank of Nigeria with the idea that it would be cheaper for the bank to allow his transport company to manage their fleet of staff buses, a proposal which was also approved.

In Nigeria today, Dangote Group with its dominance in the sugar market and refinery business is the main supplier (70% of the market) to the country's soft drinks companies, breweries and confectioners. It is the largest refinery in Africa and the third largest in the world, producing 800,000 tonnes of sugar annually. Dangote Group owns salt factories and flour mills and is a major importer of rice, fish, pasta, cement and fertilizer. The company exports cotton, cashew nuts, cocoa, sesame seed and ginger to several countries. It also has major investments in real estate, banking, transport, textiles and oil and gas. The company employs over 11,000 people and is the largest industrial conglomerate in West Africa.

Dangote has diversified into telecommunications and has started building 14,000 kilometres of fibre optic cables to supply the whole of Nigeria. As a result, Dangote was honoured in January 2009 as the leading provider of employment in the Nigerian construction industry. He said, "Let me tell you this and I want to really emphasize it...nothing is going to help Nigeria like Nigerians bringing back their money. If you give me $5 billion today, I will invest everything here in Nigeria. Let us put our heads together and work."

Mike Adenuga

Michael Adeniyi Agbolade Ishola Adenuga Jr (born 29 April 1953) is a Nigerian business tycoon, and the second-richest person in Nigeria. His company Globacom is Nigeria's second-largest telecom operator, and also has a presence in Ghana and Benin. He also owns stakes in the Equatorial Trust Bank and the oil exploration firm Conoil (formerly *Consolidated Oil Company*). *Forbes* has estimated his net worth at $5.8 billion as of 2017, which makes him second-wealthiest Nigerian behind Aliko Dangote, as well as the third-richest person in Africa with a net worth of $14.1 billion

Folorunso Alakija

Folorunso Alakija is a Nigerian businesswoman, one of the richest African women and also one of the richest black women in the world. In 2014 she unseated Oprah Winfrey as the richest woman of African descent in the world. She is a business tycoon involved in the fashion, oil and printing industries. She is the group managing director of The Rose of Sharon Group which consists of The Rose of Sharon Prints and Promotions Limited and Digital Reality Prints Limited and the executive vice-chairman of Famfa Oil Limited. Alakija is ranked by *Forbes* as the richest woman in Nigeria with an estimated net worth of $2.1 billion As of 2015, she is listed as the second most powerful woman in Africa after Ngozi Okonjo-Iweala and the 87th most powerful woman in the world by *Forbes*.

Folorunsho started her career in 1974 as an executive secretary at Sijuade Enterprises, Lagos, Nigeria. She moved on to the former First National Bank of Chicago, now Fin Bank now acquired by FCMB (First City Monument Bank) where she worked for some years before establishing a tailoring company called Supreme Stitches. It rose to prominence and fame within a few years, and as Rose of Sharon House of Fashion, became a household name. As national president and lifelong trustee of the Fashion Designers Association of Nigeria (FADAN), she left an indelible mark, promoting Nigerian culture through fashion and style.

In May 1993, Folorunsho applied for the allocation of an oil prospecting license (OPL). The license to explore for oil on a 617,000-acre block—now referred to as OPL 216—was granted to Alakija's company, Famfa Limited. The block is located approximately 220 miles south east of Lagos and 70 miles offshore of Nigeria in the Agbami Field of the central Niger Delta. In September 1996, she entered into a joint venture agreement with Star Deep Water Petroleum Limited (a wholly owned subsidiary of Texaco) and appointed the company as a technical adviser for the exploration of the license, transferring 40 percent of her 100 percent stake to Star Deep. Subsequently, Star Deep sold off 8 percent of its stake in OPL 216 to Petrobras, a Brazilian company. On 9 March 2016 she became the first female Chancellor (Osun State University) in Nigeria.

ADEOLA ODUTOLA

Timothy Adeola Odutola (1902-1995), OBE, CFR, CON, was a prominent Nigerian businessman from Ijebu-Ode, Ogun State. He was one of the pioneers of modern Nigerian indigenous entrepreneurship and the first president of the Manufacturers Association of Nigeria. He attended Ijebu Ode Grammar School, under the principal, Rev Oladotun Ransome Kuti.

In 1932, he resigned his positioning as a court clerk and entered private enterprise. He soon opened damask stores and fish stalls at various cities in western Nigeria, such as Ife, Ibadan, Ilesha and Lagos. After, his subtle beginnings as a fishing net and damask trader, he entered the Cocoa and Palm trading business and started buying lorries to transport the produce to Lagos for export. He built two large commodity storage stores during this period, one was located at Ijebu-Ode, he was also involved in the business and political community as a member of the Produce Buyers Union and the Nigerian Youth Movement. However, the establishment of marketing boards, and the subsequent power of the boards to regulate Cocoa and Palm oil trading proved to be an inhibiting factor to private entrepreneurship in the commodity produce business. Odutola, gradually, transferred his resources and energy to saw milling and gold mining at Ilesha. He also became a major agent for John Holt Nigeria. At the beginning of the drive towards industrialisation in Nigeria, Odutola extended his industrial prowess to the production of rubber goods and started the manufacturing of cycle tyres and tubes in 1967.

Throughout his career, he established various factories in the country, spanning, the transport and food industry, he also built a secondary school at Ijebu-Ode. He was a member and later president of the Nigerian Stock Exchange and the Manufacturers Association of Nigeria in the early 70s.

DELE MOMODU

Dele Momodu (born Ayòbámidélé Àbáyòmí Ojútelégàn Àjàní Momodu; 16 May 1960) is a Nigerian journalist/publisher, businessman, philanthropist, actor and motivational speaker. He is the CEO and publisher of *Ovation International*, a magazine that has given publicity to people from all over the world, mainly in Africa. In 2015, he officially launched Ovation TV and subsequently launched an online newspaper called The Boss. Momodu has received hundreds of awards and honours for his work in the world of business, politics, literature, the music industry and the fashion industry. He writes a weekly column called "pendulum", published every Saturday on the back page of *Thisday* newspaper. The articles are praised for highlighting issues in Nigeria, as well as discussing popular topics, current events and notable people, often in a polemic/critical style. Through pendulum, Momodu became a prominent voice for the APC presidential candidate at the 2015 general election in Nigeria - the current president Muhammadu Buhari.

A graduate of University of Ife, (now Obafemi Awolowo University, Ile-Ife) 1982, Dele Momodu holds a degree in Yoruba and a master's degree in English Literature (1988). He lectured at the Oyo State College of Arts and Science in Ile-Ife, between 1982 and 1983 while on National Service. Between 1983 and 1985, he was private secretary to the former Deputy Governor of Ondo State, Chief Akin Omoboriowo. In 1986, Momodu served the Ooni of Ife, Oba Okunade Sijuwade Olubuse II, managing the Motel Royal Limited owned by the monarch. Following Momodu's resignation from the Motel Royal, he went on to study for his post-graduate degree in English literature. He was during this time contributing articles to the likes of *The Guardian*, *Sunday Tribune* and other Nigerian based publications. On 30 July 2016, Dele was awarded with an honorary doctorate degree (PhD) from the University of Professional Studies, Accra, Ghana, earning him the title "Doctor of Humane Letters".

Despite the harsh terrain and business challenges involved with starting a business in Nigeria; the successful entrepreneurs listed above held their ground and fought their way to the top. In a country with a population of over 170 million inhabitants and millions of businesses; these entrepreneurs diligently carved their names in the sands of time by taking advantage of the fastest growing business opportunities in Nigeria among many <u>African businesses</u>.

The famous entrepreneurs in Nigeria are dogged in guts. They are strong willed and unrelenting. Success is not an option to these set of individuals in fact it's a must. These individuals refuse to be held down by circumstance; instead, they reached out for their inner strength and went for success. Above all, these entrepreneurs don't take no for an answer; they basically say no to giving up and that was why they succeed.

You can Read More on: <u>http://newsofnigeria.com/20-famous-entrepreneurs-in-nigeria/</u>

(GOOGLE.COM, SECRETS TO BILLIONAIRES START UP AND OTHER BILLIONAIRES IN HISTORY)

a. They started small

The industrialists listed above are rich by all standards; in fact, they are billionaires. But they were not born that way and they didn't start out as billionaires; they started small. Andrew Carnegie came from a poverty-stricken family, so also did Henry Ford but these men were humble enough to start small and risked failure. That's why they are billionaire industrialists. This should ring a bell in your head that success doesn't happen overnight, it's a process that requires hard work.

2. They concentrated

The reason I used these industrialist billionaires as case studies was because they made their mark as industrialists. They started small as industrialists, became billionaire industrialists and still remained true to their course. These industrialist billionaires did not diversify their effort; they concentrated. Andrew Carnegie, Lakshmi Mittal and Vladimir Lisin concentrated on steel manufacturing; Henry Ford concentrated on automobile production and Aliko Dangote concentrated on commodity manufacturing. Once again, I emphasize the point that these men did not diversify; they concentrated. So, if you want to become a billionaire, if you want to become a successful entrepreneur; then you must concentrate your resources, time and your effort.

3. They paid their workers well

One key to becoming a successful industrialist is to take care of your workers. Having enthusiastic workers is a key to a smooth production process and these billionaires knew that. Production is a tedious task, so be sure to take care of your workers.

4. Efficiency was their watchword

Another key secret to the success of the billionaire industrialists was their constant effort to improve efficiency and productivity. Henry Ford was the first individual to mass produce cars at a faster rate; Aliko Dangote built the largest cement factory with the latest technology just to increase efficiency and Lakshmi Mittal has increased his steel output by constantly improving on his steel manufacturing process. Efficiency is the keyword to successfully running not just a manufacturing company; but a successful business.

5. They had a mission

Of all the secrets to the success of the industrialist billionaires listed here; the mission is the most important. Why did you become an entrepreneur? Why do you want to start a business? Why do you want to build a business? Why do you want to become a billionaire industrialist?

If you take a closer observation at the entrepreneurial life of the industrialist billionaires, you will notice that they all had a strong business mission and that mission was the driving force behind their success. If you want to find success as an industrialist or a business owner; then you must have a strong business mission. Aliko Dangote became the richest black person in the world because he was on a mission to provide the basic need of over 150million Nigerians. Henry Ford became a famous entrepreneur because he had a mission to democratize the automobile and make it available to the masses. Do you want to join this list of billionaire industrialists? If yes, then you must fashion out a strong business mission for your company and stick with it no matter what.

As a final note, these are the business success secrets of the richest industrialist billionaires in the world. Just as said above, their success can be replicated. All you have to do is simply put these success formulas to work and I will see you at the top.

(NARIALAND.COM, 5 MAJOR PROBLEMS STARTUP ENTREPRENEURS FACE)

- a) What are the problems with being an entrepreneur? These are really problems that can easily become crisis in your hands if you are not an entrepreneur at heart and if you lack the relevant knowledge and skills required to effectively handle such problems:

1. Structural Problem

You will be faced with a lot of issues from the outset that are purely structural in nature. If you don't understand what I mean by structural problems, I bet you already are facing such problems or you are about to face them and won't know what is wrong. The ability to execute your technical competence very well doesn't confer organizational skills on you. Organizational skills are what it takes to build an organization in a way that puts the odds in your favour. Let me put it like this: you need two kinds of companies not one; a holding company and a trading company. Most entrepreneurs are never told when they start out. The trading company trades with clients and customers to make the ongoing profits while the holding company owns the assets in the trading company.

2. Financial Problem

By this, I do not mean insufficient capital; in fact, I do not belong to the school of thought that money is always the first thing needed to start a business. By financial problem I mean accounting, bookkeeping and financial management tactics. Most people starting businesses do not realize how much they have to do per day. You have to learn how to keep your books, bank account(s) and make financial decisions strategically. This can erupt into business failure and bankruptcy if you violate the laws guiding organizational financial management, as a matter of fact your passion and enthusiasm will not be enough at that point to keep you going. To avoid closing down your business you need to understand the financial problems you are facing and deal with it by taking drastic action/steps to fix them before it becomes too late.

3. Sales and Marketing Problem

This can be the most delicate problem of any enterprise as some are facing today. You cannot be an entrepreneur and report that you don't like selling, you're not good at marketing or that you're shy to talk to people. Let me help you out: Go get a job! You are not an entrepreneur at heart; you don't have the software pre-installed. It's often said that the MD is the Chief Seller, Chief Marketer and Chief Public Spokesman for the company. Those are unescapable responsibilities of yours. Brian Sher, in his book What the Rich know and desperately want to keep Secret, advised "Never delegate your marketing and sales to anyone else". Why? No one can sell what you produce or offer the way you can. Remember, bringing in cash flow is the most important area for any company. If you're not making profit, you're not in business. Bradley J. Sugars quipped, "You can cut costs to profit, but you can only sell your way to prosperity."

4. Employee Headache

Hiring becomes a problem when you don't know how volatile a recruitment error can be and how lethal its effect can be on the company. Managing people is one of the many headaches that come with being an employer, and if you don't have the shock absorbers for it, you can go out of control. People remain the number one most appreciable asset of any organization but they remain the number one headache of employers (especially when you hire wrongly). For small organizations, your hiring decisions are very important. One wrong hire out of two payroll staff is a 50% loss to the company and a capital down effect. Please be guided.

5. Clients Problem

The next awful set of people you will have to deal with will be your clients. I've being scorched a number of times, so I speak from a standpoint of experience. Many things it can go from wrong default in payment agreements to unnecessary difficulty in relating with them and much more. As a rule, it is wise to back all verbal discussions with written and jointly signed documents. And be sure to honour your part of the agreement. Making assumptions on behalf of clients can be a dreadful experience when the going gets tough, especially when your staff makes such assumptions on behalf of the company. Client feedback is also a great way to measure yourself but getting that feedback can be a herculean task as most clients do not want to fill forms.

These are just a few problems to be prepared for. My intention with this writing is not to discourage you from entrepreneurial quest but to affirm the level-headedness of that quest. If you should be an entrepreneur, you must have been reading with a burning excitement and figuring out what went wrong some time ago. If you read with a broken heart of confusion or I can't do it spirit, chances are you don't have the software of an entrepreneur in you. You are better off not venturing into the jungle; there are wild fierce beasts at large waiting to feast on you if you do.

So, if I am not an entrepreneur at heart and I don't want a job, what should I do? I'll would say to such person, the only reason why you are indecisive is because you have not started handling responsibilities and paying mind scorching bills, when that becomes your new reality nobody will advise you to go and look for a job or go into entrepreneurship, it's just a matter of time. Entrepreneurship is not for everyone, not everyone will be willing to pay the price of hard work to grow a business. If you feel you don't know anything on entrepreneurship, then go and learn apprenticeship(understudy) under an entrepreneur or alternatively go and work for an already established entrepreneur (employment). But the long and short is don't wait until bills and responsibility is stirring at you in the face before you make up your mind because when you let that happen believe me when I say this going into entrepreneurship would not be the first thing on your mind but rather how to pay those bills will and in the end you will eventually will have to make a choice, to either go for a job, go into petty trading (sole trader) or hawking, when the pressure for money becomes stronger, some even descend to the point of joining bad gangs to make quick money to survive which would eventually lead to their self-destruction. Note that there is a difference between entrepreneurship, sole trader and hawking; they are obviously not the same. So, my dear friend; you can choose out of any to get your life running otherwise you will become a beggar without realising. Before you know it a professional corporate beggar at that. What then is the difference between entrepreneurship, sole trader and hawking.

In Literal meaning Entrepreneurship is a person starting up a business from an idea with the sole aim of making profit with an aim/plan to build an empire from the business.

Sole trader is any business start-up by an individual with the sole aim of generating an income for its owner e.g. a kiosk owner or shop owner. **Hawker** on the other hand is any person selling units of convenience/household items with the sole aim of surviving from the money made as profit.

CHAPTER 10
NETWORK MARKETING BUSINESS START-UP

"Life will present to you many opportunities in the most common of pieces. Inspect- Respect – Expect and Prospect It" By **Matthew Ashimolowo**

The platform basis used in writing this section is Multi-level marketing system like GNLD, FLP, GREENWORLD, H2i e.tc this will help you build a better foundation on how to start and grow. Network marketing can transform your life from being broke to being financial independent with plenty of lifestyle trips to compensate for though involves hard work and a lot of referral from people basically network marketing is based on people but first to enjoy the benefits of network marketing you have to consider changing your mindset on how you want to do business in network marketing, such as:

Complete Mindset Overhaul (Mindset Change): break out from employee mindset then how do you see your past and future with regard to where you want to be?

Let your Past stay There In the Past: Many still live and dwell in past victories and defects, relive every day to accomplish something better than what you did yesterday. Never let your past determine your future, as it is popularly quoted *"Don't let your background place your back on the ground"*.

What are your Desires, Dreams and Goals for this year and for your future: Perception: This is the basis on how you see the world and what you are willing to do about it? Sit down and let things happen or make things happen. How do you perceive opportunity when you see one or how do you recognise opportunities if it's right in front of you?

Better Self-Image: Revalue your self-worth; don't allow circumstances dictate how wonderful your life will be, rather dictate it for yourself, by yourself for only in building your self-image will you truly grow and prosper in multi-level Marketing. Rate yourself higher by setting goals and achieving them and creating reward of what you stand to gain by achieving the goals that was set. Raise your values and targets each time you achieve your targets/goals. Improve your self-esteem and confidence even though you have been a looser all your life with no money or property to show for make up your mind to do something different from what you have always done, before you can change the trend.

"You might not be responsible for where you are now but you are completely responsible for where you are going tomorrow or where you will be in the nearest future".

Desire and Lifestyle Upgrade (The dream of every Nigerian): Make more money ii. Better Quality health iii improved lifestyle as to eating what you like, when you like it and how you like it and being anywhere you want to be without the money constrain or how will I survive. Living a life that not only involves you but those around you.

Sad Reality of Today's Nigeria: The Nigeria economy is an economy tied to dollar rise or fall, same applies to fuel rise and fall which shouldn't have been but sadly, it's our reality in our today's economy. **Why is these:** Attachment to past failure and future with a very bleak future ahead ii) Having a battered self-esteem as an economy and not willing to build for a better tomorrow even though you hear politicians and people wish and hope for it. iii). having falling standard of living for the poor and lowered quality of life for her citizen. Should your life be based on Nigeria's economy or should it be based on how you will make the world a better place through financial Independence.

Increased Financial Challenges: You see the truth of the matter is financial Challenges will always come but having the means to change it or solve it is completely up to you on how you achieve that means. But from these factors alighted I) Low salaries yet high expense budget ii) Delayed salaries from government and private bodies iii) No income sources for the sacked, retrenched and jobless graduates on the street making financial needs high and high competition for the few available jobs and irregular pension for the retired.

SESSION1: MULTI-LEVEL MARKETING MASTER TIPS (google.com)
Learn the secrets from MLM experts so you can follow in their footsteps.

Multi-level marketing is amazing. It's one of the few forms of business I've found that offers a level playing field. In other words, anyone can become successful in this industry. And the best part is that others have already blazed the trail to success, so you just have to look at what they've done and follow suit. There are things you'll hear over and over again as the principles to success in MLM. Here are the top five:

1. Be Coachable. MLM is a business of duplication. Those who've already being successful will share their secrets to success, and all you need to do is listen and then do what they tell you. Unfortunately, I wasn't very coachable in the beginning. I was good at traditional business and figured, I could do my normal business and still make money from network marketing. Boy, was I wrong! At the beginning but later turned out that it happened that way because of my approach and actions. Because I didn't listen to my up-line leaders, I didn't make any money at first but did later. Successful MLMers have being there, done that--and have the pay check to prove it--so be coachable, and duplicate their success.

2. Develop your dreams, goals and objectives. Studies have shown that very few people have written dreams and goals, yet those who do achieve high levels of success. Identify your dreams first. As yourself, if time and money weren't inhibitors, what would your life look like? Describe your dream house in great detail. Likewise, get a mental image of your dream cars, vacations, wardrobe, and lifestyle and so on.

From those dreams, develop your goals. A dream is the big picture, and goals are the steps that will get you to your dreams. For example, let's say your dream car is a Mercedes SL65 with a cost of $225,000 and a monthly payment of around $3,800. What are the steps you need to take to achieve that dream? An increase in your income might be necessary, so your goal would be to increase your monthly income to, let's say, $10,000.

Next, you break your goals down into bite-size objectives (in our example above, this would be the things necessary to increase your monthly income to $10,000). Each day, you should review your dreams, goals and objectives in order to determine your daily activities.

3. Work. Network marketing has probably produced more millionaires than any other industry, and although each of those people built their businesses with different companies and using different methods, they all did one thing--work. MLM isn't a get-rich-quick scheme; you'll only get rich through hard work.

One of the main differences I see in those who fail vs. those who succeed is their level of work. Most people who've failed treated their MLM businesses like a hobby, working whenever they had some spare time. The top income earners, on the other hand, work at their businesses every day.

Let's say that after a thorough evaluation of your schedule, you can only devote 10 hours a week to your business. Take a daily planner and block out those available time slots. Remember, work isn't filing, checking e-mail or surfing the web. Work in MLM is prospecting, presenting, following up, registering new associates, training and support.

In the beginning, you should spend 90 percent of your time on prospecting, presenting, following up and signing up new people. As your network builds, you can devote more time to training and support. But never, ever stop prospecting, or your business will die.

4. Be Consistently Persistent. Most network marketers give up too early. They expect to make $10,000 their first month, and when they don't, they quit. But it takes time to build an MLM business. You're going to have to contact a lot of people, give many presentations and endure a great deal of rejection. However, it's the person who is consistently persistent who will succeed.

If you're duplicating a successful system, the only thing separating you from success is time. When things are looking dark, keep going. Make one more call. Talk with one more person. Follow up one more time. If you're with the right company, you should never give up because you'll eventually be successful.

5. Make a million friends. The advice that made the biggest impact on my success in network marketing was to go out with the idea of making a million friends instead of a million dollars. You can only be successful in network marketing if you help others become successful. So, go out and find some new friends who you can help become successful in your business. Forget about your wants and needs, and serve these friends instead. This concept is called "servant leadership"--you lead by serving those you lead. The more friends you make and serve, the greater your success in network marketing.

These five principles of success are just the start. I'm sure that your sponsor and up line leaders have their own list, so make sure you ask them how they became successful. And finally, realize this: It's one thing to have this knowledge--and a whole different thing to actually do what you've learnt. So be a doer, and watch your business and income skyrocket.

GAME PLAN: Leverage on one today and make the money you have always wanted to earn

SECRET OF THE RICH: Network, Leverage, Teamwork (Your Network = Net worth, Teamwork = Investment).

FORMULA FOR NETWORK MARKETING SUCCESS

U – USE the products yourself, believe in them and love them

S – SHARE your knowledge of the benefits of the product and or business opportunities with people you know, referrals and total strangers.

E – ENROL quality people to join you to U.S.E coach and support them to invite others to do these activities

BENEFITS OF MULTI-LEVEL MARKETING CYCLE

Figure 9 Multi-level marketing growth diagram

REFERRAL MARKETING: This is a word-of-mouth conversational sales approach; Network Marketing is more than just a game of *NUMBERS* it's a game of *STRATEGY*. The strategy and the numbers is all you need to excel in network marketing. Dream it and then achieve it

SESSION2: (CRIBBS, 9 STRATEGIES TO HELP GROW YOUR NETWORK MARKETING BUSINESS)
If you are in Network Marketing and Direct Sales, you know it's a tough business. It's incredibly rewarding, but it is also a tough business. Being successful in MLM doesn't just happen, one has to be very strategic and plan for success. The good news is, this business is designed to be duplicated, so success can happen by enthusiastically following a plan and teaching others to enthusiastically follow a plan.

Below He outlined nine strategies that will help you grow your team, thus grow your business.

a) Have the Right Attitude

First and foremost, you have to have the right attitude to succeed in network marketing. Part of that attitude is being a person who likes to help others succeed. Zig Ziglar once said "You can't help someone row to the other side of the river without reaching the other shore yourself." When you help enough people succeed, you too will have success. Being able to help others succeed is one of my favourite aspects of this business.

You also have to learn that hearing "no" is not going to destroy you and that there is nothing personal in someone not joining you in business. This business is not for everyone and everyone will not see the opportunity the way that you do. It's nothing personal. You're not a failure and don't need to feel like it's your fault they don't "get it."

Every person you speak to about your business has the potential to be a customer, a business partner or someone who can refer the right people to you. You have to have an attitude that does not equate "no" with failure. Show some enthusiasm. If you're not enthusiastic about your business, why would anyone want to join you?

B) Find a Reputable Company with Lots of Promise

This may seem obvious, and to most it is. Once you find a solid company commit to it. Give it at least a year. I've heard time and time again that failure does not occur in this business. Quitting happens, but failure does not happen. If you are working, talking to people, sharing your product, sharing your business opportunity you will grow.

If you believe in the business model and understand the value of leveraging your network, time and energy but you are not with a company that has the potential you are looking for, find a new company.

3) Keep It Simple

I am convinced that some people just like to over-complicate things. This business succeeds when you duplicate what works, teach your team how to duplicate those same strategies and teach them how to teach their team. There are so many ways to complicate this business. Stick with what works.

Look to the success stories, learn what they do and duplicate what they do.

Does that mean you can't improve on what is being done? I say ALWAYS look for ways to improve, but do not forsake the tried and tested ways as you test your ideas.

4) Target People Who Get Business

Network Marketing is serious business. Entrepreneurs who understand business and see the vision of how direct sales works are much more likely to join you and partner with you. Look for people who influence and look for people who can be your "power partners." We all know people who are like magnets and who everyone wants to be associated with.

Look for people who will naturally benefit from being in your business, that's why mompreneurs have come on to the scene so strong in network marketing. They benefit because they get to balance family and business on their own terms. As you talk with others and are asking for referrals, let your conversation direct their thoughts to the kind of individuals who are ideal for your business and your team.

You want referrals that lead you to go-getters, magnets, influencers and people known to be helpful. You want to spend your time with the movers and shakers, not the ones you have to convince to join you in business. You want people who "get it" and are enthusiastic about it.

5) Talk to as Many People at One Time as You Can

The entire idea behind Network Marketing comes down to the word "leverage." How are you leveraging your network? How are you leveraging your team? How are you leveraging your time? When it comes to how you spend your time, use your time wisely.

Talk to the masses. Set up a toll-free number with a recorded message or set up a webinar that people can view. As your team grows, set up training calls where you are training multiple team members at once instead of one-on-on. Time is valuable and if you can teach people how to leverage their time, everyone benefits.

As you are doing this, you are also training your team that the best use of their time is talking to as many people as possible. You could realistically meet with five people during the day for coffee. But what if, instead, you spoke to those five people at one time…or better yet, twenty people at once, or 100 people at once.

The way this plays out may look different for different people, but the idea is the same. Leverage your time and talk to as many people at one time as possible.

6) Learn How to Recruit

If you want to grow your business, you have to grow your team. In order to do this, you have to be really good at prospecting, inviting and recruiting. I've invested heavily in these particular skills through training courses specific to cold market, warm market and social media.

WHAT YOU NEED TO KNOW

a) Cold Market Prospecting Mastery – This training has the absolute best training on posture that I've ever seen. Posture gets people to take you seriously. In this training you'll learn how to find prospects to talk with everywhere you go, how to start conversations and how to get them excited to hear about your products and opportunity. This training helped me with confidence, verbiage to use and with knowing how to get people to show up for a presentation.

b) Your First 90 Days In Network Marketing – Even though this training says "first 90 days" it's good for anyone who wants to learn how to get started and even help other people get started. Even if you've being in business for a while, you will love this training. It helped me with prospecting and recruiting. I began to get results after taking this training by immediately recruiting some new people. It helped me create habits and stick to those actions, thus the results. It shared specific language surrounding objections and how to be very conversational while handling objections.

C) 10k Social Media Recruiting Formula – This training by Jessica Higdon taught me how to recruit people using Facebook. It shared specific scripts and introductions that work. It taught me how to build a business online. After taking this training, I immediately recruited several people on Facebook because I knew how to find the right people, how to approach them online and then how to get them onto a presentation.

7) Train, Train, Train

The power of network marketing is that you utilize the time of others to leverage your time and efforts. The saying "I would rather have 1% effort from 100 different people than rely on 100% of my own" is so true to me. But those 100 people have to know what they are doing in order to help you succeed. So train, train, train.

Training is also a great way to stay connected to your team, help keep them motivated, empower them to build their teams and demonstrate leadership and duplication. Spend a greater percentage of your time with those team members who are displaying the most activity and are duplicating the steps to success.

Empower your team to duplicate what you do and encourage them to lead their teams. This goes back to leveraging your time and energies.

8) Create Goals, Benchmarks and Take Decisive Action

Where do you want to be in 6 months? Do you have a goal and a road map that will get you there? Break the six months down into intervals that will allow you to measure your progress along the way. Where do you want to be in 1 year, or 2 years? Again, you have to have clearly defined bench marks and an action plan that will get you there.

Writing your goals down is huge. Writing down the actions to get you there is vital. **But all of it is done in vain if you do not take action to make it all a reality.** You have to know where you are going in order to get there.

9) Stay on Top of Your Game

Be the kind of leader who is always working to improve your skills. Improve your presentations, improve your conversation skills, always find new ways to help and empower people. Learn from the leaders in your company and leaders in the industry.

One of the great things about network marketing is that there is always room for more growth. There's always room for more business and there's always room to improve your skills. Staying on top of your game keeps you in a position to help more people. Whether directly or indirectly, you are always going to be in contact with people so you want to make certain your people skills are at their best.

10) Know the MLM Industry

Knowing your business and the company you work with is vital. You certainly want to know, understand, teach and promote the best practices from within your company. But you also need to stay informed of the best practices and best technologies from within the entire Network Marketing Industry as well. There are a lot of Direct Sales companies out there doing very well. What are they teaching their distributors? Why are they successful? Why are they growing? What can you do that would benefit your customers and your team?

11) Have FUN!

Ok, so this is number 10. Who said business can't be fun? Building a business, building a team, encouraging a team, working with people – it all makes out for a very fun business! If you expect others to join you in your business you have to let them see that you're having fun and that you enjoy what you do. Sadly, it seems like most recruiters want to tell you how much money they make. I believe more success will come when others see that you love what you are doing, enjoy the opportunity to help others and enjoy the way you are able to leverage your time. Yes, everyone wants to make money, that's why we are in business. But I believe quality of life trumps most other benefits.

SESSION 3: INSIGHTS ON FINANCIAL IMPROVEMENT USING MLM (MULTI-LEVEL MARKETING)

EARN MORE TO BE MORE: a) Work on income increment which is very typical to get more money, which comes from getting part-time jobs or part-time business that brings money to your bank account. Which with time will become not enough so while working, income increment on a quarterly basis or annual, is the wise thing to do but will not be enough to give you the lifestyle that you desire. So, you increase your income sources.

MULTIPLY YOUR INCOME STREAMS:

i) This makes you less dependent on your current job and source of income.

ii) Makes you independent of economy recession. *If you want to be rich, then you have to create multiple income stream.*

ADD RESIDUAL INCOME SOURCES: Now imagine this if now why you are still active your full salary is not enough then asking yourself this question, will it be enough when you start collecting pension?

TERMINOLOGIES ON TYPES OF INCOME

a. Linear income
b. Residual Income
c. Active Income
d. Passive Income

LINEAR INCOME: Here your income depends on your personal effort it means the more effort you put in the more money you make meaning once your effort stops your income abruptly stops when you are still at the infancy stage but once you grow and climb the ladder of achievement. You won't need to work as hard as u used to when you started but you will earn ten times more with lesser and lesser effort the only way to earn income is to work and work.

ACTIVE INCOME: Unlike Linear income that is used in multi-level marketing this is used in the work place which is your income depends on your effort such as your time, skills, contracts, and talent and money skills.

RESIDUAL INCOME: Here efforts are at the highest at the start and proportionally rewards are small. Over time your required effort declines as your business grows and your recognition, incentives grows alongside with huge money attraction for inconveniences.

PASSIVE INCOME: This requires little or no effort to start and maintain it and grow it and you will still get incentives, reward and recognition for just doing nothing but bring people. The more people you register the more money you make.

THE GPS MAP TO YOUR FINANCIAL FREEDOM

a) Where are you Going (What are your Dreams)?
b) When do you want to get there (how quickly)?
c) How do you plan to get there?

This is based on your strategy to map actions with goals and milestone alongside spending money as a fuel to bring your financial dreams to reality.

CHARACTERISTICS OF A GOOD SALES FORCE FOR PRODUCT BASED BUSINESS

a) The ability to communicate effectively with people at different levels
b) The ability to get along with all types of people from all walks of life
c) The ability to show concern about the problems of their prospects
d) The ability to always have a positive mental altitude, not giving room to whiners and complainers because they will be too busy complaining they won't be able to sell anything

e) The ability to be humble when necessary while many sales people truly are super sales types, the ability to be humble can be an asset when the situation calls for a little humility
f) The ability to see good in people they meet
g) The ability to be self-sufficient to handle situation
h) The ability to show enthusiasm to sell, to sell successfully your sales force must not only believe in the product or service they are representing. They must be enthusiastic about it as well.

SESSION 4: LIFE STORY OF KFC FOUNDER

At age 5, his father died

At age 16, he quits school

At age 17, he had already lost four jobs.

At age 18, he got married

At age 19, he became a father

At age 20, his wife left him and took their baby daughter

He became a cook and a dishwasher in a small café

He failed in an attempt to kidnap his own daughter and eventually convinced his wife to return home

Between age 18 and 22, he was a railroad conductor as a side job and he failed

He applied for law school but he was rejected

He became an insurance sales man and failed again

He joined the army and washed out there

At age 65 he retired

On the 1st day of retirement he received a cheque from the government for $105

He felt that the government was saying that he couldn't provide for himself

He decided to commit suicide; it wasn't worth living anymore; he had failed so much.

He sat under a tree writing his will, but instead, he wrote what he could have accomplished with his wife. There was so much that he hadn't done, there was one thing he could do better than anyone he knew and that was to cook.

So, he borrowed $87 against his cheque and bought and fried up some chicken using his recipe, and went door to door to sell to his neighbours in Kentucky.

But remember at age 65 he was ready to commit suicide but at age 88 colonel sanders founder of Kentucky fried chicken (KFC) empire was a billionaire just from selling fried chicken

Note: It's never too late to start all over again

SESSION 5: BILLIONAIRE MINDSET (THE DIFFERENCE FROM OTHERS)

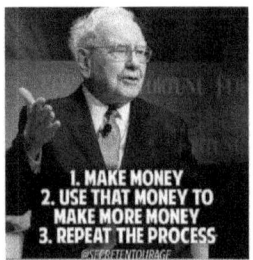

MONEY: Average people look for ways to spend money. Billionaires look for ways to invest money.

INVESTMENT: Average people invest just a little. Billionaires know that investing is the key to abundance

JOBS: Average people think of a better job that would make them wealthy. Billionaires know that a job will never make them wealthy, investments will

RISK: Average people stay away from risk because they might fail. Billionaires know if they don't take risks, they have already failed.

PROBLEMS: Average people try to avoid problems. Billionaires see problem as an opportunity to make billions

PREPARATION: Average people prepare for today. Billionaires prepare today for the opportunities of tomorrow

TIME: Average people waste time. Billionaires see time as their most valuable assets.

FEAR: average people are always afraid of losing money. Billionaires know if they don't lose money, they cannot be wiser, smarter and stronger.

CONCLUSION
6 PRACTICAL STEPS TO START THAT DREAM BUSINESS SMALL-SCALE IN SUMMARY (GOOGLE.COM)

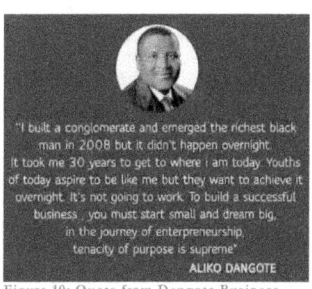

Figure 10: Quote from Dangote Business Tycoon

Step1: Discover your strength and discover a business idea that will be managed and sustained on your business strength and skills. A great man was said don't produce what you can make but rather produce what you can sell. That is the soul of business

Step 2: Formulate your product recipe and perfect your production, make your prototype and subject it to testing and evaluation. For services-based business master your hand work and know your craft.

Step 3: Formulate a business name that is unique to you and is not already in use, create your brand identity, set up an office (it can be your house) or rent an office where clients can reach you. Rent a shop if it's a product business where you can sell and customers will come and buy.

Step 4: Appoint and handle the administrative matters surrounding your business. Register your business to avoid theft of other business start-up. And also, for clients to take you seriously alongside your customers otherwise you will be taken as a joker.

Step 5: Promote and start Selling. One thing you must do before and after registering your business is to promote your product or services. Otherwise what is the point having a great product or service nobody knows about.

Step 6: Build a local Partnership from start for this will go a long way in opening new opportunities, accessing new markets, and mitigating risks.

(Kiyosaki, NETWORKING MARKETING IS AN ASSET NOT A JOB, 2016)

Robert Kiyosaki
Network marketing teaches basic, critical life skills. It teaches people how to overcome their fears, how to communicate, and how to handle rejection and maintain persistence. This kind of education is absolutely priceless.

Here's what I tell people: "Even if you don't like it, stay with it for five years and you'll be better equipped to survive in the real world of business. And you'll be a better person."

The people who are successful in network marketing have a spiritual cause. They genuinely want to help better others' lives. If you don't have that, if you just want a paycheck, then work for the post office! (Mar 05)

Figure 11: Robert Kiyosaki MLM expert

Some people would often ask, "Why do so few people make it to the top of their network marketing system? Most people join only to make money. If they don't make money in the first in the first few months or years, they become discouraged and quit (and then bad mouth the industry). Others quit and go looking for a company with better compensation plan. But joining to make a few dollars is not the reason to get into the business.

The two essential reason to join network marketing business are:

Reason one to help yourself make money then **Reason number 2** to help others make theirs. If you join for only one of these 2 reasons, then the system will not work for you. Reason number 1 means that you come to the business primarily to change quadrants to change quadrants to change from the E (Employee) or the S (Self-employed) quadrant to the B (Business owner) or I (Investor) quadrant. This change is normally very difficult for most people because of money. The true E or S quadrant person will not work unless it is for money. This is also what causes people to not reach the top of the network marketing system: they want money more than want to change quadrants.

A (B quadrant or I quadrant) person will also work for money, but in a different way. The B quadrant person works to build or create as asset-in this case, a business system. The I quadrant person invests in the asset or the system. The beauty of most network marketing systems is that you do not really make much money unless you help others leave the E and S quadrants and succeed in the B and I quadrants. If you focus on helping others make this shift, then you will be successful in the business. As a Big business owner or an investor, sometimes you don't get paid for years; this, a true E quadrant or S quadrant person will not do. It's not part of their core values. Risk and delayed gratification disturb them emotionally.

What kind of Asset is a network marketing business?

Remember, there are two reasons required to be successful in network marketing: to help yourself, and to help others. Reason number 1 means helping yourself get to the B side of the quadrant.

The beauty of a network marketing business is that your goal is to create assets, which are other B's working under you and their job is to create other B's working under them. In traditional business, the focus is for the B to have only E's and S's working for them. So, when you change your money conscious mindset to a billionaire mindset you automatically change the world around you without knowing including the people around you and the society you live in.

TIPS FOR SUCCESS IN NETWORK MARKETING

- **Have patience when starting network marketing opportunity:** Success does not come over night, you have to put in leg work in order to see the profits rolling in. Be honest with your goals and timelines to avoid giving up too early when you aren't seeing results. Don't give up, don't give in.
- **Use the internet to your advantage in network marketing:** The more people you recruit the more your network will grow. Use social media to your advantage to interact with friends.
- **Picking your spots in network marketing is incredibly important:** Find your target market, then create marketing approach to reach them and remember market the benefit not its features
- **Don't try to overwhelm people with information when meeting them:** start by giving them nuggets of info about the product. If they seem interested and request to lean more, then go ahead with additional information. Overwhelming someone is a quick way to get them to say "Thanks but no thanks".

ABOUT THE AUTHOR

Mr Austin Chuks Eneanya, - He obtained his first Degree from University of Lagos in B.sc in Systems Engineering and later went on to pursue his masters' in business Administration with Management specialisation from the same University. A principal consultant and specialist with several years industry experience in business planning and development for start-up businesses including project management and entrepreneurship Training). He has been training retirees and SMEs owners in the private sector also, involved in youth empowerment programmes in various seminars including states outside Lagos - Nigeria. Also, in addition to his credit he has collaborated with start-ups to win the following: National Robotic Olympiad (2014), Diamond Bank BET 6 competition (2016), Mind to Mind Business Initiative (2018). He is also the author of Modern-day business model.

WORKS CITED

AFRICA, A. S. (2015, December 3).

AFRICA, F. S. (2015, December 3).

CHIBUZO, U. (2016, JULY 25). THE PRICES OF ALL PRODUCT REGISTRATION WITH NAFDAC NIGERIA.

CRIBBS, B. (n.d.). 9 STRATEGIES TO HELP GROW YOUR NETWORK MARKETING BUSINESS .

CRIBBS, B. (n.d.). 9 STRATEGIES TO HELP GROW YOUR NETWORK MARKETING BUSINESS.

forbes.com. (2016). *12 FACTS YOU NEED TO KNOW FROM FORBES' 2016 BILLIONAIRES LIST*. Retrieved from Forbes.

GARY LOCKWOOD. (n.d.). SALES APPROACH.

google.com. (n.d.). *log-2-6-warehouse-sample-calculating warehouse space pdf.*

google.com. (n.d.).

google.com. (n.d.).

google.com. (n.d.).

google.com. (n.d.).

google.com. (n.d.).

GOOGLE.COM. (n.d.).

GOOGLE.COM. (2016). SECRETS TO BILLIONAIRES START UP AND OTHER BILLIONAIRES IN HISTORY.

google.com. (n.d.). 7 WAYS TO PROMOTE YOUR BUSINESS ONLINE FOR FREE .

google.com. (n.d.). HAIR START-UP BUSINESS .

google.com. (n.d.). ITEMIZING STARTING A PRODUCT-BASED BUSINESS.

google.com. (n.d.). ITEMIZING STARTING A PRODUCT-BASED BUSINESS.

google.com. (n.d.). SECRETS TO BILLIONAIRES START UP AND OTHER BILLIONAIRES IN HISTORY.

GOOGLE.COM. (n.d.). SECRETS TO BILLIONAIRES START UP AND OTHER BILLIONAIRES IN HISTORY.

Ikenna. (2016, May). 40+ BUSINESS FUNDING OPPORTUNITIES and AWARDS FOR AFRICAN ENTREPRENEURS.

Institute, F. (n.d.). WAREHOUSE AND INVENTORY MANAGEMENT.

IWERE, T. (n.d.). CHOOSING THE RIGHT FRANCHISE: TEN KEY FACTORS TO CONSIDER.

Kiyosaki, R. (2016). NETWORK MARKETING IS AN ASSET NOT A JOB.

Kiyosaki, R. (2016). NETWORKING MARKETING IS AN ASSET NOT A JOB.

Lawpadi, A. (2019, 03 3). *Lawpadi Blog*. Retrieved from Lawpadi: https://lawpadi.com/9-things-every-nigerian-know-labour-act/

LUGO, Y. (n.d.). STARTUP OPPORTUNITIES IN LATIN AMERICA.

NARIALAND.COM. (n.d.). 5 MAJOR PROBLEMS STARTUP ENTREPRENEURS FACE.

NARIALAND.COM. (n.d.). 5 MAJOR PROBLEMS STARTUP ENTREPRENEURS FACE .

OMEH, D. (n.d.). HOW TO BECOME A SUCCESSFUL ENTERPRENUR.

OXFORD BUSINESS, G. (2019, Jan. 3). *MULTIPLE WAYS TO MAKE MONEY IN AFRICA AND SUCCESS STORIES*. Retrieved from Oxford Business Group Bloomberg Terminal Research Homepage: OBGR<GO>: https://oxfordbusinessgroup.com/overview/nigerias-legal-framework-and-rules-and-regulations-doing-business

SMEBizInfo. (2015, March 24).

TopBusinessideas.com. (n.d.). 10 SMALL BUSINESS INVESTMENT OPPORTUNITIES IN GERMANY .

wikipedia.com. (2016, JULY). Nigerian's Top 21 Famous Entrepreneurs in Nigeria 2015.

www.ingramcontent.com/pod-product-compliance
Lightning Source LLC
Chambersburg PA
CBHW072130170526
45158CB00004BA/1310